HUNTING MONSTERS

They walk among us—devious, dangerous predators whose horrific acts go far beyond the boundaries of comprehensible human behavior. In this gripping, behind-the-scenes account, **Gregg McCrary**—one of the country's most preeminent criminal profilers and former Supervisory Special Agent in the FBI's Behavioral Science Unit—takes us deep inside ten of his most fascinating cases, including:

- the terrifying home invasion in a peaceful community in upstate New York that ended in rape, arson . . . and the savage slaughter of an innocent family

- the strange instance of an international serial killer who rode along with the cops who unknowingly pointed out his victims

- the heartless massacre of nine gentle souls at a Buddhist temple in Arizona

- the Genesee River Killer, who liked to revisit his victims hours after they had been slain and discarded
                          and . . .

- a final, definitive judgment on the famous Sam Sheppard murder trial—the case that inspired *The Fugitive* film and TV series.

"Gregg McCrary has distinguished himself as one of the world's foremost criminal profilers and crime analysts . . . Read this book and you will understand how his insight has helped solve many difficult crimes."
Dr. Henry Lee, chief criminalist and director of the
Connecticut State Police Forensic Science Laboratory
and author of *Cracking Cases*

THE UNKNOWN DARKNESS

PROFILING THE PREDATORS AMONG US

GREGG O. McCRARY
Former Supervisory Special Agent, FBI

with KATHERINE RAMSLAND, PH.D.

HarperTorch
An Imprint of HarperCollinsPublishers

HARPERTORCH
An Imprint of HarperCollins*Publishers*
10 East 53rd Street
New York, New York 10022-5299

First HarperTorch paperback printing: October 2004
First William Morrow hardcover printing: September 2003

The William Morrow hardcover edition contains the following Library of Congress Cataloging in Publication Data:

McCrary, Gregg O., 1945–
The unknown darkness : profiling the predators among us / Gregg O. McCrary, with Katherine Ramsland.
    p. cm.
    Includes index.
1. Serial murders—Case studies. 2. Criminal investigation—psychological aspects. 3. Criminal behavior, Prediction of. 4. McCrary, Gregg O., 1945–
5. United States. Federal Bureau of Investigation. Behavioral Science Unit—Officials and employees—Biography. I. Ramsland, Katherine M., 1953–
II. Title.
HV6505.M39 2003
363.25'9523—dc21   2002043225

HarperCollins®, HarperTorch™, and ❤™ are trademarks of HarperCollins Publishers Inc.

Printed in the United States of America

Visit HarperTorch on the World Wide Web at www.harpercollins.com

10 9 8 7 6 5 4 3 2 1

For Carol McCrary,

who cooked for us, tolerated our long hours, critiqued us,
and gave us that all-important thumbs-up when we needed it

Contents

Introduction

> We must understand how criminals think and realize
> that they have a fundamentally different view of the
> world from that of people who are basically responsible.
> I submit that this basic understanding, if it ever existed,
> has been lost in the fog of theoretical speculation and
> political rhetoric often espoused by people who have
> never even met a criminal.
>
> —Dr. Stanton E. Samenow

Death always finds its way to the basement. Morgues
aren't put in a penthouse, and the FBI's practice is no
different. The crimes assigned to the Behavioral Science Unit where I worked for ten years were dark and
gruesome. They disturbed even our colleagues at the
academy, so the administrators relocated us to an area
that was more "out of sight and out of mind."

We ended up sixty feet underground in small, win-
dowless offices in what had once been a bomb shelter.
The heavy vault door was gone, but its former frame
still stood as a dubious welcome to all who entered. It
wasn't long after we settled in before a sign appeared
over this grim entrance to announce our unit's new
identity. It read simply "The Fugawae Tribe," a name
derived from the question we were asking ourselves as
we wandered around the abandoned bunker: "Where
the fuck are we?"

Since the BSU was a relatively new unit in the 1980s when I joined, we were still forming an identity and developing our behavioral-analysis program. We'd all come into it after years of work as field agents, and although only a few of us had textbook knowledge about psychology, we certainly had street experience with criminal behavior. I had worked many types of investigations, from "disorganized" crime to bank robberies and kidnappings, along with foreign counterintelligence and organized crime.

I got into this work through serendipity. After college, I took a job teaching high school and coaching wrestling. I knew that this wasn't a lifelong calling, but it allowed me to support myself and work with many good people until I figured out what I really wanted to do. Then, in 1969, I met an FBI agent who convinced me to apply to the Bureau. I wasn't sure that the FBI would be interested in me, but I was interested in the FBI. If an applicant received an appointment as a special agent and successfully completed new agent's training at the FBI Academy, the Bureau wanted a three-year commitment. I figured I could do anything for three years, and if it wasn't a good fit, then the FBI and I would go our separate ways. I ended up staying for over twenty-five years.

After completing new agent's training, my first office of assignment was Detroit. There I was dispatched to the resident agency in Flint, Michigan, to work a wide variety of crimes, including bank robberies, kidnappings, and extortions, all of which seemed to be plentiful. After a year in Michigan, I was transferred to New York City where I worked organized crime for several years and then received an "OP" (office of preference) transfer to Buffalo, New York. In Buffalo, I continued to work an assortment of criminal cases there and elsewhere around the country. During that time, I'd also had various odd assignments, such as chasing the Aryan Nation's thugs around Idaho and Montana and working undercover assignments.

The FBI Academy training was great, but the real education of an FBI agent begins once you actually hit the street and continues throughout your career. For example, in the classroom you learn that different offenders have different thresholds of deterrability and respect for law enforcement. Your appreciation for that reality increases immeasurably when making arrests. Many offenders complied and were "arrested without incident," to use the Bureau jargon. A few were so shaken that they pissed their pants. Others ran, and some fought, and I had one who tried to detonate a bomb.

That case occurred in Buffalo. Two bank robbers had been hitting Ohio and Pennsylvania pretty hard and then decided to expand their enterprise to Buffalo where, among other things, I was the SWAT team leader. I got an unexpected SWAT call, and as the team mobilized, I was briefed on the offenders and their MO.

One would go into a bank dressed as a businessman, with a briefcase, but he was armed with a .45-caliber handgun in a shoulder holster and a bomb. He'd give the branch manager a note stating, "I have a gun and a bomb in the briefcase. You have two choices. You and I can go into the vault and get some money or I'll blow us up. What do you want to do?" Obviously that wasn't much of a choice. Once in the vault, he'd take the bomb out and fill the briefcase full of money. He'd tell the manager that he had a partner outside who would blow the place up with a remote-detonating device if the police arrived within the next thirty minutes. In a final touch of thievery, he'd relieve the manager of his car keys and quietly drive off, in the manager's car, with the bank's money. He'd drive to a prearranged switch point, dump the manager's car, and crawl into a hidden compartment underneath the cab of an old truck. Then his partner would drive them away. The police were looking for a big, clean-cut guy in a suit, but all they could see was this little guy with a beard driving a beat-up truck, so they paid him no attention. This strategy had been working quite well for them until this particular day.

FBI agents in Cleveland, who were in charge of the investigation, had identified them but lacked enough proof to arrest them. They had developed one of the offenders' former girlfriends as an informant. She was angry and only too happy to cooperate. She called and told the agents that these guys were going to pull a job the next day, but she didn't know where. Cleveland mobilized their surveillance and SWAT teams and alerted the Pittsburgh office, which went on standby. Because the offenders had never come into New York State we got the call only when they crossed the state line from Pennsylvania.

I alerted the team and we prepared our gear and sent the surveillance aircraft up. I got into one of the ground vehicles and merged with the moving surveillance being conducted by the Cleveland and Pittsburgh agents.

The offenders weren't hard to spot. They came up the thruway in an old beat-up flatbed truck, an engine chained on its back. The air surveillance stayed on them, watching as they pulled into a rest stop, where one changed into a suit. This was no scouting mission.

They were going to hit a bank, but where? They continued north, past the exits for Buffalo, and turned east, toward Albany. Then they unexpectedly exited the thruway and headed north on Transit Road. They passed a large strip mall and then made a turn and came back, toward us, on the other side of the highway. We had been careful to stay out of their sight, letting the aircraft maintain the point position, but now they were coming right back toward us. We scrambled to move onto side roads and get turned around as discreetly as we could so they wouldn't make our surveillance.

They pulled their old flatbed truck into the mall parking lot, then parked at one end. At the other end of the mall was a bank, sitting alone in the lot. Subject number one, the guy in the suit, got out and started walking in the direction of the bank. Since subject number two stayed with the truck, we divided into two teams, one for each subject. But there was a problem.

The last store on this strip mall was a Child World. This was a weekday and it was crowded with mothers and kids. We believed the "businessman" had a bomb. We didn't want to endanger anyone, so we had to wait and see exactly what he was going to do. We hoped to let him walk past all of the stores and then take him down in the parking lot.

Each team was slowly and carefully moving in, getting ready to take the two suspects down simultaneously, but you know what they say about the best-laid plans. Just as subject number one reached Child World, his partner bolted from the truck and started running toward him. He was yelling and waving his arms as he ran. We thought we'd been made. Fortunately, his partner was too far away to hear him.

The team assigned to take down the driver did so

quickly and without incident. He was completely surprised. We later found out that he was trying to stop his partner from going through with the robbery, as their truck had dropped its transmission and he couldn't get the vehicle out of the lot. Not only was their escape plan in the commode, but now there were three FBI SWAT teams from three different states closing in on them. This just wasn't their day.

That arrest was creating some commotion as our team closed in on subject number one. We were closer to Child World than we wanted to be. Two agents grabbed the suspect, one on each arm to keep him from getting to the bomb inside the briefcase, as a third agent confronted him head-on, yelling, "FBI, you're under arrest."

He shouted, "Fuck you. Let me go or I'll blow you up."

"No," they responded, "we'll shoot you."

He yelled again, "I'll blow you up." He was trying to get to his .45 in the shoulder holster as they wrestled him away from the front of the store. These threats and counterthreats went on long enough for everyone to realize he was not going to comply with our demands. We believed he had a bomb in the briefcase, and the agents could see the holstered .45. We couldn't take the chance that he would detonate the bomb or perhaps get to his gun and start firing, not with women and children in the vicinity. That left us no choice. The agent in front of him shot him once, in the head. He did so at an upward angle to avoid hitting anyone else. The subject immediately collapsed. It was a through-and-through head wound that blew out his right eye. Thick, viscous blood immediately began oozing out of his mouth, ears and nose, and he was convulsing as he lay on the ground.

The scene suddenly became chaotic. Sirens were sounding and people were coming out of stores. We were still afraid that the bomb might detonate and were trying to keep spectators back, but everybody wanted to get close to see what was going on. As the team's emergency medical technician (EMT), I began to work on him while an ambulance was called. There wasn't a lot I could do, other than make him comfortable and try to keep his airway open. I used my jacket as a pillow, but all of the blood made it difficult to keep his airway unobstructed. I was sure that each convulsion was his last. With that head wound, I knew that I was working on a dead man. He went quiet and I started to cover his body. Suddenly he opened his one good eye and looked at me. Choking on blood, he asked, "Are you an agent?"

I was stunned. A dead man was talking to me. I looked around at the other agents to make sure I wasn't hallucinating. I needed some validation here. They were as surprised as I was. I looked this guy in his good eye and said, "Yeah. I'm an agent."

"Are you the agent that shot me?"

"No, no. Take it easy. There's an ambulance on the way."

"Let me die," he said. "Let me die."

Then from out of nowhere, this priest in robes and a purple sash stepped forward and asked me if he could give this guy his Last Rites. It was a surreal moment, and I told him to go ahead. The ambulance arrived shortly after that; and the EMTs worked on him for a while, then rushed him to the hospital. To my surprise, he survived. It turned out to have been a fluky wound trajectory, where the bullet went through the front of the skull and up through the sinuses, blew out the right eye, and exited just below the temple. It never got inside the cranium. I ended up testifying against him in federal court, where he and his partner were convicted. He committed suicide in prison shortly after that.

In retrospect, that attested to the danger we were in. These guys had driven from Ohio with a fully functioning but unstable bomb. They had inserted a blasting cap into twenty-eight pounds of explosives and connected that to a mercury switch that was wired to a battery. What made it really dangerous was that the shunt of the blasting cap was unprotected. This meant that any extraneous radio transmission or static electricity could have detonated the bomb. They could easily have blown themselves up, and some of the bomb techs who dismantled the device were surprised that they hadn't. The guy we'd grabbed clearly didn't shy away from suicide, so had he been able to get to the bomb, he might very well have blown us all up.

This was the type of incident that always made me wonder what the hell had been going on inside that guy's mind. Even with the more routine stuff, and especially when working undercover, I could see that criminals just thought differently from the rest of us. I wanted to know more about the underlying reasons for that, and I was aware that the agents in the Behavioral Science Unit (BSU) at the FBI's National Center for the Analysis of Violent Crime (NCAVC) were deeply involved in this. I was acquainted with John Douglas, the BSU chief, so when I worked as a field coordinator for the NCAVC in Buffalo, I let him know I was interested in joining the unit. When a slot opened up, he contacted me, and I was one of over thirty experienced agents who applied for the job.

They narrowed it down to five or six and invited us

to Quantico for a couple of days for a final screening. That last step involved interviews about our investigative experience and our reasons for wanting to join the unit. Then we were given cases to analyze and had to present our evaluations to unit members. At the end of the process, they offered me a position in the operational wing of the BSU and I took it.

My years as a street agent were helpful, particularly my work undercover. Since I'd been in the criminal arena for years, I was able to think like they did—up to a point. As far as I was concerned, that was the most fascinating part of the job. The challenge was to outmaneuver the criminal element by thinking *ahead* of them.

I had spent years studying and practicing the Japanese martial art of Shorinji Kempo, and I had learned to discipline myself to see past a situation to a specific type of strategy. This approach was applicable to outthinking and outmaneuvering criminals as well, but it meant that I had to have a much deeper and more complete understanding of their mind-set.

The philosophy of Shorinji Kempo seems counterintuitive to some, but it's effective when you have to out-think an intelligent psychopath. It goes something like this: When confronted, you're taught to empty your mind of all preconceptions and to center yourself. This allows you to correctly read a potential attack and, without hesitation, employ the proper defense. The counterattack *blends* with the opponent's attack and uses his own momentum against him. Although your instinct when pushed is to push back, you pull instead. Because the opponent meets no resistance, he falls forward. It's analogous to when someone prepares to push open a door that he thinks will be difficult to open, and just as he starts to force it, it's pulled open from the other side.

I had used this strategy to good effect in my fieldwork, and I believed in the philosophy that mind and body are considered to be one, so you train them together. It involves the merging of strength and compassion, because neither is good without the other. What distinguishes Shorinji Kempo from other martial arts is the blending of hard (*goho*) and soft (*juho*) techniques. Some martial arts, like Aikido, are soft, with little emphasis on the offensive maneuver but with a great deal of effort spent to avoid attacks and manipulate the opponent's momentum. Typical Japanese karate is considered a "hard" art, with punching, kicking, and blocking but with little emphasis on avoiding attacks. Shorinji Kempo blends both, for a balanced approach. One is not necessarily better than the other; you learn to use what's appropriate for a specific situation.

Another tenet of Shorinji Kempo is that one's potential is achieved over time, because mastery is not an inborn talent. It's a cumulative process that depends on effort, discipline, patience, endurance, and an unbending will. Like any discipline, if you practice every day, you'll probably get better at it, and as your abilities improve, you will develop stability and confidence.

Unfortunately, the same also goes for some criminals. The more they focus on and practice what they do, the better they get at it, so we have to work harder to stay ahead of them. It's a high-stakes mind game, which appealed to me. Involvement with the profiling unit gave me daily hands-on experience with some of the most violent and devious and cunning psychopaths among us. That meant there was always an opportunity for piecing together the puzzle of the offenders' motives. It was all about using *their* process to get where I needed to go. When we were able to make them think that they were stronger than they really were, they often made mistakes.

So exactly what is the work of a profiler? In the mid-1990s, "profiling" became a popular buzzword. Since then, it's been featured in novels, in films, and on television, from *Profiler* to *Silence of the Lambs* to *Red Dragon*. While many of these stories are engaging, any resemblance between their content and the reality of the work itself is usually coincidental. Their purpose is to entertain, not to inform. Consequently, I've seen a good deal of public misperception about profiling's purpose and methods.

Criminal profiling, as the FBI pioneered it and as I present it in this book, may be defined as "a process used to analyze a specific crime or series of crimes in order to develop a behavioral composite of an unknown offender."

Profiles may be classified as either "prospective" or "retrospective," and each is the antithesis of the other. "Prospective" profiling attempts to construct a set of characteristics common to a specific type of offender, i.e., a terrorist, a child molester, or a serial killer. These types of profiles are, generally, templates laid over a specific population in an attempt to predict who within that group might have an elevated potential for committing a certain type of violence. A common problem with prospective profiles is that they become overly inclusive and dependent on stereotyping, which can result in suspicions of the wrong people while allowing actual offenders to remain free.

"Retrospective" profiling—the type we used in the

FBI—is an after-the-fact, case-specific attempt to define the personality and behavioral characteristics of the individual(s) responsible for a specific crime or series of crimes. The process focuses on the identification and apprehension of the offender, as opposed to diagnosis and treatment. It is a guide for law enforcement in specific cases.

Essentially, behavior reflects personality. This is true for noncriminals as well. The clothes we wear, the cars we drive, and the way we comb our hair are all external manifestations of underlying personality traits. In the criminal arena, profilers rely on this maxim. Our premise is that the method and manner in which a crime is committed reflects an offender's personality traits. Thus, through a thorough and accurate assessment of those details, we can draw certain logical inferences about the offender. Yet that's easier said than done.

The reality is that criminal behavior, like all human behavior, is complex and there is no "one-size-fits-all" profile for any type of offender. When I'm asked, "What is the profile of a [serial murderer, child molester, rapist, etc.]?" I reply, "There is none," because even for similar types of predators, we have no formula. They remain individuals.

Profiling can be a complicated process, and there's a misperception, even among law-enforcement officers, that profiling is all that agents from the BSU do. In fact, profiling is part of a more comprehensive behavioral-assessment program called Criminal Investigative Analysis (CIA). This is a multifaceted approach to crime, covering activities as diverse as risk analysis, false allegations, staged crimes, stalking, domestic homicides, criminal-enterprise homicides, gang violence, kidnappings, child abductions, child molestation, white-collar crime, organized crime, Munchausen syndrome, product tampering, police killings, terrorism, juvenile violence, bombings, and arson. Thus, in the interest of demonstrating a cross section of the work that we did at the BSU, I chose cases for this book that show a few more of the many facets of CIA.

In order to understand how profiling and CIA differ, we can look at the four stages of a criminal investigation.

1. First we determine whether or not a crime has been committed.
2. If so, we try to accurately identify the crime.
3. Then we try to identify and apprehend the offender.
4. Finally, we present evidence in court.

CIA can be used during any of these stages, while criminal profiling is limited primarily to the third stage and may also be utilized during the fourth stage. Within the framework of an investigation, Criminal Investigative Analysis commonly offers the following services:

- Crime and crime-scene analysis
- Profiling
- Investigative strategy
- Interviewing techniques
- Probable cause in support of a search warrant
- Trial strategy before and during a trial
- Expert-witness testimony
- Threat assessment

It should be clear that while profiling is an important skill, the FBI's behavioral program has a more widespread application.

As a subspecialty of criminal investigations, behavior analysis within the context of a crime requires an in-depth education in both psychology and law enforcement. The more one assesses motive, the greater the need for understanding criminal psychodynamics and psychopathology. FBI profilers come from within the ranks of seasoned agents who have years of investigative experience, and who then take two years of additional classes, training, and other work to qualify.

Yet the tendency, thanks to the popular media, is to believe that it's simply a matter of developing one's deductive reasoning skills. You'll even find people offering accelerated weekend seminars that promise certification as a profiler who can consult with law-enforcement agencies. However, the attempt to conduct a thorough Criminal Investigative Analysis without comprehensive training in both psychology and criminal investigation can result in costly errors. It can deflect an investigation onto the wrong track, derail it altogether, or undermine the case in criminal court.

An example of this came up for me in a rape case. A university-based psychology professor had been invited to profile the incident. He had no law-enforcement experience and little to no training in crime analysis or profiling, yet because he'd read some textbooks about rape, he offered himself as qualified to assist. The city police department gave him the details and he provided a written analysis that was over twenty pages long. He went into great detail about the offender's prior criminal and educational history, residency in relation to the crime scene, and personal habits. The police used this information to continue their investigation for another year, but had no success. Finally they came to us and asked if we would take a look at the case. We generally don't reanalyze a case that someone else has taken on, but the investigators said they had no other recourse, so we agreed.

The case went to Larry Ankrom, a colleague of mine in the unit. Larry looked over the police report and then gave it to me. Independently of each other, we both came to the same conclusion: This was a false allegation of rape. Not only was the offender unlike anyone described in the pseudo profile, there was no offender at all!

We then presented our opinion to the police, along with our reasoning. They admitted to having had similar suspicions, but this "profiler" had given them so much detail and had seemed so certain. The investigators then employed an interview strategy that we had developed and used successfully in the past with pseudo victims. Tearfully and with a sense of relief, the complainant conceded that she had never been raped.

The point of this story is that the good professor had done some research, but since he had no experience or training in the dynamics of false allegations, he didn't know what to look for. He'd spun a story that delayed getting to the truth.

Once one has all the education, training, and specialized knowledge necessary, then, as my friend and colleague, criminalist Dr. Henry Lee, has said, "One must speak honestly about what it all adds up to."

The cases I cover in the following chapters offer a comprehensive idea of what Criminal Investigative Analysis is, how profiling works in different types of situations, and how my own perspective, from training in Shorinji Kempo, influences the manner in which I go about solving crimes. From the crime scene to the courtroom, my background centers me and helps me think clearly, even as cases pile up.

The role of the "profiler" is to jump right into an on-going investigation, so let's do that now.

1: The Scarborough Rapist

The sky is darkening like a stain
Something is going to fall like rain
And it won't be flowers.
—W. H. Auden

[1]

The descriptions were vague of a rapist who stalked women as they got off the bus at night to go home. It was difficult for investigators to get a good lead. They weren't even sure they had a single offender, but several victims had described a man with light brown hair, a solid build, and a young voice. Most of them placed him in his early twenties, although one woman believed he was only eighteen. He'd started with fondling and vulgar talk, which were frightening enough, but within a year, he'd escalated to more serious offenses. As we looked over the cases, we had reason to worry.

These incidents had taken place in an east-side Toronto suburb known as Scarborough, which was just over the border of New York State. The FBI works closely with all Canadian authorities, and our office in Buffalo had frequent contact with the law-enforcement agencies along the "golden horseshoe" from Niagara Falls up to Toronto. In the fall of 1988, three years into my tenure with the FBI's Behavioral Science Unit, the Metropolitan Toronto Police Department asked for a profile of this rapist. They sent us a file that detailed seven cases they believed were linked to a single offender. Six were from Scarborough and one was from Mississauga, a city of 750,000 people southwest of Toronto. It wasn't clear that the Mississauga attack was in the series, so we prepared to analyze the crimes both with and without it to see what impact it had on our overall assessment.

As we got to work, we couldn't have anticipated that our prediction for this offender would not only be tragically accurate, but that we'd revisit him again for much more serious crimes. In fact, he was to become one of the most highly publicized sadistic psychopaths in North America, and as a rapist he was just warming up.

[2]

The first sexual offense that we examined occurred on May 4, 1987. A man followed a twenty-one-year-old woman from a bus stop as she walked home. She was petite and had long brown hair. Near her own home, he grabbed and fondled her. Ten days later, from the same bus stop, a strange man followed and attacked a younger woman in a similar manner and subjected her to a stream of vocal vulgarities. He demanded that she say certain lewd things back to him and then tell him that she loved him. On July 27, there was a similar attack, but the offender continued only to approach his victims from behind, fondle them, and use foul language. Sometimes he penetrated them with his fingers.

Then six months later—if we were still looking at

the same man—he grew bolder. In December, there was another attack in a Scarborough neighborhood. Around ten-thirty P.M., a fifteen-year-old girl with brown hair left the bus stop on Guildwood Parkway and Livingston Road, a few blocks north of the Scarborough shoreline of Lake Ontario. She was 5 feet 4 and weighed around 105 pounds. Only a few houses from her home, a man accosted her from behind, showed her his knife, and pulled her into the shadows between two houses. He assured her that he would not hurt her, and as he proceeded to attack her sexually, he kept up a stream of questions: What is your name? Do you have a boyfriend? How old is he? She answered his questions but lied about her name, which he discovered when he went through her purse and found her ID. This apparently angered him.

He pushed her face against the ground, placed a cable around her neck and tightened it. For an hour, he raped her anally and vaginally, saying things like, "I just want to have fun" and "Does this feel good?" He called her "sweetie" several times, but then ordered her to call herself a slut. After raping her, he forced her to perform fellatio on him and insisted that she tell him he was a better lover than her boyfriend. As the ordeal came to an end, the rapist assured her that even if she went to the police, he was not going to get caught. If she told, she would only humiliate herself and her boyfriend. Then he commanded her to stay down and count slowly to twenty. She did so, and when she looked up, he was gone.

All of these women described a good-looking young man who talked a lot and wanted to hear his victims say certain specific things. In other words, he was providing them with a script of a ritual set of phrases that would arouse him. By approaching and attacking his victims outdoors, in the populated Guildwood Village area of Scarborough, the offender had increased his risk of identification and apprehension, yet he appeared undaunted and confident.

On December 23, just two days before Christmas, another woman, age twenty-two, stepped off a bus very early in the morning, around one A.M. She was tall and stocky, weighing around 150 pounds—the first victim who was not small and thin. The others, too, had long dark hair, while hers was blond. She knew about the rapes but felt safe in this neighborhood.

"Don't look at me," a man ordered from behind. Forcing her into a backyard, he went through the same program he had carried out with the adolescent girl that same month, making this victim call herself foul names and give his penis lewd Christmas greetings. "Tell me that you love me," he ordered. He told her that if she screamed, he would slit her throat. Then he used her belt to tie her to a fence, and as a final gesture, he kicked her in the ribs. He let her know that if she went to the police, he would come back and find her.

She reported the incident anyway, getting her injuries on record and giving the police a good description. The man was white, around 6 feet tall and weighing about 180 pounds. He had blond or light brown hair, down to his collar, a clean-shaven face, and a mole under his nose. He had smelled clean and lacked an accent. On his right hand, he'd worn a gold ring.

The police made a composite sketch but did not publish it, and for several months, no further attacks were reported.

Then in April 1988, the rapist struck again—this time in a different neighborhood, Mississauga. The difference in geography made investigators question whether it was the same man, but the victim had long brown hair, similar to most of the Scarborough victims, and she was subjected to the same type of verbal and physical abuse. As she walked down the street one evening, a man approached her. He asked a question that she didn't understand and before she could respond, he dragged her into the shadows behind a house and forced her to lie facedown. She struggled and tried to fight him off, so he used his belt to tie her wrists. He slapped her and then made her repeat his script while he raped her vaginally and anally. Then he warned her not to call the police. She ignored him and reported the attack.

For this rape, the police arrested a courier, but when blood tests cleared him, he was released. Nevertheless, despite a similar MO and a description that matched those from Scarborough—this victim added that he had blue eyes—investigators did not see a solid connection. The attack had occurred too far away. Nevertheless, they tentatively added this incident to their growing collection.

Another attack occurred that April, against a 19-year-old woman getting off a bus in the center of Scarborough, and the offender made her say all the same vulgar or puzzling things, in particular, "I love you."

By August, the police had reports from eleven victims who might all be connected, but since the Metropolitan Toronto Sexual Assault Squad receives as many as 1,500 rape reports each year, they couldn't be absolutely sure. Spotting a pattern in hindsight is much easier than when entangled in multiple investigations.

But a pattern was nevertheless emerging, and the police wisely called a general meeting of the public. Such meetings are most helpful when information flows in both directions. Law enforcement educates the community as to the nature of the problem, while the community, in turn, provides information to the police. The police had been aggressively proactive in their response, with female decoys riding buses and officers on all-night stakeouts, but so far, they had spotted no one suspicious.

That's when they sent the seven-case file to the FBI's Behavioral Science Unit and I was assigned to do the criminal profile. I looked over the facts and then traveled to Toronto with my colleague Special Agent John Douglas.

[3]

Douglas was instrumental in forming the FBI's first behavioral science operation in the late 1970s. Tall, blond, loquacious, and a self-described hotshot, he had an amiable manner. When I joined the unit in 1985, he was forty and still recovering from a breakdown that he'd had two years earlier when traveling for work. I was aware that he had earned a reputation for reading the behavioral clues from crime scenes in sensational cases like the Atlanta child murders and the Trailside Killer in California. Although he had started as an instructor, he had helped to open up the operational arm of the Behavioral Science Unit, which he called the Investigative Support Unit. They operated out of the FBI Academy in Quantico, Virginia.

Opened in 1972, the new academy, located on the

back of Quantico's U.S. Marine Corps Base, was a self-contained facility of classrooms, laboratories, libraries, and dormitories for training new agents. It sparkled like a college campus, in contrast to the more military-type training quarters we'd had when I first became a field agent in 1969. Older agents were aghast at this pampering, coddling, and general "sissification" of new agents and were sure that it signaled the beginning of the end of the "real" FBI.

While change is often an illusion of progress, in this case actual progress was being made. It took until after J. Edgar Hoover's death the same year the academy opened for psychology to become an accepted part of the curriculum. Yet it not only happened, but psychology has made a significant contribution to law enforcement. Nevertheless, it's clear to us that there's a large gap between what students learn about psychology in the college classroom and what we must know about the criminal mind in order to deal with rapists and murderers, so we shaped behavioral science to work better for our needs.

The actual origins of the profiling method are unclear, but it's commonly believed that Dr. Thomas Bond constructed the first recorded profile of an unknown offender when he analyzed the series of murders in England attributed to Jack the Ripper. In a report written on November 8, 1888, to the head of the Criminal Investigation Division (CID), Dr. Bond drew from the crimes logical inferences about the killer's occupation, income, habits, motives, paraphilic disorder, and general mental health. Then, over sixty years later, in the United States, Dr. James Brussel constructed a profile of New York City's "Mad Bomber," which inspired and influenced the FBI's behavioral profiling program.

It all began with Howard Teten. A twenty-year veteran of the FBI, Teten had met Brussel and learned that his approach to analyzing unknown offenders was to look at the behavioral manifestations at a crime scene for evidence of aberrant mental disorders, and then use that information to make specific deductions. In the Mad Bomber case, over three dozen explosions had occurred during the 1940s and 1950s in places like Radio City Music Hall and Grand Central Terminal, and the perpetrator had sent a number of angry letters to the area newspapers and to a utility company. Brussel studied all of this material for the police and provided the man's ethnicity, approximate age, personal presentation, living situation, level of paranoia, motive, religious affiliation, employment status, and even his typical manner of dress—a double-breasted suit. When the police finally tracked down George Metesky in Connecticut in 1957, he was in his robe, so they requested that he get dressed. He came out buttoning up a double-breasted suit, just as Brussel had predicted. Most of his other details checked out as well. It was impressive.

While none of us mistakes criminal profiling for an established science, and no responsible agent would rely on a profile alone for solving a case, we know that with sufficient information, the psychological assessment from behavioral clues can be surprisingly accurate. Even so, a profile is always the end result of interpretation, which is based on the interpreter's experience and knowledge, as well as on the quality of the information provided. Not everyone will interpret the clues in the same manner. For example, in a series of murders attributed to the Boston Strangler in the mid-1960s, the psychiatric profiles were contradictory. Some insisted there was only one offender, while others said more than one. That case, also known to Teten, highlighted some of the problems with the system, but he was sufficiently impressed with Brussel's method to give it a try.

He offered his own first profile on a stabbing murder in 1970, claiming that when confronted, the guilt-ridden adolescent killer who lived close by would immediately confess, which turned out to be just as surprisingly accurate as the profile Brussel had done on Metesky. That was also the year in which Teten teamed up with Patrick Mullany, who specialized in abnormal psychology. Together, they initiated the criminal-profiling program via a forty-hour course in abnormal psychology, presenting it as one among many investigative tools.

When the Behavioral Science Unit got its start in 1972 as a teaching program for agents and police officers, it gave Mullany and Teten a chance to expand their research and its applications. They began to help solve cases for local agencies, so requests for consultations started to come in from police departments all over the country. That meant training more agents to go out and assist, and that became the Crime Analysis and Criminal Personality Profiling Program. By 1977, the unit had a clear identity, and John Douglas was eventually appointed its chief. In 1985, it came under the auspices of the FBI's National Center for the Analysis of Violent Crime.

Thus, the applied criminology course eventually grew into an experience-based investigative program. Instructors went on the road to teach around the country, and when they had free time, they got access to prisons to interview the very offenders about whom they were teaching. Among their initial thirty-six cases were Charles Manson, Richard Speck, and Edmund Kemper. A few of the agents specialized in areas such as equivocal death analysis or serial sexual offenses, but most worked to deepen the general database of information about what these offenders do, and why. With each interview and each new case, they increased their experience in analyzing crime scenes.

As more requests came in for field consultations, rather than just offering courses Douglas developed the BSU's operational arm, and that's where I applied for a position. My primary responsibility was to consult on specific crimes, and at any given time, each of us in the operational arm had as many as fifty or sixty open cases. In 1988, when I was called to Scarborough, there were only ten of us in the unit, which meant we had to be generalists. We each did it all, although we tried to stay within specific geographic regions. I had the East Coast of the United States and did a fair amount of work in Europe, but that wasn't carved in stone. Assignments were based on how busy one of us was at any given time. The cases stacked up, but we had to keep moving. Since Toronto was basically an East Coast location, the Scarborough case was mine.

[4]

We had quite a lot of documentation from the Toronto police, but you don't get everything you need from just a written report. Sometimes investigators have an informal interpretation they don't wish to put into writing, so it's generally smart to meet them and talk through the case. On the way up, I told Douglas as much as I knew from the reports about the rapist and his victims, and we agreed that the police knew this offender in some capacity; he'd been in trouble before. We had a few ideas about him already, based on the descriptions, but profiling is an open-ended process. More information can always be added and sometimes it changes what you think.

Our first objective was to get a good sense of the neighborhood where these rapes had occurred, because being physically at the crime scenes would tell us more than photographs. It was a late afternoon in November when we arrived and already a little dark, which gave us a good feeling for the place at around the time when the crimes generally occurred. It was chilly, but some of the rapes had happened in December, so we quickly realized what it must have been like for the offender to stand around in this place looking for victims. We drove through the neighborhood and then got out and walked, especially around each of the bus stops from which women were followed. We wanted to see what the victims had seen, and even as night set in, it was clear that there was quite a bit of traffic in the area. Buses came and went, and there were a number of cars. That meant a lot of potential witnesses, and since no one had reported a stranger lurking about, we thought it likely that he was from the neighborhood. He belonged there. No one would even notice him.

We walked around for a couple of hours with two members of the task force while they showed us the significant areas and answered our questions about the neighborhood. I thought the fact that we were in the midst of an upper-middle-class community was itself a factor to note. If the offender lived here, and he was young, then he'd be unable to afford a house like these, which meant that he probably lived with one or both of his parents. I also noted that while the single homes, divided by driveways or hedges, were close together, there was room enough for someone to get between them to hide and then commit a crime in the shadows. Boats on trailers were backed into some of the driveways, and several cars were parked in a way that gave cover. I also saw fences and landscaping with shrubs that might hide a man watching for the lone female coming home.

Yet the neighborhood was also well populated, and it jumped right out at Douglas and me that this man was willing to take risks. He might have been from around there, but he was still exposing himself to potential discovery. We thought that might even be part of the excitement for him. There's a theory that the nervous system of a psychopath is understimulated and so they naturally seek out the heightened thrill of a challenge. If this guy was a psychopath—which would make him even more dangerous—then he'd keep going for the stimulation. He'd keep raping women.

After our walk-through investigation, we all went out for beers. That's usually part of my agenda, so we can develop an informal relationship with the local investigators. While sharing a meal or having a drink with us, they tend to open up and say things that might not be said otherwise. We also use this to build rapport, so it relaxes them. We want them to know us better and to realize we just want to help them do their job. That makes things work well all around.

By the end of the evening, as Douglas and I returned to our rooms, we felt that much of what we'd already written in our report had been confirmed. We were ready.

The following morning, we went into a crowded conference room where a half dozen investigators awaited our opinion. Some were skeptical and perhaps thought that they didn't need our help, but others were interested in what we had to say. I went into this meeting aware of the fact that when you talk to cops about psychology, there's a general mistrust. They're quick to run up the bullshit flag. They're not interested in feeling sorry for these guys, and they're asking what the hell a behavioral profile is. The seasoned cops are generally the easiest to talk to because they have more experience with the complications of crime. In fact, all investigators profile to some extent, whether they know it or not. In order to get some direction, they have to make assumptions about an offender's behavior. We've just refined the process, so for those with experience, what we say usually makes sense. As we went on that day, the initial tension quickly diminished.

One thing we wanted to set straight right away, since there was some disagreement among the investigators on this, was the offender's probable first encounter zone with the victims. Since he was grabbing these women from bus stops, several officers had speculated that he might have worked downtown somewhere, spotted the women there, and followed them as they got on the bus to go home.

We weren't inclined to accept that hypothesis. Given the associated locations of each of the crimes, we believed he was from Scarborough. If he worked downtown and targeted victims there, we felt sure we'd see a wider geographic pattern to his attacks, because it's more likely that the victims would be from widely diverging parts of the city. Instead, they were generally clustered in Scarborough.

We then went on to say why we thought he lived with his parents. In other words, the bottom line was that he was cruising his own neighborhood. But there was more. We felt we had a good sense of this guy and of what he might do next, so we spent most of the day going over our report.

The reason for many local agencies requesting a criminal profile is to help focus the investigation and perhaps narrow down the pool of suspects. Sometimes, coming into a situation with fresh eyes and a broad experiential base provides new insights and a sharper perspective. During the analysis, we examine the method of and manner in which the crime was committed. We look at such variables as the time of day it was committed, risk factors for the victim, risk factors for the offender, and the number of crime scenes involved. If more than one, we then differentiate between the primary and secondary crime scenes. We examine the criminal MO, look for any evidence of ritualistic behavior, and in a series of crimes, we're alert to evidence of a signature aspect that may link the crimes behaviorally. Because past behavior is the best predictor of future behavior, we can offer informed opinions about the probability and nature of future attacks.

Geography is important as well, and geographic profiling is its own area of specialization. Dr. Kim Rossmo, formerly of the Vancouver British Columbia Police and currently director of research for the Police Foundation in Washington, D.C., pioneered this discipline. It involves getting a good sense of how the various crime scenes are related to one another by location and which ones may pinpoint an offender's zone of familiarity. That may help to narrow down where he lives or works, and this method has been particularly successful in urban-based serial crimes such as rape and murder.

In the Scarborough case, we knew where the attacks had occurred, but we also tried to establish where each victim had initially encountered her attacker. We worked to determine if there were any common links among the women, such as working in the same place or shopping at the same store. After a lengthy analysis, we had discovered nothing in their backgrounds or lifestyles that would elevate their risk of becoming victims of a violent crime or sexual assault. We considered all of them to be low-risk victims. That was significant, but it made things more difficult. Random attacks by strangers are harder to solve than are those that clearly link the victim with an obvious suspect.

All of these victims were white females, fifteen to twenty-two years of age, and six of them were living in the Scarborough area. Three of those lived in extremely close proximity to one another. We noted the fact that four of the victims had traveled either from or through the downtown area immediately prior to the attack, but we felt that probably meant nothing.

In addition to developing the victimology, it's important to conduct a meticulous analysis of the crime and crime scene, and to carefully review all investigative and forensic reports. In a series of rapes such as this one, it is critically important to examine the assailant's "core behavior," i.e., the verbal, physical, and sexual behavior he exhibited during the commission of the attacks. The verbal behavior is not only what he says, but also how he says it, as well as anything that he might script the victim to say. This offender's verbal behavior was profusely profane, and he often made his victim describe herself as a bitch, a cunt, or a slut.

Physically he used an excessive level of force, beating them even in the absence of resistance. As the rapes continued, the brutality appeared to be increasing. He not only broke the collarbone of the sixth victim, for example, but also poured dirt on her, rubbing it into her hair and onto her body. Could there be any clearer message about his attitude toward women?

We felt that this offender used bus stops for staking out potential victims and that he was routinely prowling the streets at night. Some of the women had simply been victims of opportunity, while others appeared to have been previously targeted.

"We believe the offender has seen victims or potential victims in passing," we later wrote in our final report, "but had no urge to attack, and at other times has seen victims and had the urge to attack, but the moment was inopportune. The successful attacks occurred when the urge, opportunity, and victim coincided." It was also our feeling that he was following them for short distances before attacking them.

The offender had approached all six of the Scarborough victims from behind, while he came up to the woman in Mississauga from the front. He gained control over them all with a "blitz" attack, or the immediate application of physical force, and he maintained control through force and threats, most of which were accomplished while brandishing a knife in an intimidating manner. We observed that all of the victims were attacked outdoors, under the cover of darkness, while they were walking alone.

We pointed out that this type of offender typically starts his attacks in an area with which he is familiar. Because he appeared to know the ins and outs and alleyways, with their potential as escape routes, this man felt he could safely act out.

"We believe your offender resides in the Scarborough area," we told the investigators, "specifically within walking distance of the first, second, and fifth attacks. Because he lives in his attack area, it's important to him that the victims not see him. This is one of the reasons he prefers to approach the victims from the rear. Upon contact, he forces them, facedown, to the ground or demands they keep their eyes closed to ensure they do not see him."

We added that the victim in Mississauga was approached in a slightly different manner. That could mean that a different offender had been involved or that this woman was an unfortunate victim of opportunity while the same offender just happened to be in her area. We believed that after he followed her for a distance on foot, he approached her under the guise of asking directions. He allowed her to see his face, but the exposure was brief, as the offender assaulted her before he finished his sentence and forced her to the ground in the same manner as in Scarborough. It was our opinion that in this circumstance the offender was less concerned about being seen because he spent little time in the Mississauga area and believed it unlikely that he would be recognized or seen there again.

One can never lose sight of the fact that human behavior is infinitely complex and that there could be other reasons for his approaching his victims from behind—perhaps he harbored some inadequacies. We thought that was clear from the fact that he scripted many of his victims to say, "Tell me you hate your boyfriend and you love me" or "Tell me you love me, tell me it feels good." He apparently had a strong need to gratify his ego, especially with women who were involved with other men. He wanted to feel superior to them. Also supporting this was the fact that he targeted victims who were alone and nonthreatening. Most of them were physically small, virtually defenseless, and could offer no real resistance.

To finish it, we pointed out one more thing: When analyzing the offender's sexual behavior, it's important to look at not just the type, but also at the sequence of the sexual acts he forces upon the victim. This offender typically had his victims perform oral sex on him after having assaulted them vaginally, then anally. This sequence of sexual behaviors serves to further punish, degrade, and humiliate the victim. We then gave the task force a framework for understanding him.

[5]

The FBI has adopted a four-part typology, as developed by Dr. Nicholas Groth, to categorize stranger-based rapists like this one. The typology involves two basic motivations: anger or the need for power. They are:

- Power-reassurance
- Power-assertive
- Anger-retaliatory
- Anger-excitation

No rapist perfectly fits any given type, but he will generally fit one better than the other three. Since the verbal behavior of a power-based rapist is not usually profane and they use little or no physical force, we believed that this offender was not a power-based rapist.

He also harbored an extraordinary amount of rage. It appeared that he intended to punish his victims, which indicated a pervasive animosity toward women in general. Also, by forcing the victims to perform oral sex on him after he had vaginally and anally assaulted them, he was degrading and humiliating them. Thus, we classified him as an anger-retaliatory rapist.

While this may seem like an obvious interpretation, its significance for the task force lay in the fact that his anger and misogyny would be evident to those who knew him. If they heard this description in some media report or town meeting, someone who feared him might come forward.

The one thing that most concerned us was the escalation in violence evident throughout this series of attacks. He used far more physical force with the victims than was necessary for control, he had broken a bone, and he had also stuffed articles of clothing into the mouths of some of these women. By rubbing dirt into the hair of the sixth victim, he seemed to be expressing his general disgust with women.

As we analyzed the interactions between the individual victims and the offender, we saw that the women were generally compliant and submissive. Still, when they misunderstood a command or delayed their obedience, even momentarily, he became enraged. Then he increased the amount of violence directed at them. We did not believe he would attack a victim with the premeditated idea of murdering her, but based on our research and experience, we thought that if someone dared to vigorously resist, he could become so enraged that he'd lose control. In other words, he was more dangerous than he might seem from the crimes committed thus far.

The increasingly sexual nature of the assaults under-scored his potential for worse violence. In the first three attacks, there had been no penile penetration, while the rest were full-blown rapes. We also noted that in the later crimes, the offender's sadistic tenden-cies were more pronounced. He asked the seventh vic-tim, "Should I kill you?" and made her beg for her life. Sexual sadists achieve gratification from their victims' reaction to the torture they inflict and from the feeling that they have dominated their victims, physically and psychologically. They relish the pain and suffering more than the sexual contact. As long as the victim is screaming and begging, they're happy.

I had one case of a sadistic rapist in Connecticut who had picked up two girls who were hitchhiking. He took turns anally assaulting them. The first one didn't scream or offer any resistance, so he kept working on her. The second one screamed and he ejaculated right away. Her reaction was his payoff. For him, the vio-lence had become eroticized, as we believed it was for the Scarborough rapist. When that happens, the doors to hell have truly been opened. A potential serial killer is unleashed, but not just any serial killer. This would be a *sexually sadistic* serial killer, the darkest and most elusive of all.

What truly worried us about him was that he demonstrated adaptive behavior, which indicated that he felt he was in control. This was evident in the de-tails of the sixth attack. While he was accosting this victim, a car pulled out of a driveway a few inches away and went right by them. He didn't panic but sim-ply forced her into some bushes near a house and con-tinued his assault.

As we continued to talk to the task force, they experienced a greater sense of foreboding, so we got down to the practical work. Who was this guy? From the crime details and the victims' various descriptions, we provided the investigators with a detailed list of his traits.

1. Some victims had seen his face, so we knew he was a white male.

2. We placed him between eighteen and twenty-five years of age, although we cautioned investigators reading the report that age is a difficult category to profile. An individual's behavior is more strongly influenced by emotional and mental maturity than by chronological age. We always say that because no suspect should be eliminated based on age alone. Yet the behavior exhibited throughout the series of assaults suggested a youthful offender rather than a more mature one, and that's how the victims had described him.

3. It seemed clear to us that he resided in the Scarborough area, possibly in the Guildwood Village neighborhood.

4. Those who knew the man would be aware of his anger toward women. He'd speak disparagingly of them in general conversations rather than keep his attitudes to himself. We thought that he'd had a major problem with a female immediately before the onset of these attacks. His anger would have been apparent not only to her but to anyone close to him. It seemed likely that any relationships he had with women would be stormy. In all probability, he had battered women and blamed them for his failures.

5. He was sexually experienced.

6. If he had a criminal record, any arrests would have been for acts such as assault, disturbing the peace, resisting arrest, or domestic disturbance, and this ag-

gressive behavior would have surfaced at some point during adolescence. We thought he might have had discipline problems in high school, and might even have received counseling for his inability to get along with others, his aggressiveness, and/or possibly for substance abuse.

7. He was bright, shrewd, and organized.

8. He was nocturnal and spent a lot of time on foot in the target assault area. Possibly people in the neighborhoods targeted had seen him standing around. People who knew him would have only a superficial acquaintance, because he was more the lone-wolf type.

9. He was probably single.

10. His work record would be sporadic, because his inability to handle authority would interfere with his ability to hold on to a job. In that case, it was likely that a relative, possibly his mother, supported him. Given his anger, we thought there was a dominant female in his life who wielded control in some area that humiliated him.

11. Some of the victims reported that he'd taken items from them when he'd left. We believed that he kept these items as trophies of his successful attack. They helped him to relive the assault when he was alone, and they were proof of his manhood, virility, and, most important, of his superiority over "every worthless bitch" in the world.

"He will keep these items in an area that is under his personal control," we said, "which he feels is secure but yet allows him ready access."

Then we offered a strategy. Our thesis was that they could either be proactive or reactive. A reactive approach would be to wait for another rape to occur and hope they got lucky and caught the guy. A proactive approach involved getting him to react to them. In other words, they should figure out his moves and put him into motion in a controlled way. They would need to challenge him, and we had a plan for this.

From our reading of the file, it was apparent that the rapist had liked a particular victim, an ice skater, because he had tried to contact her again by phone and had spoken to a member of her family. We suggested that, with her and her family's permission, the police could use her as bait. That's dicey, and I wouldn't be reckless with a plan like that, but our thinking was that we were coming up on the anniversary of her attack, so the press could run a story about how she'd been unaffected by the attack and had gotten on with her life. In this way, she could show the rapist, who might be reading the paper, that his need to humiliate her hadn't worked. Such a report would also revive his recollection of her, and since he'd contacted her once, he might do so again. The idea was to lure him out in some way. I don't think we underestimated the potential danger, but we believed we could keep this girl safe.

What we find many times in cases like this is that devising a strategy works not only with the offender in the way that we hope but also with the victims. It gives them a sense of empowerment that can be therapeutic. They feel that they're doing something positive to have an impact on the situation, and they can reestablish both a sense of control and a trust in their environment. That was the upside, but we couldn't do it without complete concurrence from the victim's family. It was just one viable plan, and we presented it, but we learned later that it was never used.

Nevertheless, our profile did help to clarify some

things for the task force and focused the investigation on a particular area. They realized that they couldn't keep thinking of the offender as coming in from some outside area. More likely, he lived right there. The differences of opinion among the investigators on this matter were resolved and everyone was on the same page. Yet as they became more focused, they could see the dangerous trajectory—that this rapist was escalating toward homicide.

We thought it was likely that the attacks would continue to be episodic and sporadic. They would occur outdoors, as usual, because he needed a sense of mobility: a place where he could easily attack and from which he could escape. The attacks might be precipitated by some stressful incident in the offender's life, and we cautioned that this man harbored no guilt or remorse for his crimes. "Attack and flee" was his attitude, ecstatic from punishing these "pieces of shit" and showing them— and more important, showing himself—who was really in charge. His sole concern would be to elude identification and apprehension, but he believed he was razor sharp and lightyears ahead of us, so why worry? Life was good, especially when he was in charge. Yet anger gnawed at him. He couldn't rest. Were the gates of hell opening? Would the darkest of monsters be unleashed? Unless he was caught quickly, we believed it was only a matter of time before their rapist became a sexually sadistic killer. That made everyone uneasy.

[6]

I had to move on. Other cases were pressing in, but I kept abreast of the Scarborough situation. There were new rapes and new victims, apparently with the same offender. Each new case reinforced my original opinion and heightened my concerns about him. He remained consistently violent and controlling. We were aware that the police had a composite drawing of the offender and that they'd been collecting DNA samples. They even had a suspect who resembled the drawing and who had voluntarily provided samples, but so far they had failed to process them. Hindsight would reveal that they had just missed closing in on the very man they were after—and that mistake would exact a terrible price.

For us, this was a classic profiling case. I assessed an offender's behavior across a series of crimes. We analyzed verbal, physical, and sexual behaviors that the offender exhibited with the victim. We looked for patterns, evidence of a signature, and any changes over time, and then made logical inferences from the information we had.

From cases like this that weren't quickly solved, I had learned that to be a successful profiler, it's important to develop a sense of perspective. Toward that end, I kept a cartoon on the bulletin board in my office at Quantico that featured an engorged dragon sitting against a tree, picking its teeth with a lance. Pieces of the slain knight's armor are randomly strewn about. The caption read, "Some days the dragon wins." For those who deal on a daily basis with the most sadistic and violent human acts, it's important to remember that we can't always stop the dragon. The work of profiling criminal behavior is toxic and we have many dark days. Even so, we keep hunting down the beast. Predators are our prey.

Yet once I'd done my part in a case, I had to move on. That was the nature of our role as criminal consultants. At any given time, I averaged about fifty open cases, which meant that whenever I was fully focused on one, I was not working on the other forty-nine. For the investigators with whom I was presently consulting, *their* case was the most important one in the world, so to operate efficiently I had to let go of the other unresolved crimes. Yet they remained on my mind, haunting me in the small hours of the night or creeping unbidden into my conscious thoughts, smothering all other concerns. As much as I worked to let go of them, they wouldn't let go of me.

This one did get solved, but only after it got worse, and I eventually returned to face the same offender again, but for a different reason. The second time, he was aware of me. He'd developed his skills and his cunning, so this time he was much more deadly. Even as I left this case, I could still see him in my mind and could easily anticipate that I would be back.

In the meantime, other agencies claimed my attention. The next major linked series of criminal incidents happened not far from Scarborough, in Rochester, New York, and this case was about murder. We had to move fast to stop this guy.

2: Fitting the Profile

> Crime is terribly revealing. Try and vary your methods as
> you will, your tastes, your habits, your attitude of mind,
> and still your soul is revealed by your actions.
>
> —Agatha Christie

[1]

Over the course of several days, New York State Police
teams had gone up in helicopters to scout out
Rochester's winter terrain. Four women were missing,
believed to be murdered, and we had reason to think
we could close in on the killer. The investigators' task
was to search for a crime scene without getting too
close, so they could find a victim to stake out. They'd
already discovered one woman's ID, and we believed
that if we located where she had been dumped, the guy
would come back. When he did, he'd walk right into a
trap.

He'd always left his victims outside, usually around
water, so we used that to guide the search. Yet after
hours spent covering the same ditches, canals, and
creeks, the police felt they'd given it their best shot. It
would soon be time to call it quits. Then one team took
off from Northampton Park for a final flight along
Highway 31, back toward the city. Almost two years

earlier, the first of eight victims had been discovered there, so they decided to have one last look. Snow on the ground was a concern, but the denuded trees made it easier to see.

They flew low over Salmon Creek, alert for anything unusual. They scanned the area from right to left and back again. To their amazement, they soon spotted something just under the bridge. It appeared to be a human figure lying facedown on the surface of the ice.

They hovered for a closer look and made out a nude white female. Her legs were splayed out and she wasn't moving. It had to be the body they were searching for. But then they noticed something else that surprised them even more, and in short order they radioed to patrol units on the ground to get over to this place *fast*. They thought that they had the killer.

[2]

It was November 1989. I'd just returned from the Bahamas where I'd successfully worked with the Royal Bahamian Police on a series of seven cabdriver murders that had occurred in Nassau. The victims had all been shot, possibly raped, and then burned and tossed into one of two piles. Their cars were then used for daytime robberies and torched afterward. With a profile based on the geographic pattern of the crimes, we'd had the police focus on a specific neighborhood and they were now running down the suspects. I was back in my underground office, about to catch up on the details of a series of unsolved murders in Massachusetts, when the phone rang.

To me that meant someone had gone through the

unit secretary and either had asked specifically for me or had asked for a profiler for a specific area. Knowing that at any moment I might be called into a brutal crime that would mean an abrupt refocus, I picked up the receiver and heard the voice of a woman I knew well.

"Gregg," she said. "It's A, in Buffalo."

I was happy to hear from her. A was Aileen Walsh, the training tech in the FBI's Buffalo office. She'd been a loyal friend during my years there as a field agent, and she always spoke the unvarnished truth. Aileen worked with the local and state police officers who had graduated from the FBI's eleven-week NA training course at the National Academy in Quantico, Virginia. These sessions inspire close relationships among attendees and strengthen cooperation between their agencies and the FBI. Aileen helped to facilitate that.

"I've had a call from Lynde Johnston," she said. "He's a captain over in Rochester, an NA grad, and a great guy. They have a situation there."

"Okay," I responded. "What's the situation?"

"They're pretty sure they've got a serial killer and they're looking for some help. Are you available?"

"Of course. I'll be in my office all day. Have him give me a call."

Aileen was efficient. Within a few minutes, the phone rang again and it was Lynde Johnston. In a quiet voice, he introduced himself and then said, "We think we have a serial killer at work here and he's targeting local prostitutes. Normally, we have about three or four victims a year, but over this past year and a half, we've had around fifteen. We'd like someone to look at these cases and give us a profile."

I asked for details and he described what they had up to that point. From what they could tell, it had started in March of the year before. The first two victims had been killed in different ways, so at the time, there was no clear reason to link them, except that both were discovered in the Genesee River. One had been bitten and strangled, and there was vaginal mutilation. She had surfaced from the river fully clothed. The other bore no signs of violation and was undressed. She appeared to have been suffocated and pushed into the water, and there was fluid in her lungs. Then skeletal remains, without a head, were found in the river gorge, another partially clothed body was found hidden in a ditch behind the YMCA, and by the fall of 1989, more such grisly discoveries suggested the pattern of a single offender. Only the fifth victim's body, tossed naked into a deep ravine, was fresh enough to gather forensic clues, but it hadn't yielded anything worthwhile.

Despite how serious the situation was, Lynde went on, it had inspired a rather ironic team: The vice cops and prostitutes, typically adversaries, were now working together. They all wanted the killer off the streets, so the cops were asking the hookers to report anything suspicious among the johns they encountered. That tenuous arrangement had turned up some possible leads.

I told Lynde I'd be glad to help, and even as he was talking, I was planning my approach. I wanted Lieutenant Ed Grant of the New York State Police, an experienced investigator I knew well, to work with me. Despite jurisdiction issues, Lynde was amenable. "We'll be happy to have him," he said. Aileen had been right; he was a great guy.

What Lynde didn't know, but would soon find out,

was that Eddie Grant is relentless, and that was one reason I wanted him along. He'd been among the top participants in our intensive police-fellowship program in criminal-investigative analysis, and while he's quick with a laugh, he idles at 100 miles an hour. Whatever he does, he does intensely. If you're a bad guy, he's the last cop you want on your case.

As I expected, when I told Eddie about the case later that day, he jumped at the chance to join me. We discussed our mutual availability in the midst of our pressing schedules. Yet before we were able to get up there, Rochester had another murder, and this one shocked everyone.

[3]

It was Thanksgiving Day, and a man out walking his dog in a marshy area by the industrial piers had come across the decomposing body of a naked woman covered by only a piece of carpet. That meant calls to the core investigation team. This looked like yet another murder in the series, making it potentially number sixteen on Lynde's list. Their hopes for just one quiet day with their families dashed, the investigators quickly assembled to brave the raw weather. They were beginning to feel overwhelmed, and with this one it only got worse: The victim had been killed more than two weeks earlier, maybe longer, and she had not only been murdered but also eviscerated. The killer had cut her from the top of the chest, between her breasts, all the way into the vaginal area. Then something else became clear: Along the wound margins, the skin was white and void of blood. That meant the killer had cut her open some time after she was already dead.

It turned out that her name was June Stott, she was thirty, and she was the only one thus far who'd been subjected to extensive postmortem mutilation. She was also not a prostitute. Whether this homicide was part of the series was yet to be determined. It was imperative now that we get there and have a look at all of the case documentation. Going to Rochester would also provide an opportunity to see the crime scenes, so we set December 13 as the day to meet with the team.

Lynde Johnston was gracious and soft-spoken. He was eager to give us whatever we needed to assist us in our assessment. The more range the offender demonstrated with his behavior, we told him, the better our chances of helping. In particular, if we decided that June Stott was part of the series of victims found in the gorge, which to that point had been mostly prostitutes, then we had clear evidence of a form of psychopathology not obvious with the other victims. That meant that if she was a victim of the same killer, he'd shifted his behavior. That wasn't great for the investigators, but as paradoxical as it may seem, such developments are good for us: The more deviant behavior an offender exhibits, the more he reveals about himself. This helps us to develop a specific strategy that can get him identified and apprehended.

Then we prepared to survey the crime scenes, and that meant going outside. Lynde, with his blond hair and fair skin, appeared to be at home in the biting-cold air, but I was less prepared. I'd grown up in upstate New York not far from there and the winters are long and often harsh. That day three inches of heavy, wet snow covered the ground—the kind that as kids we called "good packing." I should have known better, but all I had on my feet were leather street shoes. No joy there. As we slogged around that morning, moisture soaked through my shoes and raw air cut to the bone.

For many reasons, geography is important in a serial murder investigation. Commonalities among the places where the killer encountered his victims and the dump sites where he left the bodies can reveal a pattern that links cases together. Our first stop was Lyell Avenue, which was the only area in Rochester where one could get a white street hooker. It was also the last place most of the victims had been seen. As expected, it was a seedy industrial area of low buildings and old-fashioned signs covered in grime. Dirty snow hugged the curbs. By day, a number of small businesses operated there, including bars, but during the evening, Lynde told us, clusters of hookers, drug dealers, and homeless people populated these streets. As we drove along, I could imagine the women eyeing each car warily, trying to determine, should they get in, what destiny might be theirs. I also tried to envision how the killer had looked them over.

After getting a feel for how pickups were arranged, we went out to the Genesee River Gorge to traipse some more through the wet slush. This area proved to be scenic parkland, which was significant for our understanding of the predator. About six hundred feet deep and twenty-two miles long, with a river that flows north over three waterfalls, the local tourism bureau refers to the gorge as the "Grand Canyon of the East." That's a bit of a stretch, but even in the dead of winter it *is* impressive. Most of the victims had been dumped here, or nearby, and in general they were found in the area of the parkland nearest the city. We also checked out the industrial areas and the YMCA near the tracks.

While we studied the place, we made some preliminary assessments of "the Genesee River guy." Part of the routine for profiling is to just talk through what we notice and do some brainstorming about the behavior of the victims and the killer. It gets us right into the case. Eddie and I both noticed that the killer hadn't taken his victims too far—only a few miles from Lyell Avenue—to get rid of them. That was important, because it reflected his comfort level. Dumping a body outside is risky, so killers who do that will typically choose an area with which they're familiar. In a way, that's just common sense: Why go to a place you don't know and risk being interrupted or caught? Yet as close as it was to the pickup site, it was far enough away to indicate that there'd been a vehicle involved. So now we had some initial impressions.

"We agree that he's familiar with this area," I said, "but why? What's the most logical reason?"

We threw out some possibilities: You can picnic here, you can hike, and you can fish. The most likely was that he liked to fish here. He wouldn't be hunting within the city limits on state parkland—excluding his human prey, of course—and we didn't see him as a health-conscious hiker/jogger kind of guy.

So he knew the area, he had access to a vehicle, and what else?

"These weren't high-priced call girls," Eddie commented, "and he's comfortable with them."

"That probably puts him just a step above them in terms of his own socioeconomic level," I suggested. "He's probably not much above them in terms of educational level, either."

"He doesn't stand out to them, obviously, so how does he get these women to go with him when they're scared of getting killed?"

We didn't have to give this much thought. "He's probably a known customer," I said. "They've had sex with him with no problem. They see him coming back and dropping them off, so to them he's just a regular john. He doesn't scare them." That meant to us that he was transparent. They were looking right through him, because they believed the killer had to be someone else.

It was also striking that, from those remains where a finding was possible, there had been no overt sexual assault. With prostitute murders, the problem is usually just the opposite. There's plenty of indication of sexual activity, but when semen is recovered, there's no guarantee that it's the killer's. That can complicate an investigation, yet here we didn't even have that.

"If this guy can't have sex with a hooker," Eddie mused, "who can he have sex with?"

"That's more than a good question," I commented.

Eddie nodded silently. That was his point. Crimes are dynamic, not static, and the outcome of any interpersonal crime will be shaped by the victim/offender interaction. We were looking for a triggering event, something that would turn what might have been a normal sexual encounter into a violent homicide. In some cases, there appeared to be anger involved. As we thought this through, we speculated that in all probability, the killer had been unable to perform sexually. These homicidal events were times when he couldn't get an erection or perhaps couldn't climax, and, of course, that wasn't his fault, so he'd blame the woman, the incompetent bitch. These streetwalkers are tough and would not tolerate being blamed. They likely berated him, and that humiliation would only have intensified his anger. He would finally regain control of the situation in the only way he knew—through violence. We didn't know this with certainty, but we thought it a fair interpretation.

"Hey," Eddie said to one of the guys on the vice squad, "maybe you need to give these hookers a little sensitivity training."

[4]

After visiting the significant areas and evaluating their interrelationship, we returned to headquarters, where Lynde showed us into a conference room. In here, he said, we could spread out the files they'd prepared for us. He pointed to a door that led to his office and a second door that opened into a hallway with vending machines for coffee and snacks. I was relieved to be out of the cold, but my shoes were going to stay wet for some time.

The conference room was fairly large, with a dozen government-issue folding metal chairs set up around a long table. The warm air felt close and smelled of burned coffee. Interestingly, Lynde had given up coffee. His caffeine intake had escalated to dramatic proportions lately and his doctor had ordered him to reduce it just as dramatically. Since a cup or two a day would only serve as a tease, he drank cups of hot water instead.

Along one wall in the conference room we saw a long row of two-by-three-foot color photos of each of the victims—mostly enlarged mug shots from their arrests as prostitutes. Below each were hand-printed facts about the case, such as where and when she'd been found and the specific cause of death. On another wall was a map of the city with color-coded pins attached: blue for the known or suspected encounter sites, mostly around Lyell Avenue, and red for the body dumpsites. That gave us a good visual of how the dumpsites were related by geographic area.

As Eddie and I scanned the posters, it became apparent that they'd hung them in the order in which the victims were found, but that was all wrong for us.

"We need to change this around," I said. We had to look at the progression chronologically, in the order in which each of these women had been killed, not found. This kind of investigation is tricky, because a significant divergence can mean we have a separate offender or it can mean the same offender is acting out in a different manner. To observe the evolving nuances, it was important to see the crimes from the killer's perspective. So, one by one, we took the pictures down, laid them on the table, and then re-posted them according to the estimated murder times. That way we could track changes in the patterns and note evidence of escalation.

Part of our protocol is to offer the local agency a choice as to whether or not to have our report in writing. We told Lynde that written reports have a downside. He seemed surprised by that, so we explained: We won't be right on every detail, and if the case gets to court, a written report or profile is discoverable. With a guilty client, the defense team's only hope is to muddy the waters, so they attack the police and the investigation, and may launch what we refer to as a "SODDI" defense—Some Other Dude Did It. In other words, a defense team might decide to use that portion of a written profile that doesn't fit their client in order to argue that he's not the killer.

"We'll talk to you freely about it," I told Lynde, "and tell you what we think and why we think it, but in some cases, it's better not to put anything on paper." A profile is only a means to an end, we added, and not an end in itself. What's vital is the strategy that emerges for the investigation and the postarrest interview.

He saw our point, so he left us alone with the files. We had the rest of the day and part of the next before we had to be ready to present our findings to the core investigation team. That meant we had a lot of work to do in a short period of time, and the clock was ticking. The pressure was on. Eddie and I sat down at opposite ends of the table, each taking half of the tall pile of case reports, and got started.

Every profile is different, based on the information we have to work with. We never go in with a one-size-fits-all or what I call a "cookie-cutter" approach. After examining the evidence, sometimes we're sure of the race, and other times it's the level of criminal experience. In any case, we always feel more strongly about some things than others. If we turn out to be 100 percent right, then chances are good that somewhere along the way we got lucky. With that in mind, we worked hard to be as accurate as possible.

I was soon aware that it was hot in the room, but I didn't know if that was from the actual temperature or from stress. It's hard to describe the pressure in these situations—it's palpable. The police were getting beat up twice a day, once in the *Rochester Democrat and Chronicle* and once in the *Times-Union*. It was a constant drumbeat. Each of these papers was trying to outdo the other in covering these unsolved murders. They accused the investigation team of incompetence and of not caring, which was far from the truth.

It was obvious to me that they cared deeply about solving these crimes and were conducting a meticulous search. Every logical suspect they developed, they investigated and eliminated. This is a measure of objective and thorough scrutiny. Yet even knowing they were doing their job didn't alleviate their sense of frustration. It was our job to ease the pressure on them by shouldering some of it ourselves.

I was impressed by their attention in the case of Patricia Ives, a young woman whose badly decomposed nude body had been found in a ditch behind the YMCA. Unable to identify her, they'd brought in William Rodriguez, a forensic anthropologist, who used the skull to reconstruct her face. That's a long, arduous, and expensive process. From that, the police made a photo to place in newspapers and on television, with an appeal for someone who knew her to come forward. Her father called. Understandably, his emotions were mixed. He was grateful to know where she was but devastated about the circumstances.

While media attacks are aggravating, the real stress comes from within—the screws we turn on ourselves. We all wanted to stop these murders. Specifically, Eddie and I both hoped to be able to tell the investigators something meaningful that they hadn't yet thought of. They had done good work thus far and we feared that after hours of analysis, we might lay it all out and they would say, "Well, tell us something we *don't* know."

Something we don't know. That's what I'd learned about from Shorinji Kempo. You empty your mind and discipline yourself to see past the obvious situation to devise an effective strategy. The situation in front of us now involved anticipating the attack of an unseen offender. Once I had an idea of what I was dealing with, I could try to *blend* with his attack and use his momentum against him.

So telling the investigators what they "don't know" involves two steps: informing them of the offender's traits and offering an effective plan of action—one they hadn't already thought of and used.

Eddie and I worked that day until nearly ten P.M. We had to sort through thirteen detailed cases and our first task was to separate those we thought were related from those we thought weren't. During the course of the day, we would exchange the files we'd each completed so that at the end of the process we'd both reviewed all of them independently of each other. The hard metal chairs were not made for long periods of concentration, but we had to keep working.

With each case, we looked through autopsy reports, lab reports, crime scene photos, victim background details, and all of the investigation conducted to date. Our job was made easier by the thorough work that the Rochester investigators had done. They had interviewed just about every prostitute in the Lyell Avenue area and a number of suspects as well. The hookers didn't know what to make of any of this, but most had been cooperative. We noted that one woman, a heavy-set older hooker named Joanne van Nostrand, had said that she'd been with a john who'd wanted her to act as if she were dead. She'd cooperated, but had reported later that he'd given her the creeps.

"He was real nervous," she told the officers, "and that made *me* nervous. Little things kept clicking, and the hairs on the back of my neck started standing up."

Neither Eddie nor I could say that this was the killer, but after a lot of reading through these files, we believed it was the kind of behavior we'd expect him to exhibit.

The goal of the first day was to get a preliminary determination of a pattern we didn't yet know. For any case like this, it's a filtering process. We look at it in phases of refinement. We'd read a case and then keep going back to cases we'd already been through to compare details and do more analysis based on what we were learning. Throughout the day, as we consumed Coke and crackers and studied the cases, a pattern that set some cases apart did finally emerge: These victims had suffered some sort of asphyxial death but were not necessarily strangled, as there was a notable absence of neck bruising and ligature marks.

An asphyxial death means cutting off the air so the victim can't breathe, and blocking the flow of blood to the brain. It's the lack of blood to the brain that is the killer. In seconds, people are rendered unconscious and will die in a matter of minutes. Nicolas Forbes, the medical examiner, called them "unspecified deaths," meaning that we didn't know the cause, but he offered the opinion that if this guy could render them dead without manual strangulation, he would have to be pretty strong. We speculated that he might be applying a "carotid restraint" technique, or what is sometimes referred to as a "sleeper" hold, in which the killer's crooked arm is used to constrict the carotid arteries on both sides of the neck. He also might have smothered some. We just weren't sure.

To categorize the cases, we established three rings, and that was based on the totality of circumstances. We considered not just the method and manner of death but also the way the victims had lived. The innermost ring was for definite cases—the ones we firmly believed were part of the pattern. The next ring was for those we thought were probably related, and the third ring contained the cases we felt were definitely not related.

It didn't take long to eliminate about half. One victim was gunned down in a parking lot that was far from the other dumpsites and the MO was entirely different. Another had been neatly wrapped in a blue tarp, with the knots symmetrically tied. That, too, was different than just rolling someone into a river gorge. Another was clearly strangled. A fourth was hit by a car while she might have been fleeing from someone. Yet there was one, Patricia Ives, who'd been hastily rolled into a ditch and covered. That was different, too, but we thought she was likely to be in the series because the ditch was near the river-gorge area, she'd been a prostitute, no real effort was put into hiding her, and she'd suffered from asphyxial death.

The first victim, Dorothy Blackburn, twenty-seven, had been found by a hunter. Her corpse was fully clothed when it surfaced after the ice broke in Salmon Creek. That was one of the sites I remembered clearly from that morning, right along Route 31, near a bridge. She'd been strangled and kicked, and she'd also had vaginal trauma, but it wasn't the kind of evisceration we'd seen on June Stott. She'd been beaten, so there were some anger issues, but the injuries were perimortem in nature, meaning that they were done around the time of death, not after. Nick Forbes thought that the wounds looked like a blunt-force trauma that had caused a bleeding laceration. We weren't clear about the sequence of events, so we had to speculate: Had he beaten her, she'd gotten dressed, and then he'd killed her, or had she gotten dressed and then this thing had gone bad? Maybe she hadn't undressed at all. Maybe it had been bad right from the start.

As we looked together at the autopsy photos, we noticed another odd thing: Across the top of her chest, above the breasts, she had some sort of patterned indentation, about an inch and a half wide, that hadn't broken the skin. Eddie and I both examined it closely but couldn't figure out what it was.

The second victim we placed in the series was Anna Steffen, whose nude body had floated in the river until it had snagged on some construction debris, where it had been hidden from view for several months. She appeared to have been drowned, but her body had decomposed too quickly for Nick to give a clear cause of death. All he could tell was that there was water in her lungs. Then it had been almost a year before there was a third victim we could include, and she'd been a homeless woman.

It was after the fifth victim, just a few months before we arrived, that the media came up with the nickname for this faceless murderer, referring to him as "the Rochester Strangler" and "the Genesee River Killer." That was when the public pressure had started.

The vice cops had filled us in on a number of things, notably the comment from Joanne van Nostrand about a john who seemed potentially violent and who wanted her to pretend to be dead. We got to know about some of the hookers who were pretty savvy, such as June Cicero. The vice cops said among themselves that if they could make a case against June, that was a hell of a night's work. She'd literally jump out of a moving car if she thought an undercover cop was in it. That meant she was pretty aware of things and might be a good conduit for information. She'd be the most sensitive to danger and the least likely to go somewhere with a john she suspected of being a killer.

Sometimes Eddie and I would take a break and talk in the war room and sometimes we went outside. Eddie, a thin and wiry chain-smoker with an abundance of nervous energy, needed smoke breaks. I'd mention something I'd found and he'd say, "Come on, come on, let's go talk about it." Then out we'd go, despite my wet shoes, and I'd stand in the cold while he smoked. Yet whenever we talked, we made headway.

"I was just looking at this scene," I said during one break.

"You talking about June Stott?" He peered through the suspended smoke and jerked his thumb up toward the war room.

"Yeah."

"So, what do you think?" Eddie's question was strangely reassuring. He apparently also had some concerns about the case.

Her body had been found lying facedown, but the odd thing was that the lividity was fixed in her back. That was wrong. In a dead body, when the heart stops pumping, the blood settles. It's pulled down by gravity and coagulates. Then, in the area of lowest gravity, the body takes on a splotchy purple look. Lividity takes several hours to set and become fixed to the point where the blood is no longer liquid, although that varies with any number of conditions, from obesity to weather. Some research has shown that lower temperatures can affect it. So can what's in the blood, such as drugs.

"The lividity indicates she was killed and left on her

back for a while," I said, "long enough for it to set, and after that she was turned onto her stomach."

"So someone came back," Eddie suggested.

"Yes. The most logical explanation is that a few hours after her murder, someone made the incision down the front of her body and then turned her over, leaving her facedown." While there'd been no missing parts, the incise wound ran from the top of her chest, between her breasts, down to her vagina, displaying her intestines. "None of the other victims showed any indication of postmortem activity or this type of mutilation. I'm just wondering if this crime was part of the series."

I didn't have to say what we both knew. June Stott's mutilation was a significant difference and she was also not a prostitute. That tended to eliminate her, yet there were similarities with the other crimes as well: She'd been found in a wet, marshy area; there was no sexual assault; and the cause of death was unspecified asphyxial trauma.

We tossed these points back and forth, and by the time we were done, Eddie was coming to the end of his second smoke. "So, do we put her in or out," he asked, "or in the 'who knows?' camp?"

"Eddie," I said, "you agree that the guy who killed her was probably the same guy who cut her open?"

"Christ, I hope so."

"So that means . . ."

"The fucker's experienced."

"Right. The only way you get experienced in murder is through murder. He's clearly comfortable around dead bodies and was ballsy enough to return to have some more fun with this one."

"So, if it's our guy," said Eddie, "why the change?"

"He's growing into this. He's got several kills under his belt and he's really warming up. His blood lust is up. Killing Stott wasn't enough. He had to come back and cut her open. He likes this shit."

Eddie nodded. "Yeah, especially when you think about how bloodless the incision was and how dry the wound margins were. She'd been dead for some time before she was cut."

"That's right. We've seen this before." I was thinking of offenders like Edmund Kemper, a serial killer in California from the 1970s who'd murdered eight women, including his mother. At first he cut off his victims' hands and heads to prevent identification, but then he started to keep the parts around for sexual gratification. From him and others, we learned that in order to return to a body, you have to overcome two things: the fear of getting caught at the scene and the natural human aversion to corpses. These guys are quick to put distance between themselves and their victims early on, but then they get comfortable. That comes only with experience.

"This wasn't a frenzied act committed in the throes of a homicidal rage," I continued. "It was just the opposite: a premeditated, deliberate, cold, controlled, predatory act committed long after the homicide. That being the case, this little indulgence with Stott is probably just a goddamn omen of things to come."

"You're right. It's got to be him, it *is* him. Stott's in."

A cold rivulet of melted snow ran down the back of my neck. I don't know if that's what caused me to shiver or if it was the realization that our killer was in a dark, downward spiral. I walked stiffly up the steps, opened the door, turned to Eddie and said, "Stott's in and I'm going in." Eddie took a final pull off his smoldering filter and we trudged back up to the war room. We had a lot more work to do before our presentation.

[5]

By late afternoon on the second day, we'd finished going through everything in preparation for describing our findings to the Rochester investigators. In order to get as many people there as possible, they set the meeting time during the shift change. Eddie and I went into a small conference room crammed with chairs, and both uniformed officers and plainclothes cops were also standing along the sides and against the back wall. I saw a few females, too, among the more than thirty people who attended. We had the lead investigators there, but the meeting was open to any investigator available and interested.

Lynde introduced us with a little humor, and I took the lead. We first presented the cases that we thought clearly belonged to the serial killer, and then did a second presentation for a smaller group on the cases we thought were not related. We offered some ideas on those as well.

At first I wasn't sure how it was going to go, so it felt a little tenuous. I could see from some of the set expressions that we had skeptics in the room, as usual, but as long as they were willing to listen, I was happy to have them there. The atmosphere was mixed. I was sure that some thought it was a waste of time, others were curious, and a few believed we could do much more than we really could.

Over the next hour, we explained again that a profile was not an end in itself, but we could tell them some specific things about who they were looking for and offer ideas on how to catch him. No matter how experienced our audience, we always reemphasized this point. We advised them not to get locked in on any component: Don't rule someone out based on any specific item.

We believed this killer to be a white male in his late twenties or early thirties, with a history of other violent crimes. We acknowledged that the investigators had already searched in vain for links among known sex offenders, yet we insisted that this guy had some experience. There was evidence of premeditation: Someone doesn't just wake up one day and out of the blue start doing this kind of crime. He worked alone, and was controlled and methodical. There was nothing flashy or noticeable about him. It was probable that he was fairly transparent to the prostitutes and cops. He'd look normal, drive a functional car, and dress in functional clothing. The prostitutes probably expected someone weird or monstrous who would scare them, but that was a mistake and they needed to be told this. The killer was extraordinarily ordinary, probably someone they knew. It was likely that he worked, but at a menial job. Although he might have a relationship and even be married, in social contexts he'd be superficial. His economic level was similar to that of the victims, he lived and worked in the city, and because he'd managed thus far to avoid apprehension, he was streetwise, which again indicated experience.

We always emphasize that the most difficult component of any profile is estimating the offender's actual age, because based on past cases, we look specifically at developmental or emotional age, and that doesn't always correlate with chronological age. We feel more comfortable with the other traits.

We also talked about how killers like this can escalate and seem to change their patterns. "To us," we said, "the mutilation of June Stott is a significant turning point. We think it's the same killer, and up until November, he was just dumping the bodies and leaving. Now he's changed his behavior, and we believe that this will be the trend. That's important for what we're going to advise. He's used to them now and he likes to be near them, so he'll continue to return to the scenes to engage in postmortem mutilation. It might even get worse."

Based on this, we then offered some strategies.

We mentioned a past serial murder case in Delaware in which they'd used a female undercover officer as a hooker to screen potential suspects. Three prostitutes had been tortured and murdered with a hammer, each one with wounds worse than the last, and on the battered bodies they'd found blue carpet fiber from a car or a van. So when this officer saw a blue van, she went over to talk to the driver. He made her immediately uncomfortable and his van had blue carpeting, so as she talked with him, she ran her fingernails over the carpeting on the inside of the door. When she stepped back, she had fiber specimens for a trace comparison. It matched the fibers on the bodies, and they were able to identify Steve Pennell as the offender. We then advised that along with the benefits of this strategy there were dangers, and no undercover officer should get into a car with a john.

Since we felt the killer had a criminal record and

lived in the area, we believed the cops might have had prior dealings with him. We also suspected that he might be hanging out in bars or coffee shops where they gathered, so they might have already encountered him in some public place. It was not uncommon for killers to do that. With that awareness, they could devise ways to get names.

One other suggestion was to try to put surveillance on any body found in the future, which meant waiting for a day or two before going to the press. There were political consequences to not telling the victim's family, but that was a decision they'd have to make.

We found out later that one thing they did in response to what they'd learned was to persuade the owner of Mark's Texas Red Hot, an all-night bar, to raffle off a television set. That was the type of creative police work that we like to encourage. They collected names to develop as suspects, yet before they could follow through, things started happening fast.

[6]

After the conference, I left Rochester to attend to another pressing case. Yet I called Lynde frequently to keep up, and he soon delivered the next round of bad news. More women were missing and one of them was June Cicero. She was one of the most streetwise hookers in Rochester, the one we all believed would be the least likely to fall victim. The killer was so skillful at hiding his intent that even June Cicero hadn't sensed the danger. If he could get her, he could get anyone.

That was the "holy shit" moment for me.

Two days after Christmas, on December 27, Eddie

and I returned to Rochester. This time I took better shoes.

Now we insisted on a more proactive measure. It wasn't enough to just wait for a body to be found; we had to get out there and find one. With four missing women and a killer who dumped them outside, it couldn't be that difficult to turn up one. Up to this point, all of the victims had been discovered by fishermen or other people out walking. We urged Lynde to start actively looking in areas that could provide likely dumpsites. With nowhere else to go, because there was so little forensic evidence, the killer's behavior influenced our plan, and yet we wouldn't just wait for him. He was "pushing" us by coming back to mutilate the bodies and I was suggesting that we blend our energy with that. We'd use his own behavior to take him beyond where he wanted to go—to get him caught. In other words, when he pushed, we'd open the door and let him fall through.

Lynde was willing to try any reasonable idea, no matter how unorthodox. Since I had other ongoing cases, I could stay only two days. Just the day before, Eddie and I had been called to the scene of a particularly brutal family massacre about fifty miles from Rochester, and it demanded immediate attention. I went back to my family and then to Quantico, while Eddie stayed in Rochester. He and Lynde would keep me informed of any significant developments, and I'd be ready to return if needed.

Only four days later, on December 31, an alert trooper on road patrol in a rural area spotted a pair of black jeans discarded along the roadside. In the pocket of those jeans was the identification of Felicia

Stephens, a black prostitute who was missing and presumed to be one of the killer's victims. That alarmed everyone, and the search intensified with more manpower, yet it was brutally cold, with ice on the lakes and creeks, which made it risky. Some police officers crossing the snow-covered frozen water went right through.

New Year's Day came and went. On the morning of January 2, the state police resumed the search by air and ground for a body, but later in the day called it off as the winds from Lake Ontario created whiteout conditions. It seemed as if the weather was conspiring with the killer.

The following day, I was at Quantico, immersed in the details of the crime scene from the family murder I'd just taken on as part of my case load. I'd just spread out the photos, autopsy reports, and victimology descriptions when my phone rang. It was Eddie, up in Rochester.

"I got news," he said.

I sat forward in my chair. "What?"

"The guys in the choppers spotted a body in Salmon Creek," he told me. "It was on top of the ice, under a bridge."

Salmon Creek was the same area where Dorothy Blackburn's body had been found. The bridge over the creek was on Route 31, which, if followed into the city, became Lyell Avenue.

"No shit," I said. "One of ours?"

"Yeah."

Recalling the clothing recently found, I asked, "Felicia Stephens?"

"No. June Cicero."

"June Cicero? Unbelievable."

"Not only that, her vagina was cut out."

"Goddamn, Eddie . . ." That sounded like our guy. We'd been looking for postmortem mutilation, especially of a kind that spoke of anger against women.

"Here's where it gets kinky," he continued.

"What the . . . ?"

"There was a guy on the bridge."

"Are you shitting me? The fuck was a guy doing on the . . ."

"Jerking off, apparently."

[7]

I needed a few minutes to process all of this. We'd planned this strategy with precisely this goal: We'd hunted for crime scenes because we were sure he'd return. It wasn't that easy in such a large area to canvass and stake out a potential crime scene—in fact, to try to pinpoint something like that was downright radical. It's not a good way to use your resources unless you have some clear reason for doing it. Yet against all odds, it looked very much as if we'd had a payoff.

I wanted this to be our guy, but what were the chances? It was almost too much to believe that at the very moment they'd located a body, the killer was there, too, going through his postmortem routine.

Yet there was no denying that we had a suspect. Now we had to move carefully.

"Who is he?" I asked.

"They've got him identified as Arthur Shawcross," Eddie said. "We don't want to get ahead of the game, but what got our attention was finding out that he was on parole for manslaughter."

That was a surprise. "On parole?" I asked. "I thought they looked through the records."

"They did, but there's a big question now. Apparently Parole tried to place him in several small towns in upstate New York, but when the local police and townspeople heard about a child killer in their community, they ran him out. That happened several times. There's some suspicion that Parole may have slipped him into town without telling anyone. That'll get sorted out later. Right now we either got to put this guy Shawcross in, or put him out of this thing."

"Are they talking to him about the murders?" I asked.

This part made me nervous. The biggest single mistake we see in many cases is interviewing the suspect too soon. There's a strong tendency to want to sit a guy down and interrogate him right away, but that's usually a bad idea. Knowing the facts of the case is a start, but a good interviewer wants to know as much as possible about the suspect, too. What's his criminal history? Is he a confessor? If he's confessed before, what were the circumstances? If he failed to confess to prior crimes, what were those circumstances? People rape and murder for a multitude of different reasons, and understanding the motive can help shape the interview. Why take a quick shot at a confession when, with only a little more work, you can take your best shot?

To my relief, Eddy told me that they were backing off and getting more background on Shawcross and his previous crimes. The plan was to let him go, since they had no real evidence against him, watch him overnight, and then talk with him more fully the next day.

During the initial interview at the state police barracks, Shawcross had told the investigators that it was just a coincidence that he was parked over the body on

Salmon Creek, that he was just driving around and he'd stopped to take a piss when the helicopter flew over. That was possible, yes, but he also admitted that he'd been arrested previously because two kids "had died." That linked him more firmly to the crimes. Though excited, the investigators did a good job of building rapport and not pressing for details. Until they could gather more information, they wanted him to feel comfortable talking with them because they intended to question him again. While Shawcross talked freely about fishing and hunting, everyone carefully avoided the subject that was on all of their minds—the murders. Then they let him go home, but whether he knew it or not, Art was now the subject of a full-court press. There was surveillance everywhere.

Before they released him, Shawcross agreed to let them take his photograph. Investigators put it into a photo spread and showed the spread to several of the prostitutes working Lyell Avenue. One was Joanne van Nostrand, the one who had told the police about a john who'd wanted her to pretend she was dead. At the time, we'd thought that a significant comment. Without hesitation, she picked Shawcross as that guy. She also indicated that Shawcross was the john with whom Elizabeth Gibson, another victim, had last been seen. Several other prostitutes identified him as well. They all knew him as "Mitch," a regular customer who'd never been a problem. Just as we had indicated: He'd been right there but more or less invisible.

Meanwhile, the investigators were developing his background. Shawcross had committed several crimes in Watertown, New York, an old factory town where he'd grown up that was located on the Black River, off the eastern shore of Lake Ontario. I'd been there my-self several times at the army's Fort Drum to train with the FBI SWAT team.

It turned out that Arthur Shawcross had made a last-ing impression on the citizens of his hometown. He'd dropped out of school at the beginning of the ninth grade—at age nineteen. He'd then enlisted in the army and served a tour in Vietnam. He had married three times, and was now on his fourth wife. Through the years, Shawcross had accumulated some minor crimi-nal offenses for burglary and had spent some time in jail, but his violence had eventually escalated. He'd burglarized the local Sears store and set it on fire. Then he'd started to kill.

In May 1972, ten-year-old Jack Blake disappeared near the apartment complex where Shawcross lived. No one knew what had happened to him, but Jack's mother was certain that Art Shawcross was involved. Jack and his older brother had been fishing with the twenty-seven-year-old Shawcross a few days before, and he'd told conflicting stories about when he'd last seen the boy. That seemed suspicious, but with no body and no evidence, the cops were hard-pressed to do much. Searches for him came up dry, but that all changed four months later when eight-year-old Karen Ann Hill, who was visiting Watertown with her mother, Helene, was reported missing.

Karen Ann's body was found under a bridge that crossed the Black River, downtown. She'd been raped and murdered. Oddly, mud, leaves, and other debris had been forced down her throat and inside her cloth-ing. Shawcross, who'd been fishing under the bridge, became an immediate suspect. Detective Charles Ku-binski of the Watertown Police Department knew him.

With persistence and skill, he eventually got Shaw-cross to confess to the crime. He also gathered enough information about Jack Blake that the police were finally able to locate the boy's body. Due to its advanced state of decomposition, it was unclear whether Jack had been sexually assaulted, but like Karen Ann, he'd been asphyxiated. For these crimes, Shawcross had gone to prison.

His release after only fifteen years was controversial; it had been granted based on positive psychiatric evaluations, but a senior parole officer in the Binghamton area wrote that Shawcross "was possibly the most dangerous individual to have been released to this community in many years."

He was settled with his wife in Rochester, where he'd had two different jobs packing salads for catering companies. On the second one, which he worked at night, he didn't always have to complete his shift to get paid for the full time. If he finished by midnight, he was free to go, and that was often the time he exploited to visit the hookers on Lyell Avenue. His wife had no idea. He even had a girlfriend, Clara Neal, whose car he borrowed for his grisly excursions.

Now the Rochester investigators had plenty of background on him, but the officials were locking horns over who'd get the credit for solving this case. In a compromise that benefited everyone, Dennis Blythe of the New York State Police and Leonard Borriello, who'd been a key investigator for the Rochester PD, were picked to interview him together. Yet before they even faced him, there was one more development.

The morning after Shawcross was caught on the bridge, the surveillance teams put him in a Dunkin' Donuts shop, where, over coffee, he chatted with some uniformed cops. At just about that same time, not far from where June Cicero's body had been found, a deer hunter stumbled across the frozen body of Felicia Stephens, whose ID and clothing had been left along the roadside. Now Blythe and Borriello had the details of one more murder to think about.

They approached Shawcross and asked if he would mind going with them again to clear up some things. There were some inconsistencies in his story. He agreed to go, so they took him to police headquarters for the interview. Right away, they confronted him with some facts that contradicted what he'd said the day before. They also told him that he'd been spotted with one of the victims on the last day she'd been seen alive.

Shawcross didn't respond. They reminded him of his rights, but he said he didn't have any problem talking to them. As they pressed a little more with evidence they had, Shawcross bristled but revealed nothing. They tried again and he resisted. It looked as if this interview might reach an impasse, yet they had an ace they hadn't yet played. They knew that Shawcross had been sitting in his girlfriend's car the day before, on the bridge. They mentioned that they had a paint chip from one of the bodies that matched the color of that car. They also said they had tire prints that could be matched. Shawcross shrugged and said that a paint chip could come from anywhere.

Yet they were leading up to something quite specific with which to catch him off guard. He didn't see it coming. The clever tactic that put the interview over the top was when they suggested that, since the car belonged to Clara Neal, she might be involved. It was their feeling that he would not implicate her. Shawcross knew he was cornered. If they did indeed have evidence, then Clara might get drawn in. "No," he admitted, "Clara's not involved."

That's when they knew they had him. Within twenty-eight minutes of starting the interview, he'd as much as admitted what he'd done. Then he really started to talk.

He first admitted to killing Elizabeth Gibson. She'd tried to take his wallet, he said, and he'd slapped her again and again. At one point, she had looked just like his mother, so fueled by rage, he'd continued to hit her. She'd kicked at him and broken the gearshift of his car, which had further angered him. He'd put his wrist against her throat and held it there until she stopped kicking and went still. She was dead, so he'd driven around with her in the seat for a while, looking for a place to dump her. He claimed that he'd cried as he'd driven. When he found a good place, he'd removed all her clothes and placed her facedown in the woods. Then he'd thrown her clothing out of the car as he drove home. She was his ninth victim.

Elizabeth Gibson was in the core group of linked victims, so if he was good for that one, they knew he was good for all of them. They pressed for more details and showed him photographs of the victims. He identified them as women he had killed. As he confessed, Shawcross offered numerous reasons for why he'd killed these women, and all of them, he felt, were justified. It was just "business as usual." One prostitute bit his penis, one questioned his manhood, and he claimed that June Cicero had called him a fag and berated him for his inability to perform. According to his story, when he began to assault her for this, she said she now knew he was the killer and she was going to tell. Art couldn't let that happen, so he killed her. Some of them he'd smothered by putting something over their faces, and with others he'd pressed his arm across their throats. As for the postmortem mutilation of June Stott, it was merely done to "aid in decomposition." There was nothing sexual about it.

No one really bought that. We'd seen evidence of sexual mutilation with Dorothy Blackburn and June Cicero. Someone who cuts out the vagina of a corpse, as he had done with June Cicero, isn't just "aiding decomposition." The detectives knew that, and they were growing increasingly aware of how unperceptive Shawcross was about his own crimes. Apparently, June Stott had been a family friend who had come to her killer's home on several occasions for dinner with him and his wife, and he'd taken her out one evening and murdered her. Yet he couldn't see how his rationale for all of this sounded hollow.

Then Shawcross did what false confessors like Henry Lee Lucas cannot do: He led investigators directly to his hiding places for the bodies of two more of his victims, Maria Welch and Darlene Trippi, who were among the four who'd gone missing in December. One was stuffed in some bushes near the river and the other was dumped in a heavily wooded area. Both had been asphyxiated.

As the investigators drove Shawcross back from these places, they took him by the area where they'd found Felicia Stephens and noticed that he seemed to recognize it, though he initially denied it, saying, "I don't do black women." Yet they used what they'd observed of his behavior as leverage to get him to finally confess to her murder. According to him, her head had gotten caught in his automatic car window, which had nearly killed her, so he'd pulled her into the car to finish strangling her. He was adamant that there had been nothing intimate between them. Yet his very inability to see how absurd his explanations for murder were had undermined his other denials.

I was personally of the belief that Art Shawcross was good for one more murder. During this time, a black prostitute named Kimberly Logan had been killed in his neighborhood, and just as with eight-year-old Karen Ann Hill, leaves were stuffed down her throat. Yet despite the pressure from his interrogators, he wouldn't confess to that one; I think it was due to a racial hang-up, like his initial denial of the Felicia Stephens homicide.

To solve one more mystery, we did find out what the peculiar markings were on the chest of Dorothy Blackburn, the first victim. Shawcross had a bungee cord in the trunk of his car and after he'd killed her, he'd apparently sat her in the passenger seat of his car, bungeed her up, and driven around for a while with her like that. He claimed that he kept most of the bodies of his victims in the front seat as he drove to the disposal sites.

[8]

Once a killer like Shawcross is captured, we always compare him to our profile. Shawcross was much as we had envisioned him. He was a white male with a history of sexually violent crimes—including sexual homicide—who lived in Rochester and had a low-paying job. He had a wife and a girlfriend, and he frequented the prostitutes on Lyell Avenue. None of them suspected him. He'd been an extraordinarily ordinary nobody whose socioeconomic level was only one step above theirs. Also as predicted, he did fish in the Genesee River Gorge.

Yet while all of those details were correct, I was wrong in one important aspect—his age. I had estimated that the unknown killer would be in his late twenties to early thirties. Shawcross was in fact forty-three when he started killing prostitutes. My explanation for this "miss" is that the fifteen years he spent in prison was a period of arrested development. Once released, he simply picked up murdering where he'd left off. In other words, had he not been caught at the age of twenty-seven, he'd have continued to kill. As mentioned earlier, we can't always reconcile emotional age with someone's actual chronological age. We've all met people in their thirties who behave as if they're seventeen. That's why we tell investigators never to eliminate a suspect based on some inconsistent element of a profile.

However, between 1972 and 1988, there'd been a shift in Shawcross's choice of victims and this needed to be addressed; we were assisted by Dr. Park Dietz's typology for child-sex offenders. What we looked at was the difference between preferential and situational offenders:

1. Preferential child molesters are the classic pedophiles most people think of. They are dependent upon children for sexual arousal and gratification, and have little or no sexual contact with adults. They tend to have specific age and gender preferences, such as twelve-year-old boys or eight-year-old girls.

2. The situational molester is just that. He molests children when available but can also rape adults or en-

gage in other types of sexual crime. A situational sex offender is simply looking for vulnerable victims. Whether that potential victim is a child, an adult, or (as Shawcross admitted) a stray chicken doesn't really matter.

Shawcross was a situational child molester. His choice of victims supported the conclusion that he was looking for individuals who were accessible and easily controlled. Due to limited interpersonal skills, which are necessary to obtain "normal" adult victims, his pool of potential victims was limited. Whether children, prostitutes, or mentally "challenged" victims like June Stott, all were easy to approach, isolate, and control.

We learned more about Shawcross's cunning. The reason he was never picked up on surveillance was because he never drove on Lyell Avenue. He apparently parked on side streets and waited for the hookers to stray a block or two. By the same token, it might have dawned on him at some point in prison that while raping and killing kids really pisses off a community, murdering people on society's fringe doesn't. They don't tend to be accorded the same dignity and protection as child victims. Besides that, it takes longer to connect the dots among prostitute murders to see a pattern than it does with children.

[9]

When they were preparing for trial, I returned to Rochester. Eddie met me at the airport, and while driving into the city, he observed, "It feels a lot better coming into town this time."

It did. The pressure was off. The police had done an

outstanding job, and now Chuck Siragusa, a seasoned and savvy assistant district attorney, was putting the case together.

Having rolled over for these homicides, Shawcross soon wished he hadn't. He and his lawyers had now decided that he was insane and would mount a defense of Not Guilty By Reason of Insanity (NGRI). To be considered insane in New York State, he had to show quite specifically that at the time of the various offenses—every single one—he had suffered from a mental defect such that he either did not know what he was doing or could not appreciate that it was wrong.

The prosecution's strategy was pretty straightforward: Shawcross knew what he was doing, knew it was wrong, and did it anyway. A multitude of facts supported that proposition, and the more we could link the details of his confession with the physical evidence, the less likely it was that he could be considered insane. All we had to do was show that his behavior was rational, aware, and predatory.

The battle of the experts during this trial wasn't much of a battle at all. The defense had Dr. Dorothy Lewis, a psychiatric expert on organic disorders and violence from New York City's Bellevue Hospital. A small woman with short brown hair, she was apparently frustrated by the defense team's inability to get the tests she needed and was ill-prepared for the prosecution's questions. She didn't even know that another expert had questioned Shawcross at the same time as her evaluation, and had made tapes of the interviews. She had to admit that this might have influenced what Shawcross had told her.

I was in the courtroom during some of her testimony, which I found confusing. She believed that

Shawcross had been severely traumatized as a child and suffered from incomplete temporal-lobe seizures that blocked his memory. She was of the opinion that those seizures only occurred when he was alone with prostitutes at night. Despite confessing to each murder and providing details only the killer would know, including leading investigators to the bodies of two of his victims, he and Dr. Lewis were floating the idea that his memory was impaired and he didn't know what he was doing. Dr. Lewis also used the fact that he'd cut out the vagina from one victim and eaten it (as he now claimed) as proof that he had a mental disorder. Throughout the trial, Shawcross sat like a zombie, as if to make it appear that he did indeed have some kind of brain damage. That was my impression.

By contrast, Chuck Siragusa clearly showed that Lewis's opinions were inconsistent with the evidence. His expert, the renowned psychiatrist Dr. Park Dietz, was the antithesis of Lewis. He was the FBI consultant I mentioned earlier who'd made the preferential/situational distinction among child killers, and from the start, he came across as highly professional. His posture was confident and his testimony rock solid. Rather than skirt the defense claims, he admitted that Shawcross suffered from antisocial personality disorder—even to the point where he might have consumed parts of his victims—but that did not necessarily produce a mental disease or defect that disabled his awareness of what he was doing. This was an effective strategy. Yes, Shawcross was abnormal, but by legal standards, he wasn't crazy, and Dietz patiently explained the difference. Shawcross held down jobs, was married, and functioned competently in daily life. In addition, he had tried his best to avoid detection and apprehension, which clearly indicated his appreciation for the wrong-fulness of his behavior. The most damning evidence was his own detailed confession.

After five weeks of trial, the jury took less than two hours to find him both sane and guilty of murder in the second degree on ten counts, since one of the eleven victims had been found in another jurisdiction. That meant a separate trial. Shawcross was sentenced to 25 years to life on each of the counts, meaning that he will have to serve 250 years in prison before he's eligible for a parole hearing. I think we've got him this time. The second trial was scheduled, but since there seemed little reason to go at it again, he pleaded guilty on that charge.

[10]

An important part of our job is to address the after-math of a major criminal investigation. We routinely sit our contacts down and explain a few things, and we did this with Lynde Johnston.

Two post-event dynamics always follow in the wake of cases like this. First, investigators must expect to be criticized for not having caught the killer sooner. Whether he was arrested after the second crime or the twenty-second, the media critics will imply that it could have been done better. Yet the reality is that when you're in the midst of a complex case, it's like being in a pitch-black maze. There are an infinite number of possibilities and choices, and no one knows which one will lead to a quick resolution. Only after reaching the end of the maze do the lights come on, and in retrospect everyone can see how it might have been solved more quickly.

The second dynamic to be wary of is that investigators tend to tank after an intense experience like this one. They're back to investigating routine crimes—the chicken-coop burglaries and no-brainer domestic homicides—so the bottom drops out. They become bored and understimulated. We told Lynde that it wouldn't be long before he'd hear some rumblings from the troops that they wished they had another serial case, something with a little challenge and excitement. He might find himself thinking similar thoughts as well.

[11]

Cases like this are instructive. Shawcross had murdered twice, gone to prison for fifteen years, gotten out, and in less than two years had then committed murder at least eleven more times. He was a sexually violent predator. What's clear in retrospect is that no amount of prison time would have changed an offender like him, yet he'd managed to fool prison officials and the parole board. Sadly, his is no isolated case. The truth is, sexual predators are often well behaved in prison and some evaluators interpret their benign demeanor as an indication that they'll do well in society. Unfortunately, that may not be true. For offenders like Shawcross, there is an environmental context to their violence. He chose to kill children and vulnerable women, and they aren't available in a prison. He wasn't criminally versatile, so having no access to his preferred victims, he behaved. However, when returned to an environment where those potential victims were once again available, he didn't hesitate to rape and murder them. In other words, no matter what he was like in prison, he was not safe to release.

Well-meaning legislators have drafted sexually violent predator laws, but some are flawed. The goal of these laws is to allow society to protect itself by keeping dangerous repeat offenders off the street, even after they have served their criminal sentence. In many states, these laws typically specify that it must be shown that a given offender poses a continuing threat to society, which is, of course, reasonable. The flaw arises when it is also required that the offender be able to benefit from therapy. The problem is that psychopaths don't benefit from therapy. In fact, such programs may actually make them worse.

Dr. Robert Hare, the leading international authority on psychopathy, cites a study which demonstrates that upon following release from a therapeutic community program, psychopaths were almost four times more likely than other patients to commit a violent offense, while psychopaths who did not take part in therapeutic programs were less violent. As one of those who'd had therapy put it, "These programs are like a finishing school. They teach you how to put the squeeze on people."

I'm not suggesting that all therapeutic programs be abandoned. Many are intensive, well designed, and work reasonably well with other offenders, but not with psychopaths—which is what a man who calls a succession of murders "business as usual" surely is. The law creates a dilemma for those mental health professionals who must decide whom to release. If the prerequisite for continued incarceration is treatability, they're excluding the most dangerous population. At a workshop I conducted at Atascadero State Hospital in California on detecting psychopathology at crime scenes, this irony was brought home. I did a few interviews with people who were going through therapy there, and one was a psychopathic killer whom the authorities were ready to release. They told me that the law required that they could hold the guy only if he had a treatable disorder, so since his psychopathy was untreatable, he'd be sent back into the community. To sum it up, one doctor looked over the top of his glasses, raised an eyebrow, and said, "We only release the really dangerous ones."

So what do we do? That's the real question. To put it in perspective, what if you discovered that a cake had no sugar in it? Could you rub sugar into it to make it edible? No. What if you found that it had motor oil baked into it? Could you squeeze it out to make the cake edible? Obviously not. The only question is what to do with the cake. Sexually violent offenders like Arthur Shawcross either lack something they need or have something they don't need. Either way, we have no method as yet to make right whatever it is. Our current options are both flawed and limited. Yet one thing we should not do is allow these psychopaths to prowl among us freely. The results will be predictably disastrous.

Fortunately, Shawcross was stopped, and we accomplished this in much the same manner as an attacker is defeated in Shorinji Kempo, by blending with his momentum and using it against him. The crime scenes told us that he was returning to the bodies. By using a strategy that exploited that particular behavior, we effectively trapped him in his own compulsions.

Even as this case closed with his initial confession, I was already involved in an even darker mystery. Just ten days before Shawcross was spotted on the bridge, a family of four had been murdered in their home. I'd been to the crime scene right after the brutal event and now had to help interpret the behavioral evidence.

3: Who Would Do This?

Other sins only speak; murder shrieks out.
　　　　　　　　　　　　　　　—John Webster

[1]

In cases like this one, where physical evidence at the crime scene appears to contradict the behavior as profiled, everything must be reexamined. A given incident may not be what it initially seems. As I put the Rochester murders on momentary hold to consult on yet another crime in northern New York State, the investigation hit me hard on two levels: professional, yes, but also a quite personal one.

On Saturday, December 23, 1989, I left Virginia with my wife, Carol, and our two children. We were driving to the small upstate town of Waterloo, New York, to spend the Christmas holidays with my wife's family. Being natives of the area, Carol and I were undaunted by the reports of new snow and temperatures in the single digits. As a matter of fact, we were looking forward to it. At least I was. When I'd lived in the area, I'd been a member of the National Ski Patrol for nine years, but upon my transfer to Quantico, I'd reluctantly withdrawn. I wanted to strap on the boards again, do some skiing, and also do some sledding with my kids. I was more than ready for a break from the insidious stream of murder and mayhem that ran through my life. Recently, it seemed to have escalated from a challenging white-water stream to a ravaging out-of-control river threatening to jump its banks.

On Friday night, we packed up the car and in the predawn darkness the following morning, we loaded our eight-year-old daughter, eleven-year-old son, and two-year-old black Lab, Zero, into the station wagon and headed north. I knew that I would have to go to Rochester at some point during this break to work on their serial murder case, but that day I pushed it from my mind. We were going home for Christmas and that was what mattered.

As we crossed into New York State from Pennsylvania, I tuned the car radio to a local station to hear the news. Among other stories was one about a family whose members had been murdered the night before in their own home in Dryden, New York, a small community outside Ithaca. It was just a few miles from where I'd grown up, and I knew the place well, so I listened closely. When I learned that the state police were investigating, I had a strong suspicion that my holiday break would be shorter than I'd anticipated. Eddie Grant would be called in from Albany, and since he knew where I was going to be, I expected to hear from him.

This was beginning to shape up as the vacation that wasn't. Carol had heard the news as well. She knew Eddie, knew me, and needed no help in connecting the dots. We didn't discuss it, but the scenario of Eddie and me working a new quadruple homicide was going through both of our minds as we drove the last couple of hours to Waterloo. The kids continued napping, playing, squabbling, and fawning over Zero, who was in the "way back" of the station wagon, as my daughter referred to it.

We made it to my mother-in-law's house, but hadn't even finished unloading the car when my pager went off. As I grabbed it, Carol said, "It's Eddie, isn't it?"

I saw the number, looked at her, and said. "Yeah, it's Eddie." I picked up a couple of suitcases and turned to walk into the house, knowing I would be leaving shortly.

[2]

Around four-thirty in the afternoon on December 22, the mail carrier saw a man in a hooded parka riding a bicycle up Ellis Hollow Road, toward the Harris home. Tony Harris, his wife, Dodie, and their two adolescent children, Marc and Shelby, lived in a comfortable contemporary home on a couple of acres in Dryden, New York, about six miles outside Ithaca. Tony had a professional job outside the home and Dodie ran a small gift shop, the Grey Goose, in a building adjacent to their house.

It was odd, the carrier thought, to see someone riding a bike there, since it was so cold out and he appeared to be struggling. However, he seemed to have arrived at his destination, because fifteen minutes later, a neighbor of the Harrises noticed two people standing in the Harris driveway and facing the gift shop. One of them looked like Dodie, but the other person was a stranger. An hour later, at five forty-five, another neighbor noticed that the house was dark, and someone else driving by at seven-fifteen spotted a figure walking by an illuminated downstairs window.

Shelby's boyfriend called the house at seven-thirty,

but no one answered. He worried about her, calling every half hour, but still got no response; Shelby, sixteen, had failed to show up for their date.

At six-thirty the next morning, the Harris house alarm awakened the nearest neighbors, who alerted someone at the state police barracks six miles away. State Trooper John Beno, a uniformed patrol officer, was dispatched, and he arrived at seven-twenty. The front and side doors proved to be locked, but a garage door was open and the outside lights were on. He noted that the alarm was no longer activated. He went into the garage and spotted an air compressor sitting on a dark sedan. Next to this car was an empty space that appeared to be for a second vehicle. Since the door into the house from the garage was unlocked, he went in and announced his presence. There was no response, so he continued inside. He smelled smoke in the air and heard smoke detectors beeping. A man's briefcase stood on the floor in the kitchen and two sacks of groceries had been brought in but not put away. They appeared to have been there for several hours.

In the middle of the family room, where opened Christmas gifts and ripped colored wrappings were strewn about, Beno saw a red-and-yellow gas can lying on its side. It looked out of place and the smell of gasoline was strong. Hanging on the staircase banister he saw a man's blue jacket, and beneath it, on the floor, a pair of men's gloves. Disturbed by all this, the officer tried to call from the kitchen for help, but he found that the phone cords had been ripped out. Now he was worried, so he went to his car to radio for backup. Then he returned to the house.

He opened some windows downstairs to clear out

the smoke and then went up the steps to look inside the rooms. Up there, he found another gasoline can and a broken phone. Then he waited for the backup to come. Three troopers arrived and together they made a thorough search. Inside one room, on the floor, they found the charred remains of a body, with only the lower half recognizable as female. Clothing was strewn about and drawers were open. The mattress had been set on fire deliberately, and charred coils burst out of it. Nearby, in a bathroom, lay a dead dog.

In another room, they saw a fire burning, so they kept the door closed and awaited the fire company's arrival. They knew they had at least one murder on their hands, along with arson. Since a family lived here, they prepared for the worst.

It was soon discovered that while a substantial amount of gas had been spread around in the house, it had been lit in only a few of the rooms. The arsonist, obviously inexperienced, had closed the doors to those rooms, shutting off the oxygen supply and foiling his plan. The fire had not spread, as he clearly had hoped it would.

The troopers at the house did a magnificent job of preserving the crime scene, keeping the arriving firefighters in defined areas so as not to contaminate the scene any more than was absolutely necessary while they extinguished the remaining fire. Then, in one smoldering room, the firefighters found a shocking scene: two deceased adults in hunched-over positions who were so badly burned they were nearly unrecognizable as human. Their heads were covered with some kind of bag and they were bound with wire close against the bedposts. Attached to another bed, a small body lay along the wall, the head also covered. This proved to be fourteen-year-old Marc, and this had been his bedroom. It soon became clear that someone had come into this home, murdered the entire family, ravaged the Christmas gifts, and then tried to burn down the house. Who would do this?

A close neighbor supplied information that provided some initial leads. The Harris family's brown GM van was missing, probably taken by the perpetrator. In the study, torn envelopes indicated that credit cards had been stolen. Had theft been the motive? Would the killer use the cards? At the very least, investigators could trace the van.

At eight forty-five A.M., the medical examiner arrived. He found that each of the victims had been shot in the head through pillowcases, twice for each of the adults and three times for the boy, and they had all been secured with heavy shoelaces and coat hangers to the twin beds. Dodie was in a kneeling position, without shoes, and had a large bruise on her right leg. Tony had been hog-tied, also with shoelaces and wire from a coat hanger. Marc was tied to the other bed, bound at its foot end, and his wrists were strapped together. Diesel fuel had been poured over the beds and on the floor between them. A gerbil lay dead in its cage.

The fourth body, lying facedown in the master bedroom, was young Shelby. She was naked, but a torn green taffeta dress was spread over her. She had been tied to the mattress and a cord was attached to her left wrist. Her mouth was still gagged with a sock and another piece of cloth. The bed was soaked in blood and blood pooled beneath her. She had been shot three times between her right ear and eye. Red underwear was on the foot of the bed, along with an open jar of

Vaseline. Sexual assault was a likely probability. The windows of that room had been covered with towels and sheets. A woman's watch was found by the bed, stopped at 6:33.

In Shelby's room, the window shades were drawn down and the bedcovers pulled back. Investigators came across shreds of panty hose dangling from a chair, as if the hose had been cut up to use as bindings, and these were mingled with strands of human hair. The chair was ringed in cigarette ashes. A pile of female clothing and a watch lay on the floor; the girl had apparently been forced to undress and redress on the spot. Samples of Shelby's blood were taken on the assumption that her killer had gotten some on his clothing, so if they caught him, they could make a match. No murder weapon or shell casings were found.

Oddly, nothing seemed amiss in the gift shop behind the house, as if the killer hadn't even bothered to check there for money. As the identification team went in and got to work, they quickly realized the futility of what they were doing: Surfaces where they expected to find prints had been wiped clean. This awareness of evidence collection suggested a more experienced offender, one with a record. He might not have understood how to burn down a house, but he did know the value of a fingerprint. Just in case he had missed something, surfaces were dusted everywhere, including on the two gas cans. It was Trooper Dave Harding who took charge of the evidence collection. He wanted this case to be closed quickly and the perpetrator brought to justice, so he stated his intent to give it all he had.

At 10:38, the missing van was located near a bank, but it was empty. Footprints in the snow suggested that someone had left the van, at a run. Witnesses said they had seen the van parked there on Friday night at various times, but no one had noticed who had driven or parked it. Yet, oddly, Trooper John Beno had noticed fresh tire tracks in the snow on Saturday morning, running over the lawn. Had the killer gone out and come back?

Less than a mile from the crime scene, the century-old Ellis Hollow Community Church was set up as a command post and every available officer called in for duty. All had to be prepared for a media onslaught. The public's reaction to any crime is directly proportional to their ability to identify with the victims. The dead prostitutes in Rochester created a stir, but not much fear among the majority of residents. After all, most women weren't prostitutes and therefore were not at risk. But when a member of an all-American family is raped and all the family is murdered in the sanctity of their home, then everyone becomes a potential victim; that possibility quickly terrorized the entire community. No one was safe while this predator prowled the streets. The case had to be solved, and solved quickly.

[3]

Eddie and I had agreed to meet at the C-troop barracks outside Ithaca on the morning of December 26. Around six A.M., I left my sleeping family at my in-laws' house in Waterloo, had a quick breakfast at Connie's Diner on Main Street, and then made the hour-long drive south to Ithaca, arriving around seven-thirty. Eddie was already there and he introduced me to the investigators working the case.

Dave McElligott, from the New York State Police Bureau of Criminal Investigation (BCI), was in charge of the operation. Nearly six feet tall, with salt-and-pepper hair, he was a cop who wanted to get the job done, but he also proved to be autocratic, turf conscious, and abrasive. Once he was assigned to head the investigation, he didn't want anyone else getting involved, in particular, the FBI. In his eyes, I was an interloper. In fact, Eddie was also something of an outsider here. While he was a lieutenant with the state police, he wasn't C-troop. He was from Albany. We realized it could be tough getting our points across, but we intended to give it our best shot. We were there to help, not to interfere.

After meeting with McElligott, we left the barracks and drove to the crime scene, on Ellis Hollow Road. It was still being processed and would be for several more days. Sipping barracks coffee as he guided the car on the icy road, Eddie brought me up to speed on the investigation. "It's too early to know exactly what physical evidence we have at the scene, as it's still being collected," he explained, "but there's a good deal of offender behavior to work with. Victimology is pretty much a flat line. There was nothing going on in their lives that elevated their potential for being murdered. No family feud, lovers' triangle, big insurance money, weird boyfriends or stalkers, as far as we know. Nothing. Just a normal family."

To be sure, we quickly reviewed the facts. Tony Harris, just six days short of forty, was a marketing director for an electronics distribution company who, from all reports, had made his family his first priority. He was a hard worker who had succeeded, and most acquaintances who had been questioned thus far thought well of him. Dodie Harris managed the antique and gift store and was recovering from several serious bouts of breast cancer. In fact, they had moved from Georgia to New York three years earlier so she could be closer to her extended family. Her father had built this home for them.

Young Shelby was athletic and active in school clubs and had a strong Catholic faith. She avoided drugs and drinking and even participated in the group Students Against Drunk Driving. She got along well with her parents and she had a steady boyfriend.

Marc, a sixth-grader, kept his hair short and his clothing neat. There was no indication that he'd been a discipline problem or that he had hung out with the wrong crowd.

In short, there was no reason to believe that they had attracted a killer. The one potential risk factor was the gift shop. We thought it was likely that the gift shop had been targeted, robbery the initial motive. Since it was Christmastime, Dodie was probably doing a brisk business and a would-be robber might think he could intimidate her quickly, grab her ready cash, and go. Yet something had changed his plan.

Everything thus far pointed to a stranger having done the killing. While stranger killings can be more difficult to solve, they can also be more amenable to the process of criminal-investigative analysis and profiling. The key lies in how much behavioral and forensic evidence is available.

"Here we go," said Eddie as he turned off Ellis Hollow Road and into the horseshoe-shaped driveway. We identified ourselves to the uniformed trooper maintaining the perimeter around the crime scene and then followed the driveway around to the house. The state police evidence van was parked out front, along with a couple of other state police cars. We expected to find a lot of activity inside.

The Harris home was a two-story gray New England–type clapboard house sitting in open acreage on a quiet country road. From the lack of trees and shrubbery, it appeared fairly new, and about fifty yards away was a smaller two-level building that looked about the same age. I surmised that it was the gift shop. As we walked from the car toward the house, Eddie gestured to a neighboring home not far away, saying, "The couple that live there were the ones who called in about the alarm sounding."

Inside I saw where the phone lines in the main living area had been ripped out. Eddie told me that the killer had overlooked one phone, which was located in the basement, so he had not been thorough. As we went farther in, I noted on the walls and fireplace mantel the emphasis on country decorating, with geese as a prominent theme. In the family room stood a large Christmas tree decorated with bows and what looked like handmade ornaments, a loving task. Next to the tree the family's gifts to one another had been torn open, presumably by the killer, who was probably searching for something valuable to take.

I learned quickly about the nature of the violence: All four had been shot in the head, but Shelby was the only one who had not been shot through a pillowcase. In every way, she had been treated differently from the others. There was evidence that she had been tied in a chair, untied, retied, made to wear a new dress that looked to me like something for a prom, then undressed, sexually assaulted, and murdered.

Cigarette ashes had been found throughout the

house and they circled the chair where she had been tied. After the murders and assault, the killer made a largely unsuccessful attempt to obliterate the evidence by setting the house on fire. Gasoline was spread through the interior of the home and on Shelby's body and bed. The offender had apparently lit the fire upstairs. That set off an audible fire alarm, which may have panicked him.

I went up the steps, decorated with red bows and green pine sprays, and into the bedroom where three of the family had been murdered. I could see on the floor the areas where they had been tied, shot, and burned, and the place still smelled of smoke and charred material. I walked around, careful to avoid evidence markers, and went over to the closet. Hanging there was a Boy Scout uniform, much like the one that hung in my son's closet. Quite suddenly, I felt blindsided. I stood utterly still in that fire-ravaged room, with the lingering smells of death and the sounds of men working, momentarily paralyzed by the sight of that neatly pressed Boy Scout uniform.

Hanging there in its innocence, it not only symbolized what had been but also what could have been. That empty scout uniform belonging to a murdered boy slammed into my emotional defenses like an armor-piercing bullet and transmogrified the scene into something much more personal than I was prepared for. Was that Marc Harris's uniform or my son's? I experienced a wrenching visceral identification with these victims, which threatened my ability to process the scene.

But I knew I'd have to deal with any residual emotional issues later. This was not the time. Eddie and I were scheduled that evening to give Thomas Constantine, the New York State Police superintendent, a comprehensive preliminary assessment. I needed to stay focused.

Eddie was looking around the room at other things, and I didn't tell him what I was feeling. As we left the bedroom to go downstairs, he turned his head slightly and said, "I heard that you worked another family murder recently, somewhere in New England. Is that right?"

I said, "Yeah. It was about three months ago in Warwick, Rhode Island." Downstairs in the house where one family had met their horrifying fate, I laid out the other case to Eddie.

[4]

In September, just over three months earlier, in a white middle-class neighborhood, a mother and her two daughters were found murdered in their home. Joan Heaton, 39, Jennifer, 10, and Melissa, 8, were stabbed and slashed multiple times, and the knife had actually broken off in Jennifer's neck. The mother and older daughter lay in the hallway, partially covered by blood-soaked bedsheets, and the younger daughter was found in the kitchen. It appeared that she had seen her mother struggling with someone and when intercepted had been running for the phone. She'd been stabbed repeatedly and her head had been bashed in with a footstool, covered in blood, next to her. In the hall, there was blood everywhere. Jennifer lay closer to the bedrooms, and Joan lay on her stomach in a short nightshirt and underwear, blood soaking into the carpet beneath her. It would later be determined that she had sustained fifty-seven stab wounds. The murder weapon was from a set of knives she'd recently bought, but the woman had also been bludgeoned and strangled. The bodies had lain there for two to three days before being found.

The intruder had entered the house by forcing open a window in the kitchenette area, and when he had stepped on a table inside, his weight had broken it. Outside, the distance up to the window was fairly high, so he had to be athletic.

Detective Bill MacDonald called me for help, asking for some immediate direction. He described this awful, bloody scene, with a forced entry and more than 120 stab wounds among the three victims, and asked if I could offer some ideas right away, over the phone. That's not typical protocol, but they were desperate, so during my conversation with the detective, I asked if they'd had anything like this anywhere else. It seemed to me a very disorganized scene, the use of a weapon of opportunity indicating an offender in the neighborhood.

They could think of another such incident. Two years earlier, they said, a twenty-seven-year-old woman had been stabbed fifty-eight times. She had gone to sleep on some blankets in front of the TV on July 27, boxes piled around her. The next day she was moving to a new home. Her two children had spent the night with their father, and her brother, with whom she shared the house, was at his job as a night security officer. He came home at dawn to find her dead. She had been stabbed with the packing knife that she had used to cut twine—again, a weapon found at the scene. That murder, they told me, had not been solved.

I asked where it had been in relation to this one, and it turned out to have been about five houses away. So I said, "You've got someone in the neighborhood doing this."

From the fact that he'd covered his victims, I believed that he'd known them and did not want to have to look at what he had done. He might even have had some earlier contact with them on the day of the murder. He probably knew their habits and accessibility, as well as the fact that there was no adult male present. From the frenetic manner of the stabbing, I thought that he'd probably cut his hand, so using my term for psychopaths I asked, "Who's the asshole around there with the cut hand? That's who you want to look for."

I pointed out that the detectives would already be familiar with him. Since it was a predominately white Irish-Catholic neighborhood, and no one had noticed someone who didn't belong there, the offender was probably white. He'd be in his late teens, strong, and have had past problems. He'd be living within walking distance of the murders. I urged them to examine blood types at the scene because I felt sure there would be one that did not match any of the victims.

MacDonald then told me that additional blood had been found in the hallway, apart from where the bodies had bled from the stabbings, and that there was blood in a bathroom.

They overnighted a copy of the crime scene videotape to me, so I could have a look, and then sent a package of crime scene and autopsy photos. I examined all of this material in detail, but my opinion remained the same.

They presented my ideas in the war room at an investigators' meeting, and came up with some strategies. With the idea of looking for a neighbor with a cut hand, police officers went door to door to ask questions and get a good look at the people inside. Then out on the street, one officer spotted a black kid he knew, Craig Price. He was fifteen, six feet tall, athletic, and friendly. He lived a few blocks away and had a bandage on his hand. It turned out that he also had a record of breaking and entering, theft, and peeping into houses to determine easy targets for routine burglaries. In addition, he had been arrested two months earlier for assaulting his sister, indicating a propensity toward using violence against people who were weaker than he was.

They called me again to tell me about this new development, adding that they had a size-thirteen shoe print and had developed a large handprint on the refrigerator door. "You've got to consider him a suspect," I said. "Assuming the latent print belongs to the offender, it will be easy to either eliminate him or put him at the scene. The blood work might take a little longer, but everything will likely come together to identify him."

It turned out that although Craig Price was black, he had grown up in white neighborhoods and had plenty of white friends, so that made him a more viable suspect than I'd originally thought. We all agreed that they had to get hard evidence, such as DNA or fingerprints, to link him to the crime scene.

The fingerprints from the refrigerator door matched Craig Price's, and he failed a polygraph test about how he had cut his hand on a broken car window. There was also no evidence of broken glass where the car had been parked. Soon, the blood analysis linked him as well. Since he was fifteen now, that meant that his first brutal killing had occurred when he was only thirteen.

By the time he was fifteen, he'd murdered four people in two separate homicides.

This became a major case in Rhode Island, because under their law, he couldn't be tried as an adult, so he'd get out when he was twenty-one. Afraid of having him back in their midst, they ended up rewriting their laws, and a coalition formed to warn other states about the possibility that their laws were also inadequate.

Several years later, when Craig Price was nineteen or twenty, I got a call from the attorney general's office. They wanted me to write a report on predicting the future dangerousness of this kid. They had psychologists doing the more traditional psychological assessment, but what I could offer came from an area with which the psychologists had no experience. The work that we in the BSU have done has been unique. We've developed an unusual degree of expertise in crimes that were unexplored until we started plowing into that area. It's the only organization in the world that specializes in the investigation of bizarre and brutal crimes. Even the courts have taken note of this. Testimony by members of the unit is generally considered to be credible evidence.

So in a six-page analysis, I talked about the fact that as a juvenile, Craig Price would get out with no record. That meant he'd have increased access to weapons, diminished parental control, greater mobility once he got a car, and increased criminal sophistication from his exposure to other criminals in the prison environment. He'd shown no remorse and had resisted therapy, so whatever had caused him to kill in the first place hadn't been treated. He'd joked with his friends about his "conduct disorder," and told them he'd soon be back out to smoke joints. He wasn't good while locked up, so there was every indication that he would continue to cause trouble and be violent. In the future, I said, he would be much more difficult to detect and apprehend.

I felt that the kid was a developing serial killer, and since he'd used overkill, he was probably driven by uncontrollable rage. From our data, we could point out that less than 1 percent of homicide cases on record reach that level of violence: Price had an established pattern of predatory violence and there was no reason to believe that he would not act out again against more victims. Past violence is the best predictor of future violence. Craig Price, I believed, would continue to pose a grave threat to society.

In 1995, the judge gave him seven more years for another offense, and then he assaulted two prison guards and got twenty-five extra years altogether.

Profiling doesn't solve crimes, investigators do—as they did in this case. If my analysis did anything, it was to help keep the investigation focused in the immediate neighborhood and looking for a troublemaking kid with a cut hand.

[5]

When the Harris murder occurred, Craig Price had already been identified and linked to the Rhode Island killings. He was still going through the legal process, and it had been jarring to see a kid so young do such a rage-based murder, so it was fresh on my mind.

Eddie shook his head. "A single, then a triple two years later, all by the age of fifteen," he commented. "What a goddamn monster. But this guy's different."

"Yes, he is," I agreed. "The callous brutality is similar, but this offender is more evidence conscious. Plus, he either spent the entire night at the crime scene, which is high risk, or he left and returned to set fire to the house, which is also high risk. All of that suggests an older, confident, more criminally experienced offender. Maybe not a murderer, but somebody who's been through the system before and is trying like hell to avoid going back."

Eddie nodded. "Right," he said. "Now let me fill you in on the rest of the investigation so far."

Bringing me up to speed, Eddie dropped a bombshell. Immediately after the murders, a younger black male accompanied by an older black female had used the victims' credit and ATM cards to get money. Then the credit cards were used at a mall near Syracuse to make several expensive purchases, with the cardholder's signature forged. The male had bought diamonds and women's clothing, which suggested a female in his life. In a case like this, we ask the credit card companies to keep the cards active so we can track every charge. This strategy typically yields a good deal of additional evidence, and sometimes the perpetrator's picture is captured on the store's surveillance cameras. While unquestionably dangerous, these two weren't the brightest of predators.

Eddie and I looked at everything that was known thus far and came up with a profile to present to investigators. Tom Constantine, the director of the New York State Police, flew in from Albany and we met him early that evening.

As he greeted us, he shook his head. The first thing he asked was, "Who would do this?" That was a question I was to hear over and over during this investigation. It seemed unthinkable in this quiet little town, especially at Christmas.

Even though it was a single-scene crime, we had a lot of behavior to analyze—more than some multiple-scene crimes. The whole point is whether there are behavioral clues that can help us to narrow down the scope of potential offenders. For starters, we had rape, an amateur attempt at arson, shooting of individual victims, a lot of time spent at the scene, the violation of the gifts, and the theft of the credit cards. It was different from someone who runs into a 7-Eleven and shoots the clerk in the head, then runs out again. That's limited behavior, but here we had a lot going on that we could read. If you have enough to analyze, you can come up with a pretty tight picture as to what happened.

We reiterated to Constantine that we believed the crime had begun as a robbery and had escalated to rape and murder. The cut phone lines suggested that whatever the initial plan was, it may not have included murder. Why cut the phone lines if the plan is to kill everyone? The dead don't call. The sexual assault appeared to be unplanned and opportunistic, yet it involved undressing and redressing one victim, which revealed a good deal about the offender's sexual fantasy.

There was the possibility of a second offender, but it was too soon to tell. Even in that event, we profile the lead or dominant figure, because that person's behavior will be most evident at the scene.

We profiled him as a convicted felon who was probably on parole and who had preselected the victims for robbery. He probably knew the area from some personal association and had no doubt watched the victims' routines. Like the sexual assault, the murders were not planned and were probably an attempt on the offender's part to leave no witnesses. This is typical of those released felons who decide that the way to avoid going to prison again is to kill the witnesses. Instead of just abiding by the law, their thinking instead is to commit a better crime. We see this over and over. I was involved in a case where a convicted thug and his girlfriend robbed a video store in Albuquerque and murdered three teenage clerks. The grandparents of one kid were out front waiting, and the offenders abducted them from the parking lot, drove them to an isolated area, and shotgunned them to death. The male involved had been sent to prison before, based on eyewitness accounts, so now he knew better and was not going back the same way. Criminals adapt, so we have to always be learning how *they're* learning. Eddie and I said we believed that the wanton murder of the entire Harris family within the context of a robbery was another indication that their killer had a record.

In our profile, we stated that his criminal history would include violent crimes, but not murder, and that he lived in a financially dependent situation in rental property somewhere near the crime scene. It was unlikely that he was an experienced arsonist, as he had bungled his attempt to burn the Harris house. If he worked at all, it would be in a menial capacity. He was likely to have a girlfriend or common-law wife. We did warn investigators that his emotional volatility and propensity for violence, coupled with his desire to avoid detection and apprehension, made him more dangerous than most murderers. He was the type of offender who was likely to resist arrest violently, if given the opportunity, and clearly he was armed.

They understood completely. They would have to be careful, so they devised a plan for closing in on him decisively and denying him any opportunity of harming them or others, including himself.

[6]

A few days later, Eddie and I went back to Rochester for another meeting on the investigation there, but I kept in touch with what was happening in Ithaca. Even as Shawcross was being arrested for eleven murders in January, the Harris massacre case was developing quickly and was to take a rather disturbing turn.

A drive-in bank customer told police about a black man and woman, in line in front of him in a beat-up old car, who had used an ATM card in the machine and had lost it. Since Tony Harris's ATM card was found stuck in that machine, that proved to be a viable lead. The man gave a description to a forensic artist, noting that the tall, thin man had been smoking a cigarette. The woman was attractive, but older.

A professor who lived near the Harris home came forward to say that he had seen an older black woman and a young black man driving a van at six forty-five Saturday morning, December 23. They went by him slowly and he got a good look.

The offender was subsequently identified through several key tips from people who knew him as Anthony Turner, aka Michael Kinge. He lived in a rented duplex not far from the crime scene with his Caucasian girlfriend, Joanna White, and their one-year-old son. His mother, Shirley Kinge, lived in the other side of the house, with her mother.

Michael Kinge was always in debt. He owed past rent and he owed on utilities bills. He wasn't able to keep a regular job, so he did odd jobs like cleaning apartments or bowling alleys. He generally got what money he could through petty robberies. On parole from Fishkill State Prison where he had been sent for armed robbery, he nevertheless found crime to be the only way to keep his small apartment. A high school dropout lacking self-control, he developed a certain charm in order to get his way. He was seventeen when he was first arrested for burglary, and he spent sixty days at Rikers Island. He then tried the marines, but was court-martialed. Nevertheless, he managed to go to a community college and come out with a business degree. Still, he could not find a decent job. He assumed he was not hired because he was black, so he developed an attitude and continued to rob grocery and liquor stores. With the money, he would buy drugs.

His mother had raised him on the Upper West Side in New York City, and though she made little money herself, she had a string of boyfriends who kept her in style. She was a poor role model for him, and both of them developed a penchant for having more than they could really afford.

Late in January, the police went to the duplex, which was not far from Ellis Hollow Road, and knocked on the door. They saw a black man with cornrow braids, holding a baby, peek out from behind a curtain. They introduced themselves and said they were checking for people who might have seen something on the night of the Harris murder. The black man offered his name, Michael Turner, and his date of birth, but nothing else. He mentioned that his wife, who worked at night, might have seen something. Then he moved away from the window and would not open the door. An older black woman looked out from the next apartment, and when the police asked her name, she told them it was none of their business.

They went back to the barracks and plotted surveillance. They knew they were dealing with a very dangerous man.

While they were keeping watch on the house, they matched Shirley Kinge's handwriting to the signatures of Tony and Dodie Harris on the fraudulent credit card receipts, and knew they were on the right track. However, they hadn't matched any of the few prints they'd lifted at the crime scene to Michael Kinge, which could mean he'd worn gloves. He had also recently purchased equipment at Sears that could be used to modify firearms and make silencers.

Someone alerted Michael to the fact that he was a suspect in the Harris murders, so apparently he prepared himself. He kept a sawed-off shotgun with him in the house, along with his Doberman. He also strapped on a knife and covered the windows with sheets. Joanna was sent out for pizza each day, but Michael never left the duplex.

Trooper Dave Harding met with Shirley Kinge and for a comparison, tricked her into giving multiple samples of her handwriting. He spent a lot of time with her and gathered information pertinent to the investigation. He also collected glasses and other items she had touched and asked for employment records, on which her fingerprints had been recorded. He said that he wanted to get a very good print, suitable for comparison, so it would hold up in court.

In early February, Harding said he had gotten a match between prints on file for Shirley Kinge and two prints that he had lifted off the gas can. Another expert verified them, which gave more weight to the case against the Kinges.

On February 7, the police picked up Joanna White from her place of employment to search her truck. She was read her rights and then taken to the barracks for questioning. They let her know their intention of searching the duplex and arresting Michael. To avoid harming anyone, particularly her baby, they needed to know the layout of her half of the duplex. They were aware that Michael was heavily armed and that he might resist them with violence. He might also use his own child as a hostage. She cooperated only after they assured her they would see that the baby was taken out safely. They also wanted Michael to be taken alive because they wanted to learn from him about the events on the night of the murders.

Two entry teams were formed, seven men on each. One was to arrest Michael and the other would go after Shirley. Patrol cars blocked both ends of the street on which the duplex sat. A helicopter stood by, at the airport, for emergency transport.

As investigators dismantled the locked front door, they spotted a figure behind a curtain, who jumped away. They identified themselves, broke in, and ran after the man. Michael Kinge went into an upstairs bedroom and grabbed his twenty-gauge sawed-off shotgun. When they came in, he sat on the bed, stuck the shotgun between his legs, and pointed the barrel at his own head. One officer tried to talk him out of it. Michael held the police at bay for a few minutes, and then when one man reached for the gun barrel, Michael jerked the gun away from his own head and fired fast at some of the officers in the room. The police returned his fire with lethal accuracy, but he kept standing up and turning toward them. Finally, after they had fired nine shots, he fell to the floor, dead. They also had to kill his Doberman. Then they found the weapon used to kill the Harrises right there in his apartment, along with other associated evidence.

Back at the barracks, they learned from Joanna that she and Michael had faced eviction that December and were also fighting with each other. On December 22, they were out driving, and Michael had Joanna stop driving so he could take his bicycle—one that he'd stolen—out of the truck and then told her to keep driving. She did not know what he was planning, she later said, but she knew he had a gun in his knapsack. He had met her early the next morning, around seven A.M., where she worked. From there, they'd gone to several banks and she'd noticed that he had several credit cards, one of which bore the name Harris. When she heard about the murders on the radio and realized that the house was near where she had dropped Michael off, she was too afraid to ask him about the credit card. He had threatened to kill her if she ever went to the police about his activities, and for that day he forced her to give him an alibi.

The other team took Shirley out of her duplex apartment without harm to anyone and placed the child in protective custody. With the primary suspect dead, it was time to look into Shirley's part in the crime. Now, a case that should have gone smoothly started to unravel.

[7]

A review of the evidence by the FBI laboratory confirmed that two fingerprints from Shirley Kinge were found on the gasoline can recovered at the crime scene.

In addition to being charged with the fraudulent use of the victims' credit cards, to which she had admitted, she was also charged with the murders. This she vehemently denied.

When I heard about this development, I talked it over with Eddie. It rang false to us that Michael had raped a young girl with his mother right there at the scene, especially in the manner in which he had sadistically played with her. Yet the police said they had a fingerprint on the gas can from the crime scene. Physical evidence is more conclusive than behavioral considerations. How else could it have gotten there? The most logical explanation was that Shirley Kinge aided her son in his attempt to destroy the crime scene.

Despite our concerns, that fingerprint seemed to close the case. Apparently the prosecutor also had some doubts about Shirley Kinge's fingerprints, but did not pursue it because Dave Harding enjoyed a good reputation and work record, and the FBI had confirmed his discovery. Still, there was something unsettling about it all.

Shirley Kinge was found guilty and sentenced to thirty-five to fifty years in prison for forgery of a signature and for her part in the Harris murders. She and her mother both insisted that the verdict was unfair.

Then, about a year later, something else occurred that opened the case back up. Dave Harding applied to the CIA. In the process, he had to take a polygraph and was asked if he'd ever done anything illegal. He said, "Yeah, let me tell you how we did this," and then opened up about how he and other officers had fabricated evidence in a case. He indicated that there had been other cases as well in which this was done.

So the CIA agents thought his work on certain cases

in New York should be investigated. They also went to the Bureau and said, "It looks like we have a criminal case here." They talked with me about how Harding had faked evidence, planting fingerprints falsely to ensure a conviction, and I told them what our own concerns had been at the time. Despite his claim of having physical evidence, with what we knew from experience, it just hadn't squared.

As it turned out, Harding had apparently felt certain that Shirley Kinge had been in the home—just gut instinct—and since he was in charge of the fingerprints, it wasn't difficult to lock up the case with physical evidence. To his mind, it wasn't dishonest, it was simply a way to make sure that a guilty person went to prison. Shirley had, after all, been seen in the van that morning. So a fingerprint on the gas can simply proved what Harding suspected, that she was at the scene and was therefore an accomplice to murder. He had done the same thing on a few other cases, believing that he had played an important role in ensuring that justice would be done.

However, the judge did not see it that way. In a 1988 assault case in which Harding had supplied a false print, he was charged with four counts of first-degree perjury, six counts of tampering with evidence, and one count of making a sworn false statement. It was the first step in an investigation of more than fifty cases in which Harding had been involved. The Kinge case was one of them, and her lawyer called for a new trial.

The state settled with her on the forgery charges, and when Harding finally plea-bargained his own case, he admitted to planting the evidence against her, which gave her the basis for a lawsuit. He got two sentences of two to six years, to run consecutively, and a ten-thousand-dollar fine. In all, he admitted to tampering with evidence in five separate cases. He had been a vigilante, a self-perceived hero who had devastated the public trust, not only in the New York State Police but also in police investigations across the country.

It became a major civil-rights investigation into the New York State Police, and that opened Pandora's box. Once they looked at that case, they found others, and then Harding began to talk. Convictions were overturned and several state troopers ended up going to prison, including Harding's partner, who admitted to tampering with evidence in twenty-one cases. Both claimed that their superiors had pressured them into doing it. After that, New York changed its investigation practices.

Harding thought he was creating evidence to strengthen the case against a guilty person, which is both wrong and stupid. I have seen various cases in which an investigator tried to tighten a case by tampering with the evidence. In presentations for law enforcement, I make this point: "The evidence is what the evidence is, whether we like it or not. Don't fuck with it. If you try to tighten the case against an already guilty person, more than likely they'll end up free and your sorry ass will be in prison. Don't throw your career and life away trying to frame a guilty person. Take the long-range approach and don't let your ego get in the way. If you don't get them today, you'll get them tomorrow."

Generally I agree that physical evidence trumps behavioral evidence, but in this case, it just didn't look right. As it turned out, our instincts on the behavioral evidence were correct. Had the primary investigators given more weight to the profile, they might have been more suspicious of this convenient "proof." Not that a profile solves a case, but the behavior in this incident was clear, and given the offender's past relationship with his mother, investigators could have seen that the behavioral evidence, if manifested as the fingerprint suggested, would have been dramatically inconsistent with that. Our instinct about the crime had been correct.

And speaking of instinct, our prediction in Scarborough in 1988 had also come true. The profile that John Douglas and I did there had warned investigators of worse crimes to come. We did not realize it at first, but the Scarborough Rapist had become a killer.

4: The Kidnapping of Kristen French

Many a good hanging prevents a bad marriage.
—William Shakespeare, *Twelfth Night*

[1]

In Scarborough, the Metropolitan Toronto Sexual Assault Squad was still investigating the series of unsolved rapes, which had climbed to fifteen but recently had not gone any higher. Nearby, the Niagara Regional Police had several murders to clear up, so at different points we were invited into more consultations. This time when the offender was flushed out, we got more than we bargained for. To my surprise, I would find that I had already brushed up against him and had even predicted his lethal behavior. He turned out to be one of the most sadistic offenders I'd ever profiled, and his partner in crime was just as bad.

In less than a year, that same golden horseshoe area of Canada that borders New York State had experienced a cluster of murders that involved four young women. It wasn't clear that these incidents were related, but the possibility had to be considered. The first one occurred on June 15, 1991, when fourteen-year-old Leslie Mahaffy went missing from Burlington, which was halfway between Scarborough, in Toronto, and Niagara Falls. After attending a memorial service for a schoolmate killed in a car accident, she had gone to a store called Mac's Milk. Then she went home, quite late, in the company of a male friend but found the doors locked. No one responded to her knocking. Her friend went home, and Leslie was never seen alive again.

By some reports, Leslie was a girl who had abused alcohol, skipped school, and run away from home. These activities elevated her risk for violence somewhat, but there were numerous possibilities, all of which made it more difficult to know exactly what might have happened to her. She did call a friend that night to say she had no money and no place to go, but she did not reveal where she was. The police identified the phone booth from which that call was made, but that generated no significant leads.

Two weeks later, on the evening of June 29, her dismembered body was found along the shore of Lake Gibson, in St. Catharines, a town close to Niagara Falls and about thirty miles east of where she had lived. Her body was in separate pieces. Seven concrete blocks containing her body parts were pulled from the water, each of which measured approximately two feet by two feet by one foot. One block contained a foot and a thigh, and a second block contained a severed foot and a calf. Oddly, the block containing her head was spray-painted black. Only her torso was missing.

The next evening, in another area across the lake, a fisherman stumbled across the missing torso. It had floated free from its concrete coffin, which was larger in size than the others. Forensic examinations concluded that the girl had been sexually assaulted and dismembered with a power saw. The black paint was of an industrial grade. The exact cause of death was unclear.

The investigating officers crushed each block and methodically sifted through the pieces, bit by bit, looking for trace evidence. Some hair was found that might help identify the offender, and it was stored for later reference. Investigators were also able to determine the type of cement used, but that wasn't terribly helpful, as it was commonly available at many hardware and home-improvement stores. However, the cement blocks were important for other reasons.

The offender had made two separate pours. He'd apparently made an initial pour, placed the body parts in the cement, waited, and then made a second pour. This created a poor bond between the first and second pours. When kicked or struck with force, the two sections would come apart fairly easily. That meant we had an offender who was comfortable with building materials such as cement and power tools, but probably wasn't a pro. If he worked in the construction trade, he wasn't very good at it, especially cement work. More than likely he was just a weekend dabbler.

The lengths to which this killer had gone to conceal the victim were quite unusual and indicated an intelligent offender, one who would be appropriately placed at the more capable end of the organized/disorganized continuum. Dismembering a body takes time and effort, especially when the only tool used is a power saw. The offender had to have taken Leslie Mahaffy to a place over which he had total control and complete privacy; a place where he did not have to worry about being interrupted or discovered, where he could take all the time necessary to complete the task and clean up as he saw fit. Adding this up, we felt it was more than likely he had a home shop outfitted with power tools.

He was comfortable with the dumpsite near a lovers' lane, and he knew he wouldn't seem out of place if anyone spotted him there, especially if he had a woman with him. The cement blocks weighed a lot, so it was likely that he had help. However, the police pointed out that he clearly was not familiar with the way the lake was routinely drained. In a different part of the lake, not far away, his handiwork would have gone undetected.

Over the next few months, I had several conversations with members of the task force, along with Special Agent Chuck Wagner, who was our field coordinator in the Buffalo, New York, office that handled the Canadian liaison. This incident had all the markings of a crime of opportunity, one in which the victim had tragically crossed paths with the offender. I suggested that on prior occasions the assailant had been in the area where Mahaffy had lived, possibly for legitimate reasons, or for surveillance, or for both. He probably saw her out alone at night and took advantage of the situation. The primary motive seemed to be sexual, with the murder secondary.

We also looked at the second murder. Not long after Leslie Mahaffy's funeral, eighteen-year-old Nina de Villiers disappeared on August 10. Her body was later found in a creek, which spurred public fears of a serial killer. However, her assailant was eventually identified. His hair was inconsistent with the hair found in the concrete blocks encasing Mahaffy's parts, which, combined with other evidence, appeared to eliminate him as a viable suspect in the Mahaffy murder.

Then in November of that same year, Terri Anderson went out with friends on a Friday night and disappeared. Her body was discovered almost six months later in the Port Dalhousie harbor in St. Catharines. Her death appeared to be accidental, possibly due to recreational drugs, but having three girls missing so close together, with two bodies quickly found, raised an alarm throughout the community. We at the FBI did not know about this third young woman until after she was found, right around the time we were consulted about a brazen abduction that was to draw the attention of the entire country, and then the world.

On April 16, Kristen French, fifteen, began her daily walk home from Holy Cross secondary school in St. Catharines. It was only a few weeks before her birthday. She was an honor student and an athlete, popular at school, and she had a boyfriend. Her half-mile walk home along busy Linwell Road usually took about fifteen minutes, and a friend driving by had seen her there at 2:50 P.M., near Grace Lutheran Church. Nevertheless, she never made it home that afternoon.

The Niagara Regional Police acted quickly. Within twenty-four hours, they had set up a command post, called the press, assigned a team, and searched both sides of Linwell Road from Kristen's school to her home. Based upon the thorough neighborhood investigation they had completed, they developed several witnesses to Kristin French's abduction. Each had observed different aspects, but together they provided a good account of what had happened.

A woman described two men riding, near the church, in a yellowish-green Chevy Camaro. The driver had rolled down his window and was talking to a girl with long brown hair and in a Holy Cross uniform. She spoke back to him. The witness said that the driver was twenty-four to thirty years old, with light brown hair.

Around the same time, another witness saw a man pushing someone into the backseat of a yellowish Camaro-style car in the church parking lot. She dismissed the incident as teenagers fooling around, yet in this parking lot, the police found a brown loafer, identified from the special arch support as Kristen's, a torn section of a map, and a thick lock of permed brown hair that had been cut off. Possibly she had been lured with a request for directions and then abducted.

An additional witness later said that she nearly ran into a car of the same description—an older Camaro, she thought—driving fast and recklessly out of the church driveway. It went east on Linwell Road, and she noticed that the windows were dark. To help recall details, this witness allowed herself to be hypnotized and remembered that the car was yellow or beige. She had seen the driver's face because he'd looked at her, but she had failed to notice the car's license-plate number.

Then a man came forward with his own account of driving on Linwell Road. He'd seen a cream-colored car going east. It sped through a red light, turned a corner, and started to fishtail. He saw someone in the passenger side turn around and push another person down in the backseat. They were struggling and he had seen flailing arms.

The offender's behavior was significant. The abduction was a high-risk crime in the middle of the day in an area with plenty of traffic, so he was bold and supremely confident, an arrogant risk taker. Left behind were Kristen's shoe and the lock of hair, and a partial map of Scarborough. That was careless, indicating that the offender was in a hurry. Upon questioning more people, it appeared that prior to Kristen's disappearance, the car had been cruising the neighborhood, so this person was a stalker watching for an opportunity. On another day, a man in a car like this was seen staring toward the school at the time Kristin would have been leaving; just minutes before she disappeared, the car had circled the parking lot of a nearby school half a dozen times. This behavior pointed to the possibility that he had specifically targeted Kristen and had planned the abduction. But a school is a target-rich environment for a sexual predator interested in adolescent girls. He may have been looking at other girls as well, and all of that had to be investigated.

I was only peripherally involved at this point as we had minimal offender behavior to analyze. Then two weeks later, on April 30, Kristen's body was found, unclothed and lying on its side, on Number One side road, in Burlington. Her hair had been cut short and she was partly covered with branches, leaves, and other debris. It was clear from extensive bruising—especially on her face—that she had been repeatedly assaulted and then strangled or asphyxiated. Dried blood ran from her nose to her upper lip. Her body was pink and clean, suggesting that someone had washed her before dumping her, and the limited decomposition indicated that she had been kept alive for a period of time before being killed. There were maggot larvae in her body cavities, but with no entomology database for the conditions in that area, it proved difficult to rely on them as a measure for the time of death. A few hairs and fibers were collected from the body to use as trace evidence in case the police acquired items for comparison. Many of the investigators were of the mind that Kristen was held captive for most or all of the two-week period.

This new information was brought to our attention, and we had to determine whether any of the murders—specifically those of Kristen and Leslie—were related. It wasn't immediately obvious. Mahaffy's body had been completely dismembered, put in cement blocks, and sunk in a lake. That body was never supposed to be found. French's body was not dismembered, was not encased in cement, and was disposed of in a manner that virtually guaranteed discovery. One was taken during the night, the other by day. Yet they'd both been kidnapped and sexually assaulted, and they had been close in age.

Because of the proximity of these crimes to the U.S. border, some investigators speculated that an American was coming into Canada to commit them. This was a variation on the common theme of denial, i.e., "No one in our community is capable of such a crime," so it must be an outsider. Our feeling was that these murders had been committed by someone who was comfortable with the area, and thus more likely to be a local. The police looked at the Shawcross case we'd handled recently, not far away in Rochester, and I said that this was actually a good example of what I meant, because he had killed where he lived and worked—it defined his area of predatory activity. I felt that we had the same pattern in Canada and therefore a Canadian offender.

I did note an odd connection between the incidents, which made me lean toward the possibility that these two girls had been abducted and killed by the same person. Leslie Mahaffy was grabbed in Burlington and her body left in St. Catharines; Kristen French was taken in St. Catharines but left in Burlington. In addition, Kristen had been left just over five hundred yards from Halton Hills Memorial Gardens, the cemetery where Mahaffy had been buried. This seemed more than coincidental. The killer might even have stopped at the grave before or after dumping Kristen's body.

For a comparison of the bruises, they exhumed Leslie's body parts, but failed to find evidence of the kind of physical abuse that was evident with Kristen. Yet both girls appeared to share one similarity: On either side of the spinal cord were two small marks, as if someone had used his knees for leverage while he strangled or smothered them from behind. Around Kristen's throat were bruises, but not clearly from a ligature, and the bluish fingernails and intact bones in the throat were consistent with other forms of asphyxiation.

The dissimilarities between the cases were troubling, and the similarities were not compelling enough to make a positive link, yet we continued to keep both cases in mind as we considered how to catch Kristen's killer.

[2]

Inspector Vince Bevan was in charge of Project Green Ribbon, named for a campaign launched at Kristen's school after she'd disappeared. Project Green Ribbon, also referred to as the Green Ribbon Task Force, had been assembled to find the killer.

Vince always listened to what I had to say and always had questions. Yet he knew the limitations of a profile. He realized that a profile wasn't going to solve the case for him. As the case developed, I offered not just profiling but also other aspects of criminal-investigative analysis. I stayed in the case all the way through, but my role changed, and Vince welcomed everything I or my colleagues had to offer. One of my roles was to help with investigative strategy, and that came about in an unusual way.

The phone in my office rang one day and I recognized Vince's voice from our numerous prior conversations. This time he had a different question. A local television station, CHCH Channel 11, had approached the task force to offer help. They wanted to work in conjunction with the authorities in producing a program that would assist the investigation.

"Have you had any experience with anything like that?" Vince asked me.

"No, I haven't," I replied. All too often, law enforcement's relationship with the media is adversarial, I went on, and Vince agreed that his experience had been the same. He told me how in a recent interview a reporter had said to him, "If another dead girl shows up, the media is going to come down here and shit on your head—and I'll be the first one! Are you prepared to accept that?" Vince had restrained himself, but his fiery-eyed look was enough to burn a hole through the reporter. The divide between the media and the task force there was widening by the second, he told me, and this might be a good opportunity, so I encouraged him to explore it further.

It turned out that Steve Harris, the show's producer, had come up with the idea when driving home one evening with his teenage daughter. Aware of recent events, she had said, "Hey, Dad, you're a big TV executive producer. Can't you do anything?" So he'd thought that maybe he could.

After some guarded preliminary meetings between the Green Ribbon Task Force and CHCH Channel 11, they eventually coordinated their efforts to present a program about the case, which was aired on Tuesday, July 21, 1992.

I said that we'd like to see it used on two levels: to inform the public and also to communicate with either of the offenders. We wanted to hit every possible emotion that we could. We did everything from "just the facts," to an appeal through a reward, to some very emotional material. Then I wanted to scare the second offender with the idea that the first one would kill him and the people around him. We just hoped something would resonate with somebody. As we put it together, it developed from the thirty-minute program that was originally planned to a ninety-minute one.

The show involved a reenactment of the crimes, and discussions with Kristen's parents and the investigators. A phone bank with forty-one trained volunteers was set up to take calls. Host Dan MacLean repeatedly appealed to the public to come forward with any information they might have. There was also the hope that someone acquainted with the offender would recognize him or his accomplice from our profile and would inform the police. Everyone was ready.

Vince Bevan provided as much information as he could, and a cream-colored Camaro was displayed on the floor to show the audience the kind of car the police were looking for, including the rust spots witnesses had described. Bevan, a soft-spoken, slender man with dark hair and a mustache, pointed out a recent repair on the driver's door, evident from gray primer paint, and he said that the interior was believed to be maroon or red.

The task force, he recounted, had checked and marked vehicles in surrounding towns that were similar to this car to eliminate them one by one as the suspect vehicle. Investigators were uncertain about the model and year, and Bevan mentioned the possibility that the offender had given it a new paint job. They were checking gas stations, auto recyclers, and body shops and asking them to look into this. It was a daunting task, since at that time there were about 125,000 Camaros registered in Ontario.

Bevan also indicated that the eyewitnesses had reported the presence of an elderly couple in matching beige jackets who clearly had watched the crime occur and knew it to be something serious. They had not yet come forward, but they were encouraged to do so now. Every piece of information helped, and they might have seen something significant. The *Toronto Star* offered a reward of $100,000 for information leading to the arrest of Kristen's killer.

Kate Cavanaugh, a Canadian profiler, was featured on the show, along with Special Agent Chuck Wagner. I offered my profile via satellite connection, relying on the general feeling that the witnesses had offered an accurate rendering of what they had seen. As it turned out, this would be another case in which well-meaning but flawed eyewitness information led the investigation in the wrong direction.

I said that this incident was clearly a stranger homicide, which, as I mentioned earlier, is more difficult to solve, but I was confident it would be solved because the team had made a lot of progress. From the offender's point of view, it had been a high-risk crime, and sexually motivated. Offenders who commit this kind of crime, I explained, have a rich fantasy life; this involves a process that makes them increasingly more aggressive, and they often make mistakes. It was likely that he had stalked her, getting himself ready to approach her, and it was also possible that, since the time the crime had occurred, he and his accomplice might have watched teenagers in other areas. I urged people to report any man or men who tried to lure girls to a car.

Where there are two offenders, I added, one is usually dominant and the other subservient. We profile the dominant offender, because it's his fantasy that's manifested in the crime scene. In this case, the offender was a predator and a psychopath. He was manipulative, and he exploited people for his own gratification, without guilt or remorse. He didn't care about the suffering he caused. If he had a wife or a girlfriend, his behavior with that person would be consistent. He'd be in total control. There was a high probability that this would be an abusive relationship as well, because he clearly hated women, and the primary woman in his life would suffer for it. He'd have a history of criminal sexual offenses like flashing, exhibitionism, obscene phone calls, or rape. The people around him knew what he was like, and he might even have spent some time in prison on a sexual offense.

"One thing we see consistently," I said, "is that an offender will act out in one situation but not in another, due to some environmental trigger, such as a stressor, that will provoke him. It could be a fight with his wife or the loss of a job—something that bucked his sense of control, so he'll go out and force someone to come under his control."

I went on to point out that we felt the offender was employed in a semiskilled capacity, possibly working with his hands. Based on the Mahaffy murder, which by this time we felt was linked, there was a high probability that he worked with power tools and had a shop at home.

Then I turned to the fact that he had held at least one of the girls captive for a period of time. That would have been disruptive of his regular routines, and someone close to him might have noticed. Over the two-week period since April 16, he would have had to monitor the girl night and day. He might not have missed work altogether, but he would have been preoccupied. At home, if he was married, his wife would not be allowed to ask questions, but she'd have known that he was gone for unusual periods of time.

Then Dan MacLean asked me, "If he is watching tonight, what do you think he's experiencing?"

I hadn't anticipated that question, but saw it as an opportunity to make a point. I said, "If he is watching, I want to tell him that he *is* going to be apprehended. It's just a question of when." I wanted to keep the pressure on him because under stress, everyone—including murderers—makes mistakes. I also consciously used fear as a weapon, warning those around him that they were in danger.

I referred to the case of Edmund Kemper, "the Coed Killer," in Santa Cruz, California, in the early 1970s. He had been killing and dismembering young girls, and as the investigation closed in, he murdered his mother and also killed a neighbor.

The submissive offender, I said, was a follower and was likely to be experiencing guilt over the crime. It probably hadn't been his idea to kill anyone. He'd be having problems coping, and the people around him would notice behaviors such as troubled sleep, interrupted eating patterns, or substance abuse because he would be trying to blot out the memory of the crime.

With sexual homicides, I said, we were usually dealing with a lone predator, and I used the Arthur Shawcross case as an example. While there had been cases of male-female teams, they were rare in sexual murders. Eyewitnesses had described the two offenders as male, and we had no reason to dispute that. However, no one had gotten a good look at the second person, so we had to go by what seemed most likely. I noted some notorious team killers, such as Leonard Lake and Charles Ng, who had lured their many victims to a cabin outside San Francisco and had turned them into sex slaves before killing them. I talked about the Hillside Stranglers, Angelo Buono and Kenneth Bianchi, two cousins who were responsible for a string of sex murders in Los Angeles and Washington State.

Sometimes two psychopaths do work together, I explained, and in that case they would have a close relationship, like brothers. Quite often, where you see one, you'll also see the other. They may have met in prison, because they would probably have a criminal background. "No one goes from being a normal productive citizen to being a sexual predator and killer," I said. "It doesn't happen. People escalate to that point through lesser crimes." However, I also knew that this person could have been committing crimes but thus far avoiding arrest.

I hoped to play to the weaker partner by saying that *his* motive might have been the thrill of abduction and rape, but not the desire to kill. The dominant offender would be more cold-blooded and predatory.

When asked about why Kristen's hair had been cut, I offered two possibilities: It had been done to humiliate the victim, because the offender felt a lot of hostility toward women. She had long hair and probably took pride in it, so it might have been done to make her feel disgraced. The second possibility could be the offender's having a psychosexual disorder, known as a paraphilia, or hair fetish. People around him would certainly notice this, because he would take unusual interest in their hair, from sniffing it to asking for samples.

I pointed out that this offender might be someone whom others saw as a nice guy. However, if the behaviors we'd suggested seemed to fit, they should alert police officials. With this program, we hoped not only to get more information from someone who had not yet come forward but also to drive a wedge between the offender and his partner.

We found out later that the offenders had indeed watched the program, and had even recorded it. The dominant partner believed that nothing we said had linked these crimes to him and he was sure he would never be caught. He did not drive a yellow or beige Camaro—it was a gold Nissan—and he had no male accomplice. When I said that this was a white male in his late twenties who had an abusive relationship with women, he called that bullshit—although he was twenty-eight and did beat his wife. The submissive partner, who came forward more than six months later, felt the profile had gotten right some key aspects about the dominant partner. He was abusive, he'd had a power saw, he had a history of crimes against women, and he'd definitely had an accomplice. She was ready to talk.

[3]

On January 5, 1993, a doctor working at St. Catharines General Hospital called the police to report a domestic assault. The victim's name was Karla Homolka. She had been severely beaten about her face and body with a flashlight and was being admitted. Paul Bernardo was arrested that same night and charged with assault. After Karla left the hospital, her mother sheltered her from her abusive husband, placing her with relatives to keep her safe. Then, on February 1, the crime lab finally processed the last of the samples taken for the Toronto Metro Police on the Scarborough rapes. Starting with 224 samples, they had narrowed it down to five possible matches and finally to one. It was Paul Bernardo.

He'd volunteered samples in November 1990, but the crime lab had only now finished the DNA analysis— more than two years after receiving the sample and six years after the first rape. There was a meeting of the Metro police, the Niagara Regional Police, and members of the Green Ribbon Task Force to discuss Bernardo. He'd lived in Scarborough, and after he'd moved to Port Dalhousie on the Lake Ontario side of St. Catharines, the Scarborough rapes had stopped. However, a rape had occurred in his new neighborhood, and then the murders had begun. It seemed reasonable that he had escalated into sexual murder and could be responsible for the Mahaffy and French killings.

He fit the profile we'd developed—he was in his late twenties, residing in the area of the crimes, and having a history of both domestic violence and increasingly violent sex crimes. He did have a power saw in his basement workshop, but working with his hands was an avocation, not a vocation. His formal education was that of an accountant, but he wasn't employed as one. As for a criminal history, it would turn out that he was involved in smuggling cigarettes between the United States and Canada, which he'd found to be surprisingly lucrative.

The task force set up surveillance on him, and combined with their continued investigation, learned that his wife had moved out and had charged him with assault. Karla needed to be interviewed, but how best to go about it? The strategy the investigators developed was to imply that the interview was going to be about the domestic assault, but have investigators from the Metro Toronto Sexual Assault Squad and Project Green Ribbon also appear. In order to induce stress for Karla, the purpose was to imply through their combined presence and a few strategic questions that they knew a lot more than they were revealing.

They arrived at her aunt and uncle's apartment, where she had been staying since she'd left Bernardo. She was confused as to why four investigators appeared, and became visibly unsettled when the investigators from the Metro Toronto Sexual Assault Squad and the Green Ribbon Task Force identified themselves. Initially, they questioned her about the domestic assault. Then they asked her if she was at all familiar with the Scarborough rapes. She denied knowing anything. Was she familiar with the Grace Lutheran Church in St. Catharines? Had she ever been there, perhaps with Paul, to help him in some way? She tried to avoid answering the question by saying that she wasn't religious. They asked her if she knew why they were asking her these questions. She said she had no idea. And so it went. It was an artful and brilliant piece of police work. Inexperienced officers might have revealed everything they knew about the case, and then when Karla denied knowing anything, they might have confronted her. Instead, these officers were nonconfrontational and utilized the power of suggestion, a softer but stronger approach. The unknown is always more disturbing than the known.

When they left, Karla, who had barely been holding herself together, fell apart. She blurted out to her aunt and uncle, "They know everything." With support and pressure from them, she admitted what she knew about the Scarborough rapes, the abductions, and the Mahaffy and French murders.

One of the detectives called back later that evening to see how Karla was doing. Her uncle told him that she was getting an attorney. That was a welcome development. That meant their strategy had worked. They were driving a wedge between Homolka and Bernardo.

She retained a lawyer named George Walker. That was good, too, because as an experienced criminal attorney, Walker would understand the dynamics involved. He would have only Karla's interest at stake, not Paul's. Walker approached Murray Segal, a senior official in the Canadian ministry, and wanted to cut a deal for his client: In exchange for total immunity, she would reveal the identity of the killer of Kristen French and Leslie Mahaffy. She knew every detail because she had been present. The killer was her husband, Paul Bernardo.

The DNA evidence definitely nailed Bernardo for the Scarborough rapes, but there was little evidence linking him to the murders. It would be difficult, if not impossible, to convict him for the murders without a

witness like his wife, someone who could provide cor-
roborating details and perhaps even physical evidence,
so they agreed to work out a deal.

Then Karla began to talk . . . a lot. She was just seventeen when she met Paul Bernardo, who was twenty-
three. To friends these two good-looking blondes had
seemed the perfect couple—they'd even been nick-
named Ken and Barbie—but behind closed doors at
their rented home at 57 Bayview Drive, things were
different. Karla spent five days giving a videotaped
confession, admitting to the fact that she knew Paul
was a rapist and she had helped him to lighten his hair
after the police had initially questioned him. She had
also prepared alibis for his whereabouts. She presented
herself as a simple, middle-class girl who had been attracted to Paul from the moment they'd met. She had
let him do anything he desired with her, even when his
demands became disgusting and brutal. She had to allow him to do things to other women, she said, or he
would have left her and might even have killed her and
her family.

She knew about the murder of Leslie Mahaffy, pin-
pointing it to June 17, 1991, three days after Leslie was
abducted, and saying, "She was afraid. I think she
knew she was going to die." Karla gave her a stuffed
animal named Bunky to comfort her before Paul strangled her. She said she had seen some discoloration in
the girl's face, so she'd turned away. But Mahaffy
didn't die right away, and it took more effort than either one had anticipated to kill her, but they did it.
Karla helped Paul wrap the dead girl in a blanket and
carry her down into their root cellar, because it was Father's Day and her parents were soon coming over for
dinner. As the dead girl lay downstairs, the couple en-

tertained Karla's parents that evening. Karla even went down to get some potatoes from beside the corpse to use in their dinner.

Two weeks later, she married Paul in a lavish storybook ceremony replete with a horse-drawn carriage ride through the quaint village of Niagara-on-the-Lake. Paul had paid some of the expenses with his lucrative cigarette-smuggling business. As they flew off on their honeymoon in Hawaii, the blocks containing the parts of Leslie Mahaffy's body parts were found.

Karla also knew about Kristen French and claimed that Paul had forced her to get involved with the assault. After only a few days of keeping the girl in their home, Paul had killed her; he later made Karla go with him to dump the body. The state of the body's decomposition suggested that Kristen had been held captive for a longer period, but Karla insisted that it was for only a few days. She said that Paul had chosen Burlington to make the police think the killer lived there, and had even considered dumping Kristen's body on Leslie Mahaffy's grave. Instead, they'd rolled her into a ditch.

Those investigators who came into contact with Karla Homolka had a difficult time believing that she was the helpless accomplice she claimed to be, but she had read quite a lot about the battered-woman syndrome. She knew how to do what people expected of her. And despite the fact that she had witnessed two murders, there was no evidence in her behavior of a guilty conscience. Upon leaving her husband, she had gone out to a club and within a few hours had had sex with a man she'd just met in a private room at the club.

[4]

The Crown attorneys, along with members of the task force, immediately began to draw up arrest and search warrants. They pressed forward carefully and methodically, ensuring that their legal work would withstand the most rigorous defense challenges. Bernardo was under an around-the-clock surveillance and would immediately be arrested if it looked as though he were about to rape or abduct again. The surveillance crew reported that he was definitely on the hunt, so this was a concern. The task force would be in touch with me first thing Monday to assist with part of the affidavit for a search warrant. Everything appeared to be under control. This was a good way to end the week—establishing the identity of a dangerous rapist and killer.

It was Friday and my son was competing in a sporting event the next morning in Virginia Beach, about a three-hour drive from our home in Fredericksburg. We decided to drive down Friday night, as it was an early morning event. We arrived in Virginia Beach around nine-thirty P.M., and I had finished carrying the last bag into our room when my pager went off. I looked at it and saw Vince's direct-dial number at the task force. I called immediately and his pressured tone of voice told me as much as his words.

"The genie is out of the bottle," he said. "The press knows."

"Holy shit, Vince." This was bad news.

"We haven't lost control yet," he assured me, "but we've got to move fast on this or we may. They've agreed to hold off for a few days, but we can't be sure, and there's no telling who else might know. We've got to move quickly."

I envisioned a scenario like the one we'd had in 1984 with Christopher Wilder. He was a sexually sadistic serial killer who had raped and harassed women in Florida before finally turning to kidnapping and murder. Alerted by a press report that he was being sought, he left town, torturing and killing several women as he went across the country. That got him on the FBI's "Ten Most Wanted" list, and state troopers finally spotted his car in New Hampshire. He went for his gun, and during the struggle, he badly wounded one officer and shot himself in the heart.

We didn't need another manhunt like that.

Vince wanted to know whether we could help. I told him that we could apply the research that the BSU had done on sadistic sexual offenders, which would bolster his probable cause for getting into the suspect's house.

"I can do that," I said, "but all the case materials are locked up at the academy. I'll have to drive to Quantico first."

"If you could, we would be very appreciative." The Canadians are always so damn courteous and respectful. What's even more incredible is that they're genuinely sincere about it.

Despite my family plans, I told Vince, "I'm on my way. It's going to take me a bit over three hours to drive to Quantico. I'll call you once I get in my office."

"Thanks, Gregg, I really appreciate—"

"Vince," I interrupted, "just buy me a lager the next time I'm in town."

It was around one A.M. when I arrived at the academy. I made my way through the gun vault and went down in the elevator to my office. I retrieved the case materials from the locked file room and got Vince and the Crown attorney on the phone. Then the three of us went to work.

In preparation for this, I had been linking what the Metropolitan Toronto Police knew about the rapes in Scarborough with what the Green Ribbon Task Force knew about the French and Mahaffy murders. I had recently become aware that there had been seven more rapes in Scarborough, and the task force had narrowed a suspect list to five men. Bernardo had been on that list. He closely resembled both the behavioral profile we had constructed and the composite drawings from eyewitness descriptions. He'd even been questioned and let go. Bernardo, who had lived with his parents in Scarborough (as I had predicted in my initial profile), had moved to St. Catharines, at which point the rapes in Scarborough had suddenly ceased.

I hadn't known about that significant development when I'd worked up a profile of the offender for the murders of French and Mahaffy—the very type of crime I had predicted for the Scarborough rapist. It was rather uncanny. Having profiled him twice within four years for two different law-enforcement agencies seemed surreal, but it did underscore the fact that a profile is a snapshot in time. The behavior of violent serial offenders is dynamic. Their crimes and their MOs can and do change over time, usually for the worse. As Benjamin Franklin noted, "Many foxes grow gray; few grow good."

Since Bernardo had been identified as the Scarborough Rapist, we already had plenty of material about him from our previous investigative analysis, and since that time, he had added a few things to his act. One woman claimed that while he'd raped her, a female accomplice was there recording the whole thing on videotape. He bit the breast of another victim and pulled out pubic hair. That woman had gotten a good look at her assailant, and her description had matched Bernardo, as well as being consistent with the descriptions offered during the earlier Scarborough rape series. These behaviors were a good indication that he had gotten bolder and more brutal—and that he'd involved Karla.

The most important point I had made with Vince over the course of the investigation was that sadistic offenders tend to memorialize their crimes in various ways, such as keeping journals, ledgers, diaries, videotapes, and photographs. I felt sure that this offender had videotaped his assaults and possibly the murders of his victims. Those tapes could, essentially, be all the evidence necessary to convict him. Put the videos in, press the Play button, and let the jurors see the crimes for themselves. It was critically important that we establish all the probable cause we possibly could to allow the investigators to search for and seize those tapes. Like other sexual sadists, Paul would be drawn to violent pornography, as it would be both sexually stimulating and would validate his own fantasies and sexual behaviors. He would want those tapes for repeated pleasure.

In my affidavit, I noted that when Bernardo had moved from his parents' home in Scarborough, those rapes had stopped. Within nine weeks of moving to St. Catharines, a rape occurred near where he lived. In every significant respect, this rape demonstrated similarities to those in Scarborough. I also indicated that, "Once he moved to St. Catharines, he had a home of his own over which he was able to exert complete control. This change in his circumstances aids him in the escalation of his offenses to the point where he can now take his victims home." Sexual sadists prefer to hold their victims for hours, days, or weeks. Now that he had a place to take his victims, and a place where he could more fully act out his sexually violent fantasies against these women, abduction became a predictable progression for Bernardo, and that virtually guaranteed a murder.

The ultimate fantasy of a sexual sadist is to totally possess another person, both physically and psychologically. The definitive possession occurs by playing God, by exercising the power over life and death, deciding how, when, and where a victim will die. The homicide itself can be the ultimate sexual experience for the offender, as the violence has become eroticized. A secondary gain is that the murder conveniently eliminates a witness.

I added that by now I expected that the unrestrained and sexually sadistic Scarborough Rapist could easily have escalated to murder. The killer of both Mahaffy and French was also a sexual sadist, and since sexual sadists account for less than 2 percent of all sexually violent offenders, the chances of more than one operating in a localized area is remote. That meant that it was highly likely that the Scarborough Rapist and the killer of Kristin French and Leslie Mahaffy were one and the same.

The specific behaviors of the offender narrowed the pool down even further. The Scarborough Rapist collected hair from two of his victims, and the offender who murdered Kristen French had also cut her hair, possibly for collection. Taking hair satisfies the sexual sadist's need to punish and degrade others, while also providing him with a trophy.

I then pointed to Bernardo's history, which demonstrated almost all of the characteristics of a serial sexual sadist. He was a white male with a background of parental infidelity and abuse—he was the product of his mother's extramarital affair, while his father had been arrested for abusing Bernardo's sister. The sexual sadist would be married at the time of his offense—as Bernardo was—and would have above-average intelligence. Bernardo had completed a four-year university degree in three years. He was neat and well groomed, presenting himself well in social settings, and he used his social skills as a facade to cover for his predatory impulses.

During the early stages of a relationship, as reported by several former girlfriends, Bernardo was initially attentive, generous, and caring, but he gradually escalated into verbal and physical abuse. One had said that Bernardo was unable to achieve an erection without inflicting pain on her or making her afraid. This is a classic indication of sexual sadism, as it is the suffering of the victim that is sexually arousing. Bernardo placed ligatures around her neck while forcing her into anal intercourse, and would insert foreign objects into her. If she resisted, he got violent and verbally abusive. The sadist's need to completely dominate, control, and humiliate is also often observable outside the realm of sexual activity.

Karla described how Bernardo would dictate her hairstyle and clothing, and how he eventually isolated her from family and friends. For the sexual sadist, this isolation makes his female partner completely dependent on him. There is often an idealization/devaluation quality in the sadist's relationships with wives and girlfriends. First she's idealized. She is all important to him and he showers her with gifts; then he becomes contemptuous, angry, and violent and sexually degrades her. She's nothing to him and she's nothing without him.

Since known items were missing from the victims, which indicated that the offender collected trophies, I noted this for the warrant. If Bernardo felt secure in his home, it was likely that he would store these materials there. Since he had given biological samples more than two years earlier, and nothing had happened to him as a result, he had probably developed an increased sense of immunity and invincibility. In his mind, he was "bullet proof."

I also indicated that just as there was a high degree of probability that the rapist was also the killer, it was highly likely that this offender would kill again, since sexually sadistic offenders were known to do so. After being questioned for the Scarborough rapes in the fall of 1990, he laid low for a period of time, but the following summer had started up again in a different area. Only external forces, such as death or arrest, can stop such offenders.

We worked on this until approximately four-thirty A.M. At that point, I locked everything up and headed south again to Virginia Beach, arriving around seven forty-five A.M. With the help of a couple of shots of espresso, I managed to stay vertical during my son's competition that morning. Things were working out, just not quite according to plan.

[5]

The initial plan had been to serve the arrest and search warrants simultaneously, but that didn't happen. Due to extenuating circumstances, Bernardo was arrested on Wednesday, February 17. The affidavit in support of the search warrant was nearly a thousand pages and wouldn't be ready for a couple more days. It didn't really matter, as the house was sealed after Bernardo's arrest.

On February 19, 1993, the warrant was executed at 57 Bayview Drive. Forensic technicians entered the house in moon suits and began a search that would last for over two months. They used state-of-the-art forensic tools, including alternate light sources and chemical fuming agents. There was concern about the quantity and quality of the physical and trace evidence in the two murders as, respectively, they were over ten and twenty months old, and Karla had indicated what great care she and Paul had taken to obliterate the evidence.

The technicians did find wood flooring and a wall with spatters that appeared to be blood. A piece of stained carpet was also discovered in Paul's otherwise neat closet. Lab tests would conclude that it contained both vomit stains from Kristen French and semen from Bernardo. This was important, as it indicated sexual contact between them. A collection of tools were located in the basement and secured for testing. Among other items found were news accounts of each of the crimes; a stash of pornography; one brief videotape of Karla having sex with an unidentifiable woman; numerous true-crime books; and a list authored by both Karla and Paul that detailed each of the Scarborough rapes.

By now, Karla had agreed to start divorce proceedings so that she could testify against her husband. When pressed about the issue of whether or not there were videotapes of the rapes and murders she confirmed what we had suspected. Paul had made several eight-millimeter tapes of both Mahaffy and French, and Karla had insisted that they were hidden in the house. However, the police did not find them.

We then reasoned that if Paul didn't keep them in the house, he must have them somewhere else, perhaps in a safety-deposit box or a storage area, but those leads came up dry as well.

While all of this was going on, Karla admitted to one more thing. It seems that they had killed even before Leslie Mahaffy, and this one gave everyone pause.

[6]

Paul was living at the Homolkas' home in 1990, sleeping on a couch. During the Christmas season, they had a party and Karla's sister, fifteen-year-old Tammy Lyn, was allowed to stay up after Mr. and Mrs. Homolka had gone to bed. She had a few drinks, and then Paul and Karla put a plan into action. Paul had expressed to Karla a desire to have sex with the younger girl, so Karla had helped him break some of the blinds in Tammy's room in order to videotape her undressing. Several times, Karla had pretended to be Tammy and let Paul have sex with her on Tammy's bed. But clearly this was not enough for him. He wanted the real thing.

As a Christmas gift, she decided to let Paul rape her sister. That night, they set up a camcorder and crushed Halcion into Tammy's drinks. Eventually she fell asleep, and onto a soft cloth Karla put halothane that she had stolen from the veterinary clinic where she worked. She held that against Tammy's face to make sure that the unconscious girl did not wake up. Paul undressed her, and as he held the camera on himself in close-up, he raped the unconscious girl vaginally and anally. Then he told Karla, who obeyed him, to suck on her sister's breasts and have oral sex with her. His commands became increasingly more vulgar, and Karla refused him several times, but eventually complied and sexually assaulted her sister.

Then Tammy vomited and stopped breathing. She was making a choking noise. Karla pulled the girl's tongue out and pumped on her chest, but she couldn't revive her. They dragged her into Karla's bedroom, alarmed that things had gotten out of control and that someone might hear. They redressed her and Paul tried to revive her while Karla hid the drugs. Then they called for help and the paramedics arrived to take her to the hospital.

The paramedics noted a terrible burn on Tammy's face, from her mouth down to her neck, but since Karla and Paul denied that any drugs were involved, investigators let it go. However, as soon as Tammy was pronounced dead, in the hospital, and the news was delivered back home, Karla began to put the blankets on which Tammy had been lying into the washing machine. In their story to the police, they claimed the marks on Tammy's face were rug burns, but the pathologist indicated that this was not the case. Nevertheless, he concluded that the death was accidental, caused by Tammy's aspirating her own vomit.

At Tammy's funeral, Karla said later, Paul wouldn't leave her casket. He called her "my angel" and played with her blond locks. He also kept a photograph of her prominently displayed.

Then Paul and Karla had moved into their Port Dalhousie home, and Paul had gone out and raped a woman in the area.

After Karla's confession, on July 20, 1993, Tammy's body was exhumed for a more thorough analysis. The first thing found were notes that Paul and Karla had stuck inside the casket prior to the burial, apologizing and declaring their love for her. The toxicology tests confirmed that she had been drugged, as Karla had alleged. The pathologist examined the large stain on the side of her face and determined that it was a burn caused by stomach acid. He also saw evidence that she had been raped. Otherwise the report added nothing to Karla's confession.

[7]

After the investigators finished the search at 57 Bayview without finding the videotapes depicting the rapes and murders of Mahaffy and French, Bernardo sent his attorney, Ken Murray, into the house to get some of his "personal effects." He had drawn a map for Murray showing where the six eight-millimeter tapes were hidden. They were between two rafters, under some insulation inside a drop ceiling behind a recessed light. The light had to be removed from the ceiling to gain access to the tapes.

Murray was allowed into the house unescorted. He followed the map, recovered the tapes, and kept them to himself for fifteen months. In September 1994, Clayton Ruby, a lawyer acting on behalf of Bernardo's new lawyer, John Rosen, delivered a package containing the six tapes to the Crown attorneys who were prosecuting Bernardo. The tapes virtually locked the case against Bernardo. It was a dramatic and exciting moment for the prosecutors, but an embarrassing one for the investigators who had searched the house for seventy-two days without finding the videos.

So the tapes had been in the house after all. That made me feel better. As I'd indicated, even when he knew the police were closing in, Bernardo could not bring himself to destroy his ultimate trophies. For Bernardo, it was a case of emotion overriding logic. He kept the trophies because the emotional needs that the tapes served outweighed their devastating evidentiary value. This has happened with other preferential sex offenders as well.

Investigators who were working with Karla as their star witness against Paul viewed the tapes and realized that she hadn't been as forthcoming as she had promised. In the videotape of Paul's assault on Tammy Lyn, Karla claimed that she had told him that the whole thing was disgusting. Yet on closer examination, it was not the rape scene that appeared to disgust her but the fact that Paul wanted her to stick her finger into Tammy and taste the girl's menstrual blood.

Karla and Paul had made a sex tape together, after Tammy Lyn's funeral, that was truly shocking. In it, as Karla stripped Paul, she told him that she had loved it when he'd raped Tammy and that she was happy he had wanted her to do sexual things with her sister—the sister they had just killed together. She suggested that he should get even younger girls for them to play with together—a line clearly not scripted by him. She then rubbed a red rose over his genitals and said they would place it on Tammy's grave. After that, she used her dead sister's panties to rub him into an erection, all the while encouraging him to continue to rape young girls. In a different scene on the same tape, she put on Tammy's clothing and pretended to be her sister making love to Paul.

Another video showed them giving the same treatment to a fifteen-year-old girl who resembled Tammy and who was unconscious throughout her sexual assault. Karla had "forgotten" about this episode and she excused herself by saying that bringing in other girls was the only way to keep Paul interested in her, but the tape showed her full and enthusiastic participation. This girl was lucky; she was let go.

Next was Leslie Mahaffy, who had been blindfolded. She said her name for the recorder as she removed her clothing. Paul filmed her urinating and then had sex with her. The next day, he had her take a shower and then Karla joined them for sex play. At the point during which Paul anally raped her, she screamed for Karla to help her, but Karla continued to hold the camera steady on her fiancé. Then he covered the camera lens and there was no more of the doomed girl.

On this same tape, Paul had recorded Kristen French urinating and then manipulating his genitals, obeying his commands to tell him sexual things, even as she cried and begged to go home. As Bernardo forced the girl to perform oral sex on him, Karla took pictures, directed her in what to do, and ran the camcorder. The two of them dressed her in Karla's schoolgirl outfits and had her apply makeup for the camera. Then Bernardo had them make love on the bed before he joined them, threatening to kill Kristen with a knife if she messed up what she was supposed to do for him.

She was clearly inexperienced and afraid, but she tried. He then urinated on her and tried without success to defecate. He continued to do degrading things to this frightened girl, forcing her to please him, while Karla insisted that Kristen do whatever Paul wanted.

Yet Kristen finally resisted and Paul beat her harshly for her spirit. That explained why she had more bruises than Leslie did. The murders themselves had not been recorded, but it was clear that both Karla and Paul had forced these girls into sexual activities against their wills, and that Paul and Karla were the last two people to see them alive.

[8]

Despite Karla's obvious involvement in three separate murders, her deal was sealed. It was too late to change the terms, so the prosecution presented her as a battered woman who had been forced to comply as an accomplice. They had no other choice, although it was clear that Karla's confident demeanor, future plans, and string of lies hardly fit that profile. She certainly did not suffer from low self-esteem, she had frequent contact with her family, and she had participated in the sexual assaults with apparent enthusiasm.

For her cooperation and a plea of guilty to two counts of manslaughter, Karla was sentenced to two ten-year terms, to be served concurrently, along with two more years for her part in her sister's death. She was never again to own any firearms, explosives, or ammunition. Then she went to prison but returned to court in May 1995 to testify against Paul, from whom she had gained a divorce.

Bernardo was charged with two counts of first-degree murder, two counts of kidnapping, two counts of sexual assault, two counts of forcible confinement, and one count of committing an indignity to a human body.

During the trial, both sides showed graphic images from these videotapes of the way in which Bernardo had assaulted and tormented French and Mahaffy. While their deaths had not been recorded, his threats to them had, but something else was apparent as well—Karla's smiling cooperation. Bernardo's lawyer attempted to pin the deaths on Karla, since she was the only other person there and since the marks on the backs of both victims appeared to match the size of her knees. She could have done it in a fit of jealousy while Paul was gone. There was no conclusive proof, he pointed out, that Kristen French had been strangled with an electrical cord, as Karla had claimed. She might just as easily have been smothered with a pillow while tied up.

The jury didn't go for it. They convicted Bernardo on all nine counts and he got a sentence of life in prison, with eligibility for parole in 2020. Karla returned to prison to serve out her time as well.

The trial riveted the community and taught us more about the unique dynamics of male/female killing teams. Up to that point, much of the research in this area—including interviews with Karla—indicated that the females were compliant victims, feeling they had to do as told or else get beaten themselves. However, when Karla wasn't acting the part she had learned from therapists and books, she seemed more like a female psychopath who enjoyed the victimization of others. She was certainly caught on tape spontaneously telling Paul that she would help him to find and rape fifty virgins, and there was no indication that this remark was scripted. Even Paul had seemed surprised. It appeared to be her own unique inspiration for pleasing "the king." That she could kill her sister and then continue to participate in more rapes and murders indicated a truly deviant personality.

Karla believed that she would be released on parole after just four years, but at her parole hearing in 1997, it was determined that she was too potentially dangerous to be allowed back into society. The same was true as of 2001, so it's likely that she will serve her entire term, until 2005. What will happen once she's released is anyone's guess. Because she fears for her life in Canada, there's some talk that she will emigrate to the States.

Once the prosecution was completed, the Honorable Archie Campbell undertook a major judicial review of the investigation. Upon a thorough evaluation, suggestions were made for improving case management, such as getting more and better computers and developing better media relations. Regarding my involvement in the case, Vince Bevan testified that from the investigative perspective, the profile was "significant" because "we couldn't make it clearer to our people that it was someone who was fairly smart, fairly organized, would have a methodical way of going about things [and that there were] different stresses that we could look for and apply."

Judge Campbell noted that the behavioral evidence cited in the search warrant application was "a good example of the state of the art and evidentiary value of profiling in serial predator investigations." While gratified by his remarks, I would respectfully argue that the evidence set forth in the affidavit was not "profiling" evidence in its narrowest sense. Rather, it was an example of successfully integrating behavioral research into an ongoing investigation.

I was astounded by the seemingly relentless flood of venomous criticism aimed at the Green Ribbon Task Force, mostly from the media. While there is no such thing as a perfect investigation, Vince and his team had solved the case. They had slain the dragon. It might not have been pretty, but dragon slaying never is.

My work on this case was finished, but the onslaught of unwarranted criticism motivated me to write Vince and the Green Ribbon Task Force, and with my letter I enclosed the following quote from Theodore Roosevelt:

> It is not the critic who counts, not the man who points out how the strong man stumbled, or where the doer of deeds could have done better. The credit belongs to the man who is actually in the arena; whose face is marred by the dust and sweat and blood; who strives valiantly; who errs and comes up short again and again; who knows the great enthusiasms, the great devotions and spends himself in a worthy course; who at the best, knows in the end the triumph of high achievement, and who, at worst, if he fails, at least fails while daring greatly; so that his place shall never be with those cold and timid souls who know neither victory or defeat.

Every day that Bernardo wakes up behind bars is a great day for the rest of us. For that we owe Vince Bevan and the Green Ribbon Task Force a continuing debt of gratitude. Let's save our criticism for those investigations that really do go bad, and for reasons that could be avoided.

From cases like this, I came to understand that the work of doing a profile must stay open and flexible. As I knew from my martial arts training, you can't anticipate your opponent's next attack. You know there's going to be one, but you don't know if it's going to be a punch or a kick. If you start defending against a certain type of attack that you think might be coming, you're going to get hammered because something else might come instead. You leave yourself wide open. You have to stay focused and remain fluid, not prejudging anything. You wait for it to come and you deal with it when it does. You just have to stay centered.

Even as I kept track of the Canadian investigation and offered what I could during each stage, I was called into another case that unfolded in a way that felt all wrong to me and was dramatically inconsistent with the profile I had compiled. Following the wrong track during the weeks following the crime allowed one murderer to kill again and nearly let him and another killer go free. For this case, I went to the Southwest, to Phoenix, Arizona.

5: The Buddhist Temple Massacre

Though I think not
To think about it
I do think about it
And shed tears
Thinking about it.
—Ryokan

[1]

At times, our profiles point to a certain type of offender, but the police arrest someone completely different. While this raises questions about the process, the answers aren't always about flaws in the analysis. In this case, when investigators ignored our suggestions, the track they followed exacted a high price, and it required physical evidence to finally show that the profile had been on target.

I don't try to overestimate the importance of a behavioral profile in an investigation, but had our suggestions been given more weight, it could have resolved the case quickly and prevented another murder two months later. In fact, within ten days, the police could have had the murder weapon in their hands, but because they hadn't organized the search, they didn't. They then went in the wrong direction, because suspects misled them by falsely admitting that they'd committed the crime. With an incident like this, we see how pressure from many sources can corrupt an investigation, punish the wrong people, and damage trust in public officials.

[2]

Early on August 10, 1991, in the Wat Promkunaram Buddhist Temple near Luke Air Force Base, outside Phoenix, Arizona, nine people from Thailand were murdered. A few hours later, a temple workman, arriving to help with breakfast, noticed that the irrigation water for the vegetable gardens was still running. Thinking that was odd, he let himself in and went into the living quarters. There, in the middle of the room, lying on their faces like spokes in a wagon wheel, were the monks. One of them, only seventeen, was a monk-in-training; another victim was a temple worker; and one was a nun. All of them lay deathly still, and the carpet was soaked in blood. The workman ran out to call for help.

I was in my office when John Douglas approached me and Tom Salp, a colleague at the BSU, and told us to get on the next plane to Phoenix. "Don't pack," he said. "Buy a toothbrush when you get there. Just go."

On the flight, we looked over the brief teletypes about the incident, but it was still breaking, so we didn't know much. It had quickly become an international political issue. Thailand had never experienced such a violent mass murder, much less one that targeted their monks. It was inconceivable to them. Our government was assuring the Thai ambassador that we were doing everything we could, and then asking us at the FBI to make sure that we were, in fact, doing everything we could. The FBI agent assigned to the U.S. embassy in Bangkok handled the liaison between the FBI, the Maricopa County Sheriff's Office and the Thai authorities. The sheriff's office had also requested that an FBI profiler be dispatched to assist them in this investigation.

We landed in Phoenix, and after a brief meeting at the sheriff's office were driven to the crime scene. It was August and the dry heat felt like the interior of a furnace. There were a few white clouds in the sky, but the sun beat down mercilessly. The land around Phoenix was perfectly flat, with brownish-red mountains in the distance. Multiarmed cacti in the otherwise arid landscape confirmed that I was in the desert Southwest.

The local law officers with whom I worked were grateful to have us and seemed eager to hear what we had to say. Everyone looked a bit overwhelmed. They were used to more traditional homicides, those with lower body counts and understandable motives, such as domestic murders or the occasional gang- or drug-related shooting, not something like this. They were trying to fit this crime into one of those traditional boxes, a revenge shooting or perhaps some drug connection.

We drove west for a while until we reached the intersection of Cotton Lane and Maryland Avenue. I noticed that the ranch-style and adobe houses were getting farther apart, and there were no immediate neighbors near the temple. They were situated out in the country amid cotton fields and subject to the overhead roar of F-16s from Luke Air Force Base.

We got out of the air-conditioned car and into the

blast of heat and went right into full-blown chaos. Officers from several different agencies were milling around. There we met Russ Kimball, from the Maricopa County Sheriff's Office. He was a well-dressed, athletic guy in his thirties with a full head of dark hair. He seemed to be a clear thinker, but he had never before confronted a crime of this magnitude. Few detectives would ever have this experience.

The temple itself was an L-shaped, barnlike building. Somehow I had expected a more traditional Asian style of architecture, so it surprised me. Next to the building was a large garden where the monks grew their own food, and I saw a simple outdoor shrine where they made offerings to the Buddha. The violence I'd been reading about made no sense in this placid environment.

It was with a mix of anticipation and foreboding that I walked toward the front door. I knew what waited inside and I wanted to begin my analysis, but I somehow felt strangely vulnerable. Certain images never leave us. They come back to haunt when least expected, and I often reexperience them at scenes like the one I expected to find inside.

We entered through the front door, into a big, open, carpeted room dominated at one end by a large altar. I noticed that there were no chairs. I imagined that the worshipers would sit or kneel on the floor in there as part of their ceremony. In front of the altar was a patterned rug, and on the blue altar cloth were plants in vases and an array of shiny gold religious implements. In their midst sat a nearly life-size gold statue of the Buddha, and nearby was a donation tree with one- and five-dollar bills attached. All of this appeared to be undisturbed, but we would check that more carefully later. The primary crime scene came first.

On each side of the altar were two doors that went into the living quarters. It was here, in that next room, near a couch and a flowered chair, that the victims lay in their blood-spattered orange-yellow saffron robes. It was one of the more striking crime scenes I'd ever seen. They were huddled together on this low-grade carpet, tagged as "Victim A," "Victim B," and so forth. The evidence technicians had finished processing the scene, so as we entered we tried to avoid stepping on the blood-soaked carpet. I saw three yellow shotgun shell casings clustered together on the floor, near the door, and a number of .22-caliber shell casings were also recovered. I learned that these items had been strewn randomly among the bodies. Two guns, fired from two different locations, usually meant two offenders, at least.

The victims appeared to have been forced to kneel in a circle with their hands on top of their heads, fingers interlaced. The unknown offender with the .22 then methodically shot each of them in the back of the head two to three times. They were in such a tight circle that when they fell forward, their bodies came to rest partially on top of one another. As each victim was murdered, the remaining victims had to know they were about to die and it appeared that they had all accepted their fate peacefully, with the possible exception of one monk who had drawn the attention of the shotgunner. This monk had grazing shotgun wounds to his arms, which indicated to us that he may have raised his arms in a defensive manner and perhaps tried to resist. But he was the only one.

It was chilling. Here were monks, who were probably more spiritually pure than most of us will ever be, calmly accepting their destiny, absorbing the utter depravity in their midst. Accepting one's own murder is quite un-American. I realized that this cultural difference was something we'd have to understand as part of the victimology.

We learned that some drug dogs had searched the place and had "hit" on one area of the temple. Although no drugs were found, this gave rise to the possibility of a drug motive for the crime. Was there one drug-dealing monk who had brought this devastation upon the temple? Or could a monk have been unwittingly used by narcoterrorists to move drugs into the country and it somehow broke bad? Shipments of opium and heroin came in from Thailand, but had these monks been involved? That was one theory being bandied about. Not a likely one, but as with all investigations, every lead must be pursued to its logical conclusion. We'd check with DEA and with our sources in Thailand.

As is the case with all crime scenes, this one told its own unique story. On the floor, in the middle of the circle of bodies, was an ashtray filled with four cigarette butts and some ashes. Four cigarettes, two different brands. The monks didn't smoke. The two different butts, like the two different guns, reinforced the "two-offender" hypothesis. Taking time to smoke a couple of cigarettes each, as well as evidence of other activity, indicated that the offenders had spent a fair amount of time at the crime scene.

The shotgun was a 20-gauge and the rounds were birdshot, something you might use to shoot quail. If it had been 12-gauge double-ought buck instead of 20-gauge birdshot, that would indicate a more criminally sophisticated offender, one who appreciated the increased lethality of the 12-gauge weapon and ammunition. That would be more consistent with the professional drug dealer "hit-men" theory. But that wasn't the case. To me, it looked like guns and ammunition that a kid got out of his father's hunting collection, just whatever happened to be lying about. These were weapons of opportunity, not professional grade.

Other things as well pointed to kids. Down the hallway, on the wall, the word "Bloods" had been roughly carved with something sharp, and as an act of vandalism, several fire extinguishers had been discharged around parts of the temple. Isolating such extraneous acts, i.e., those things that an offender didn't have to do to commit the crime, can be among the most revealing. Why discharge fire extinguishers? Why carve "Bloods" on the wall? The answer, to my mind, was youth and stupidity. This wasn't a gang-related homicide; it was someone who wanted us to believe that it was a gang-related homicide, someone who had no idea of what a gang-related homicide looked like.

One other odd thing was a pile of keys on the dining room table. The monks had a communal van and apparently everyone had a key to it. It looked to us as though someone might have been sorting through the keys looking for one to something else—a safe or a storage area, something like that—but it wasn't clear at the time what that was about.

In profiling a crime scene, things that might not make sense right away may make sense to us later. We have to observe and consider the totality of the circumstances, the overall pattern, and stay alert to what fits and what's odd or out of place. At the risk of oversimplification, an equation for profiling is that if you know *this* about the crime scene, then you can say *that* about the offender. So we had to determine what was the "this" in this crime scene—and for me the totality of the circumstances kept coming back to three things: disorganization, youth, and stupidity. These characteristics were abundantly apparent. The overall scene also suggested more than one offender, and that this was something other than a random crime of opportunity. The offenders had specifically targeted either the place or the victims, but why? Regardless of motive, the disorganization at the scene and the apparent link to kids strongly suggested that the investigation should focus on the temple's neighborhood.

[3]

Russ Kimball liked what we had to say. He listened and took notes. We told him that he needed to have a way to organize the information he'd be collecting, and that he ought to get a single 800 number so that people with leads would have just one place to call. He'd also need a good retrieval system, such as our Rapid Start system, so that he could put everything into a single database and be able to cross-reference it. If they interviewed "David Jones," for example, they could look him up and see that he'd been interviewed three separate times. That would ensure maximum coordination and streamline the investigation.

They immediately got an 800 number and implemented some of the other suggestions we made.

Some facts were easily discovered. The temple abbot, among the dead, had been thirty-six. Most of the other monks had been in their thirties or forties, although the nun had been seventy-one; the teenager had been related to her. The temple helper had been twenty-one. We could also clearly see the simplicity of their lives, which I found striking.

All of the victims, with the possible exception of the nun, had lived there at the temple. They each had a room, because we saw eight or nine separate single rooms within the communal setting. The place was very Spartan. I saw a television and a VCR, but mostly just a few pieces of furniture to sit or eat on. I came across a book or two, and some plants, but it appeared to me that they had no real possessions. If you went into each of their rooms, all you would find was one or two saffron robes hanging in the closet and perhaps a small bed or a mattress on the floor. In every sense, the living was monastic. Their lives revolved around devotion to their religion. We learned that they owned some cameras and that those cameras were not at the scene. Taking items of dubious monetary value that could link someone to the crime scene was another checkmark for youth and stupidity.

As we learned more about the victims over the next two days, we discovered that their neighbors had liked them, so it seemed improbable that this had been a hate crime. In fact, we found nothing that elevated their risk for becoming victims in this collective manner. They weren't doing anything to attract it. They weren't involved in any obvious criminal activity.

Besides working the drug theory, investigators explored the notion that this violent act had been retaliation for a love affair. One of the monks had apparently been carrying on with a married woman. Yet such retaliation is usually victim specific, and in this incident no one victim appeared to have been targeted more than any other. In addition, it was unlikely that a jealous husband could find someone else who would agree to commit mass murder just because his wife was cheating on him.

[4]

After the task force had gotten under way, we left Phoenix but continued to look for more information on our own. Nothing of note happened in Arizona until a month later, on September 10. Two significant incidents occurred on the same day, each pointing the investigation in a different direction. Had the sheriff's office given more weight to our analysis, they would have followed the more likely lead.

From Tucson, the investigators received a call from a man in the Tucson Psychiatric Institute who claimed he could tell them who had been involved in the massacre. The sheriff, Tom Agnos, sent men down there to follow up on it.

The Phoenix lead was more solid but was taken less seriously. The Office of Special Investigations at Luke Air Force Base had called to report that base police had come across a rifle similar to the weapon suspected of being used in the slayings. They had seen it in August, ten days after the event, during a routine traffic stop, but had not realized its significance. While higher-ranking officers at Luke were on the task force and were aware of what to look for, they had not passed this information on to the base police.

At the time it was first seen, the rifle had been on the passenger side of a vehicle driven by Rolando Caratachea, 17. Driving in a car behind him was Jonathan Doody, 16, of Thai descent, and they'd been stopped for "suspicious activity." The next day the police again stopped the boys, only this time they were in the same car. The officers asked Caratachea where the rifle was. He told them it was in his car, which was parked at Doody's mother's house on the base, not far from there. They went to search the car and found the rifle. Since it was partially concealed, a violation of state law, they called in a sheriff's deputy.

He arrived, but there seemed to be nothing amiss and Caratachea was not suspected of any crime, so the deputy gave the rifle back and failed to report it.

At some point during the next few weeks, the Office of Special Investigations had looked through the police-incident records and spotted the reference to the rifle. On September 10, they passed along to the task force what information they had, and those investigators got a search warrant and seized the weapon.

They now had a .22-caliber rifle that had been in the possession of two adolescent boys who had lived in close geographic proximity to the temple. Doody's mother would occasionally invite the temple monks to dinner. Had the Phoenix investigators paid attention to the behavioral analysis, they would have seen all kinds of red flags. However, rather than expedite testing on this rifle, they placed it in line, behind other evidence at the Arizona Department of Public Safety. It was one of about eighty rifles collected for testing in the case, and they would not get the results back for six weeks.

In the meantime, they had extracted confessions for the murders from four other men in Tucson. The man who appeared to have made the initial phone call, Michael McGraw, 24, related details about the temple massacre to the investigators and implicated four other young men: Mark Felix Nunez, Leo Valdez

Bruce, Dante Parker, and Victor Zarate. Investigators searched their homes and brought them in for questioning, to pressure them, using what McGraw had described. The interrogations lasted for many hours, and the exhausted men finally gave in. Each of them admitted to the crime and provided more details. Sometimes what one man said conflicted with someone else's account, but what the confessions agreed on was that on the afternoon of August 9, the men had driven to Phoenix in two cars, a Ford Bronco and a Chevrolet Blazer. Parker had even described a ring taken from one of the monks that the deputies did not even know was missing. It was shaped like a spiral. He also said that one monk had resisted the intruders and had been thrown to the floor, and he mentioned that he'd been startled by a nun coming into the room where they were holding the men.

That was good enough for the interrogators.

On September 13, the task force, comprised of sixty-six investigators, announced the arrest of the five Tucson men, two of whom were ex-cons. The case had been solved, and the task force expected to find physical evidence to link all of them to the crime scene.

I heard about this and was a little surprised. I always experience a painful shot of self-doubt when they nail someone who is at odds with my analysis. I certainly don't believe that I'm infallible, and we're always learning from crimes and crime scenes, but this one bothered me. I was confident of the "youth and stupidity" analysis of the scene, which in turn implicated someone nearby. If the Tucson subjects were responsible, then there must be some local connection. The monastery had been specifically targeted and that would be difficult to do from Tucson. Just to be sure, I reviewed everything again, looking for something that I might have missed, but couldn't find anything. I was convinced that if I had to do it over again, I would have called it the same way. Something about the Tucson connection just didn't add up, and it wasn't long before the case started to unravel.

The next day, after the announcement, the suspect named McGraw called the press to say that his confession had been coerced and that he had not done any of the things to which he had admitted. The police had fed him information and shown him diagrams, and had insisted that he draw the same diagrams and repeat everything they said back to them. "I did exactly what they told me to do," he said to a reporter. There were as many as thirty investigators questioning him, for over forty-four hours, wearing him down, and he alleged that some of them had repeatedly threatened him. He denied that he'd called the police in what they had described as a suicidal urge to clear his conscience. He said he'd checked into a psychiatric institute for a drug habit and that someone else from there had called and falsely implicated him. The investigators had denied his requests for a lawyer, forced him to urinate into soda cans, kept him from sleeping, and bullied him. He'd confessed just to get away from them.

Indeed, records would later show that McGraw had been at work at the time he admitted driving to Phoenix, and if what he said about being shown charts and other information was true, that was a major flaw in the interrogation protocol.

Then the other men recanted their confessions, claiming they, too, had been coerced. They were weary and confused after being denied food, sleep, and phone

The "war room" inside Rochester Police Headquarters, where Lt. Eddie Grant and I examined the victim files and offered suggestions that contributed to the capture of serial killer Arthur Shawcross. *(Private collection)*

The bridge over Salmon Creek, where police in helicopters spotted June Cicero's body, as shown, under the bridge. Her killer was there having lunch. *(Courtesy of the New York State Police)*

My partner, Lt. Eddie Grant (in trench coat) with the New York State Police, assisting with the removal of June Cicero's body from under the bridge. *(Courtesy of the* Demo-crat and Chronicle, *Rochester, New York)*

Mugshot of Arthur Shawcross soon after police apprehended him. *(Courtesy of the New York State Police)*

The Harris family home with a gift store behind it. Near the Christmas of 1989, the entire family of four was murdered and the house was set on fire in a failed attempt to destroy evidence. I came in to profile the scene. *(Courtesy of the New York State Police)*

The exterior of the Wat Promkunaram Temple outside Phoenix, Arizona, where I would find a devastating crime scene inside. *(Courtesy of the Maricopa County Sheriff's Office)*

The sight that greeted the temple worker who found the murder victims. On August 10, 1991, six monks and three others associated with the temple were placed into a circle and shot execution style. *(Courtesy of the Maricopa County Sheriff's Office)*

I noticed this altar when I first entered the Buddhist temple. Although the killers meant to rob the monks, they failed to see the value in these ornamental items. They also missed the dollar bills on the symbolic money tree. *(Courtesy of the Maricopa County Sheriff's Office)*

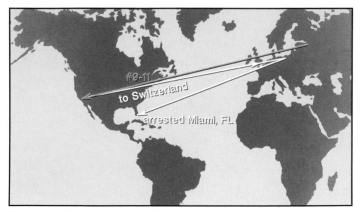

Using a world map, I could see the vast distances that Unterweger covered during his yearlong spree. He was an unusually mobile serial killer. *(Private collection)*

Jack Unterweger, displaying his prison tattoos in a photo, learned in court that his macho bravado revealed a dark side that unsettled the jury. *(Courtesy of the Austrian Federal Police)*

Jack Unterweger's defense te[am] used photos like this to sup[port] their idea that he was so pop[ular] with women he did not ne[ed to] consort with the prostitute[s who] were the victims. *(Court[esy of] the Austrian Federal Poli[ce])*

A unique and complicated knot, cut from one of Unterweger's victims, which helped to link his multiple crimes and convince a jury that he was a serial killer. *(Courtesy of the Austrian Federal Police)*

After Unterweger was convicted of murder, he committed suicide in his jail cell. His body, under the cot, is partially exposed. *(Courtesy of the Austrian Federal Police)*

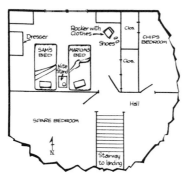

Sketch of the Sheppard crime scene, showing where Marilyn Sheppard was found bludgeoned in her bed. Her son, in the next room, slept through the attack. *(Courtesy of the Cuyahoga County Prosecutors' Office)*

Marilyn Sheppard lying bloody and bludgeoned on her bed. The stain on the sheet next to her indicated that her arm had been there, which suggested to me that her body was moved from its original position. *(Courtesy of the Cuyahoga County Prosecutors' Office)*

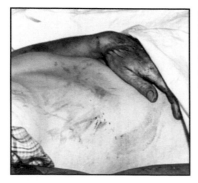

Marilyn Sheppard on the bed, her hand near a smear stain on her body, which also suggests that she was moved. *(Courtesy of the Cuyahoga County Prosecutors' Office)*

Mugshots of Sam Sheppard, arrested on August 2, 1954, for the murder of his wife, Marilyn, on July 4 in Bay View, Ohio. *(Courtesy of the Cuyahoga County Prosecutors' Office)*

The daybed where Sam said he was asleep at the time his wife was being attacked upstairs. When he heard her cry out, he raced up the steps, but not before neatly folding and placing his jacket on the daybed, as pictured—a strange behavior.
(Courtesy of the Cuyahoga County Prosecutors' Office)

Sam Sheppard's desk, which shows that the "ransacking burglar" was unusually careful to leave items intact on top, inside a drawer, and in a pile dumped from another drawer. Though he was covered in blood, he left no blood on the items or anywhere in this area. *(Courtesy of the Cuyahoga County Prosecutors' Office)*

Sam Sheppard's overturned medical bag with items spilling out. I thought it was strange that the killer, supposedly looking for drugs, didn't just take the bag with him. *(Courtesy of the Cuyahoga County Prosecutors' Office)*

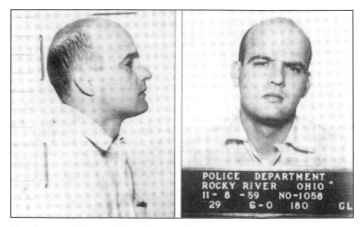

Mugshot of Richard Ebberling, the "bushy-haired stranger" who was a suspect in the murder of Marilyn Sheppard. He died before he became the centerpiece of the civil suit brought by Sam Sheppard's son on behalf of Sam Sheppard against the State of Ohio. *(Courtesy of the Cuyahoga County Prosecutors' Office)*

calls, and they'd confessed because they were tired. Two of them said that before the interrogation, they were placed in a room containing charts and photographs associated with the murder, which gave them information to feed back to their interrogators; they had finally used it to get a break.

On September 17, Zarate was released when videotapes showed that he was in Tucson at eight-thirty that evening.

Like I said, something didn't add up.

The other four men were kept in jail, and three grand juries believed that there was enough evidence to hold Bruce, 28, Nunez, 19, and McGraw for trial. A judge decided that Parker, 20, should also be held.

Then something happened back in Phoenix. Ballistics finally tested the gun belonging to Caratachea and found a match between the casings found in the temple and the ones fired by this .22-caliber semiautomatic rifle.

This was real news. This discovery was closer to what I had anticipated—local kids—so I paid attention to what happened next.

[5]

The task force got another warrant to search the apartment where Jonathan Doody had moved in with Alessandro "Alex" Garcia, 17. They were companions at Agua Fria High School and fellow U.S. Air Force ROTC students.

The search turned up a 20-gauge Stevens shotgun, which was soon matched to the shell casings found at the crime scene. Now the task force had both weapons. They also found two knives, a camouflage hat, two face masks, and gloves. In Garcia's parents' home, they located duffel bags, one filled with miscellaneous army equipment, and they got some tips that certain items had been pawned. It wasn't long before they linked one of the boys with a brother who had once lived at the temple, and they were charged with multiple counts of first-degree murder.

They made several statements that implicated them, although each pointed the finger at the other. At first, Garcia said there was no one involved but the two of them, and he drew a sketch of the temple to show that he had been there. Later he said that others had taken part. He was aware of the Tucson men who had been arrested and were under interrogation, and he offered two names, "Willis" and "Bruce," and mentioned a "black man," but said that only he and Doody were involved in the actual murders. He added, "I think I saw Parker"—the name of one of the Tucson men—but would offer nothing more.

Doody, too, offered a lengthy confession and described events quite differently. He said that they were part of a larger gang. They had initially met on Camelback Road, by the Agua Fria River (west of Phoenix, not south, where the Tucson suspects had indicated), around eight-thirty that evening and had then set off to rob the temple. One of the victims recognized someone in their party and called him by name, so Doody said he "was sent" outside to make sure the walls were soundproof. When he returned, "someone" was already firing. He himself had nothing to do with the murders. The crime began as a "challenge," Doody said. They were going to see if they could beat the sensor-alarm system at the temple, although he offered no reason for why they needed guns, knives, and military gear for that. "It just went downhill," he stated. They then drove back to the Agua Fria, where Doody claimed the group threatened to hurt him and his family if he ever told what had happened.

He also named two other friends, George Gonzales and Rolando Caratachea, as accomplices, but they denied any involvement. Doody had borrowed the .22 from Caratachea, but Caratachea said he had not known what it was to be used for. He and Gonzales weren't charged. Several other people whom Doody named were never located, and another boy who supposedly had arranged to sell some of the stolen goods was also subject to a search of his home. They found latex gloves—something investigators had determined from lack of suspicious prints that had been used in the temple—but no cameras. The stolen cameras were later recovered at a pawnshop.

Both boys got lawyers, while a judge decided whether they were to be waived out of juvenile court and tried as adults.

Yet astonishingly, these two arrests still did not free the Tucson suspects. Sheriff Agnos argued that there was a connection between them and the Phoenix teenagers, and he insisted they be held until evidence could be gathered. He hinted that he had a source of information who would back away if the men were released, and he pointed out that the FBI crime lab was still analyzing hair and fibers collected at the temple. Until those results were in, the men should stay in jail. He insisted that the confessions had been good, because streetwise men—especially men who'd already been in prison, as they had—would not have admitted to something they didn't do, knowing the dire consequences.

However, County Attorney Rick Romley felt they

had no evidence with which to hold the men and questioned how the confessions had been obtained. Reading them all, word for word, raised considerable doubt. There were conflicts among the accounts, the confession of one suspect had been read to two others before they confessed, and some of the material was vague or inaccurate. For example, one suspect said they'd passed a number of houses before turning into the temple driveway, but there were no houses out there.

On November 22, the men were finally released. Only Parker was kept, due to a parole violation for a prior burglary conviction in another state. The charges were dismissed without prejudice, meaning that the men could be charged again should evidence warrant it. They were free to go.

While there was a public outcry against this, and Garcia did vaguely mention that other men were involved, to hold these men any longer would be a clear violation of their rights. As it was, the county would soon pay dearly for their initial mistake.

After Doody and Garcia were both ordered to stand trial as adults, Garcia struck a plea-bargain deal that involved testimony against Doody. In an interesting, but not totally unexpected, development, it turned out that for Garcia, the temple murders were apparently just a beginning.

In October, two months after the massacre, Garcia goaded his fourteen-year-old girlfriend, Michelle Hoover, to prove her love for him by helping him kill a woman they had seen in a campground. Hoover cooperated, and they murdered fifty-year-old Alice Cameron.

Hoover's admission meant that the police had to free

someone else for Alice Cameron's murder: George Peterson, a mentally disturbed, forty-seven-year-old man who after sixteen hours of interrogation had falsely confessed to the crime. He'd spent over a year in prison, awaiting a trial that could have sent him to death row.

The only imaginable excuse for how the temple murder investigation was run was that it had involved a high-profile case of international proportions under intense media scrutiny, so investigators had felt pressured to get a quick solution. In a single night, they'd gone from working routine crimes to suddenly being under the world's scrutiny for a brutal crime, with no apparent motive, against gentle people.

The danger with this kind of pressure is that you begin to ignore the fundamentals of investigation; the minute you do that, you're on a slippery slope that can slide you right into disaster. You can lose your objectivity. In fact, there were deputies who had questioned the direction the investigation was taking when they went to Tucson, but they had been treated with derision. Those who were on the fast track to solving it had a theory, and they weren't willing to give it up just because the facts failed to support it. When that happens, you get two negative results: You victimize innocent people and you lose your reputation as an investigator.

I'd seen this before. In a case I'd once reviewed, a woman had been beaten to death and her body left in a shed. Based on a tip, the police had arrested a young punk who supposedly had bragged that he had done it and had shown the body to friends. It seemed to me that he'd just found her and had used her to act macho, but that he hadn't actually killed her. In fact, a gay couple who had gone into the barn had also seen her and had brought back some of *their* friends. In other words, finding this body had become a tourist event. It wasn't a stretch to believe that a person discovering it might use it to impress a friend. Then someone told the police and they made the arrest.

Pretty soon investigators found evidence at the scene that interfered with their theory. They had a bloody fingerprint, but they didn't bother to make comparisons. They did find semen, and they ran a DNA test, but it didn't match their suspect's. His defense attorney got a copy of the bloody print and had a fingerprint analyst check it against that of the accused. It wasn't his print. So in terms of physical evidence, they had a fingerprint and semen that didn't belong to the man who was charged, and they even had another viable suspect.

The victim's boyfriend would beat her up routinely; she had an order of protection against him. The police did interview him and he said that the place had been trashed when he'd come home one night, but he'd attributed it to a stranger. His tale was unlikely, but police failed to follow up on him. He was a likely suspect, but they had their own ideas, based on thin evidence, at best, and none of it physical. In this case, they had let their theory decide the facts.

In the Buddhist temple murders, the string of false confessions and false arrests pointed to a similarly flawed investigation—one that had almost allowed the real thugs to remain free to continue to prey on the rest of us. That Garcia had killed again so soon and so callously indicated how dangerous he was, and once he started to talk, the story chilled us all. We finally learned what had happened that night in the temple, although the full story and motives may never be clearly known.

[6]

It allegedly began as a plan for a robbery, Garcia admitted in his self-serving statement. They had plotted it for two months after hearing from Jonathan Doody's brother David about the solid-gold Buddha and the safe that contained $2,000. The monks also had cameras, and some of them kept money under their mattresses. It had seemed easy pickings. Doody had visited the temple with Garcia and a boy named Angel, and they had seen the altar and a money tree, the offering to the Buddha. After that, they became obsessed with robbing the monks and turned it into a "war game." The idea of going in for plunder excited them and they became predators.

Doody and Garcia purchased military clothing and gear, including snow boots, camouflage hats, scarves to hide their identities, goggles, and harnesses with knives. Doody borrowed the rifle and Garcia smuggled the shotgun, which belonged to his uncle, out of his father's house. They took the guns out to the White Tank Mountains to test their homemade silencers, which failed. They decided to go for it anyway.

On the evening of August 9, they went to a party and then drove to the temple between ten and ten-thirty in Doody's 1983 Ford Mustang. They checked it out and then left, returning around fifteen minutes later. Then they burst in and ordered the monks to the floor. They arranged them in a circle, kneeling and facing one another, and for the next hour they took turns holding them at gunpoint and ransacking the place. The monks had offered no resistance. At one point, a nun came in, which surprised them, and she was forced to join the men.

They placed what they took into two military duffel bags, amounting to $2,650 in currency, $140 in coins, two stereos, six cameras, a video camera, binoculars, and a bullhorn. Garcia recalled a set of dentures, which had belonged to the nun, on a nightstand. The temple did have a safe, but they couldn't find a key for it.

Doody said they wanted to make sure there would be no witnesses, which meant killing everyone there. Garcia alleged that he had tried to dissuade him from that plan, but Doody was determined. Standing on a couch, above the monks, Garcia said that Doody just began shooting them. He went from one to another, and if the first shot appeared not to have killed the victim, he'd shoot again. Garcia used the shotgun to wound some of them, but he insisted that he had not killed anyone. Then he used the back of a knife to carve the word "Bloods" on the wall in the hallway. Together they had sprayed the place with the fire extinguishers.

While he did not admit this in his statement, apparently he had told his girlfriend afterward that there were more people involved than just him and Doody. She didn't know how many, but she remembered his saying "a whole bunch of us." He said a group from Phoenix had met with six other people, whom he did not describe, and they had traveled in three cars to the temple. Whether she based her report on what she had heard in the media, with the hope of diffusing the blame, is anyone's guess. Her account seems unlikely, because under pressure, conspiratorial crimes don't hold up well. Once one person rolls, everyone starts pointing the finger at everyone else. If there were other players, they would probably have been identified and blamed by Doody and Garcia in some way, and those participants would have had their own stories to tell. The two boys whom Garcia and Doody did implicate had nothing to say.

On July 12, 1993, Jonathan Doody was convicted of nine murders and eleven other criminal counts, and sentenced to 281 years in prison. Although the prosecutor had sought the death sentence, the judge felt that it could not be determined which young man had actually pulled the trigger on the rifle, so this ambiguity made him cautious. Nevertheless, the sentence ensured that Doody would never again walk the streets.

Alessandro Garcia was sentenced to 271 years in prison, the maximum possible under his plea agreement. Judge Gregory Martin stated that it was his intention to see that Garcia was never released from prison. His cooperation had allowed five innocent men from two separate incidents to be released from jail, but both the judge and the prosecutor felt that his crimes were of such a magnitude as to preclude leniency. It was just too frightening to let such a person back into society.

Michelle Hoover pleaded guilty to second-degree murder and was sentenced to fifteen years.

Those men who were falsely arrested sued Maricopa County, resulting in a settlement of $2.8 million. George Peterson, who was convicted of killing the woman in the campground, also got a settlement for false arrest and imprisonment.

In 1996, the Arizona Court of Appeals, looking into allegations that Doody's confession had been extracted without a parent present, upheld the convictions and the prison sentence.

Given how badly the investigation had been run, Arizona authorities now impose higher standards on how confessions are obtained. Even so, this case does highlight important issues regarding interviews and interrogations, in particular the perplexing notion of how people can admit to a crime they didn't commit, fully knowing its significant penalties.

[7]

There are different types of false confessions, and sometimes people just confess spontaneously to something they did not do: In 1932, when Lindbergh's baby was kidnapped and killed, over two hundred people admitting to having committed it. A decade later, more than thirty people confessed to the murder of Elizabeth Short, "the Black Dahlia"—including a man who had not even been born when she was killed. It happens, and it's usually in response to a high-profile case in which fame is a possibility. It may also be done to protect someone or to exacerbate one's own sense of guilt, but it's not as common as confessions that are coerced.

Ironically, it was in Arizona, in 1966, where the case of *Miranda* v. *Arizona* established the rights of suspects to have a lawyer and to remain silent. In part, these rights were established to prohibit getting confessions with the use of brutality or extreme psychological ploys. If the person does not want to talk, interrogation must cease. Any statements that are made are subject to an evaluation as to whether they were made knowingly and willingly after having waived the right to remain silent and to have an attorney. If the subject decides to talk, the police are free to use deception and various forms of manipulation to elicit the information they seek, but are not allowed to coerce with force. Mental disability is an important factor to consider in evaluating whether or not a statement is voluntary, and the interrogators obviously are prohibited from exploiting a suspect's mental illness.

Yet the interpretation of these laws is not always clear, and while the vast majority of investigators want to get the right person and only the right person, a few just want to close a case. Getting a confession means they've done their job, regardless of whether the confession is true. They're also aware that nothing relieves doubt for a jury like a confession, and even if the court rules it to be inadmissible, the jury may still give it weight. Sometimes the only way to get guilty parties to talk is to use deception or to wear them down, yet it's not always clear when that becomes coercion and which people may be more prone to buckle under the slightest pressure.

Some people anticipate that the interrogation will be too stressful so they give in quickly, but there's another phenomenon that can also occur: People may internalize messages of guilt from the police and come to believe that they committed a crime in which they actually had no part. That happens when the interrogator shows a great deal of confidence in the suspect's guilt during a long and emotionally intense interrogation and can demonstrate reasons for the suspect's not remembering. When the suspect does internalize guilt, it actually changes his memory of events. He firmly believes in his guilt.

An astounding example of this type of confession is found in the case of a sheriff's officer, Paul Ingram, in Olympia, Washington. Toward the close of 1988, one of his two daughters was pressured by youth workers at a church retreat to admit to having repressed memories of sexual abuse, so she accused her father of molesting her. He vehemently denied it, but then his other daughter made a similar accusation, saying she had been raped at his poker parties. He was arrested and interrogated by men he trusted who suggested he had repressed memories. Even his minister insisted that he confess, and since he believed in the devil's influence and could not imagine his daughters lying, his self-confidence wavered. Ingram could say only that he had no memory of such episodes. By the end of twenty-three separate interrogations over the course of five months, in which he was berated and told he would go to hell if he didn't confess, Ingram began to think he might be guilty after all. With the help of a psychologist who taught him trance work, he started to experience fleeting images of the things his daughters had claimed.

Eventually he did confess and soon he was providing numerous details of the activities of a satanic cult in which he was involved. While no physical evidence corroborated what he said, investigators were not only eager to accept his confession but to believe they had a child-abuse cult in the area. In fact, one of Ingram's daughters accused thirty prominent people in the community of sacrificing babies to Satan, and as a result several people's lives were ruined.

In preparation for the trial, prosecutors hired sociologist and cult expert Richard Ofshe, from the University of California at Berkeley. They wanted him to interview Ingram and demonstrate that his retrieved memories matched the facts. Ofshe talked first with the daughters, who he felt were not truthful, and then with Ingram. It seemed to him that Ingram had been manipulated into a confession, which he realized could happen when trance work is coupled with suggestion and intensive questioning, so he tried an experiment.

Over the course of two days, he picked out events at random and added a few that no one had yet described that he knew to be false, and then asked Ingram to talk about them. At first Ingram did not recall the fake incidents, but after some time spent in prayer, he was able to do so. He then offered a written confession of these events, in embellished detail. Ofshe realized that Ingram had to be making it up. That suggested that the entire confession could be false. He tried to get Ingram to understand this, but to his surprise, Ingram refused to budge. He insisted he had done these things. Ofshe concluded that Ingram's "memory," far from being true to events, was the product of extreme social influence. It was a phenomenon that he labeled "hypnotic story creation." Ingram had inadvertently been taught to visualize numerous crimes in which he believed he was involved.

For something he never did, he was convicted and sent to prison for twenty years. Only there did he begin to realize that his visualizations were not real memories, but it was too late for him. He remained in prison.

Familiar with many cases around the country, Ofshe cites the Buddhist temple murder incident as "one of the century's most dramatic and disturbing false confession cases." While the men involved did not buy into the guilt that the police officers imposed, they did admit to something they did not do and which would put them in prison and possibly on death row. And they did more than just say that yes, they had done it, whatever it was. One man had supplied more details. Coercion, even without hypnotic trance work, can be quite powerful.

False confessions of this kind commonly occur under certain conditions: sleep deprivation, feigned friendship, isolating the suspect by refusing him a lawyer, using leading questions, excessive use of threats, exposure to graphic crime scene photos, and the suggestion that law enforcement already has evidence against the person. Also, if promises are made in the event the person starts talking, or if there's a way out by blaming an accomplice, he or she may do so just to relieve the stress or get out of the interrogation room. In the moment, the consequences of what they say may not occur to them.

The characteristics of those most likely to offer up a false confession include youth, a low IQ, mental illness or confusion, a high degree of suggestibility, a trusting nature, low self-esteem, high anxiety, and the possession of a poor memory. Some of these traits are exacerbated by the fatigue that occurs during lengthy interrogations, and anxiety may become confused with guilt.

It's also true that when the suspect repeats information that officers have discussed, as the Tucson men said they did, it may be recorded in the police notes as a confession when in fact it isn't. Had the police never picked up the murder weapon, those men and George

Peterson could have been falsely convicted and imprisoned. With nothing else to go on for a crime that *must* be solved, innocent people can get hurt.

From the perspective of profiling, this mass murder was a case of a more disorganized crime and crime scene. In such circumstances, the offenders typically live in close proximity to the crime scene and that should have focused the investigation primarily in that area. Thus, when the military police at Luke Air Force Base, which was located virtually across the road from the temple, did stop a kid with a gun that was the right caliber, they should have confiscated it for immediate testing. That should have become a priority. In other words, the police should have been more interested in pursuing a lead like that than in rumors from a Tucson psychiatric hospital.

Yet how much weight a local department gives to a profile is always an issue. Profiling does not solve a case, investigators do, but different investigators have different attitudes. For some it's a matter of "checking the box," i.e., yeah, we did that, we got an FBI profile in the case, so what? I was once involved in the analysis of a double homicide of a male and female who were both active in the military. We provided investigators with a pretty clear sense of direction, but the lead investigator took the "file it and forget it" approach. The case went unsolved for a couple of years, until a new investigator took charge. He went through everything and found the profile buried in the file. Dusting it off, he read it carefully, moved in the direction we had suggested, and solved the case.

[8]

Yet we're still faced with trying to understand the motive for such a seemingly senseless mass murder. Was it as simple as witness elimination, or might that explanation be too utilitarian? Is the truth somehow darker? In *Thus Spoke Zarathustra*, Friedrich Nietzsche addressed this very issue:

> Thus speaks the red judge, "Why did this criminal murder? He wanted to rob." But I say unto you: his soul wanted blood, not robbery; he thirsted after the bliss of the knife. His poor reason, however, did not comprehend this madness and persuaded him: "What matters blood?" it asked; "don't you want at least to commit a robbery with it? To take revenge?" And he listened to his poor reason: its speech lay upon him like lead; so he robbed when he murdered. He did not want to be ashamed of his madness.

Today, a simple monument with the pictures and names of those slain in the massacre sits atop a lily pad–covered pond at the Wat Promkunaram temple. Every morning platefuls of food and drink are left for the dead:

Chalerm Kittiipattap, 29
Boonchuay Cahiyathamuo, 37
Suthichai Annutaro, 32
Siang Mahapanyo, 28
Somsak Sopha, 47
Pairat Phromwaro, 36
Foy Sripanpiaserf, 71
Matthew Miller, 17
Chirasak Chirapong, 21

Not all of my cases involved me inside an active investigation. Sometimes I went in after the fact to try to better understand the dynamics of the crime. This, too, was part of our program at the FBI, and among those types of cases, one offender really stood out.

6: Duping Delight

He entered the territory of lies without a passport for
return.

—Graham Greene

[1]

When a successful businessman becomes a murderer,
that gets our attention. In the BSU, we collected data
about serious offenders from those who were serving
time in prison, particularly when they helped us to
learn about the most unique facets of the criminal
mind. One of my own interviews involved a particularly educated and clever psychopath, said by many
document examiners to be one of the greatest forgers
of all time. Once again, I had to prepare myself to bait
someone who had spent his life baiting others and do it
without his seeing through my game. I relied on my
ability to remain centered and use the opponent's energy in my favor.

On October 15, 1985, in Salt Lake City, Utah, two
different people picked up large packages wrapped in
brown paper and addressed by the same hand. The
homemade pipe bombs inside exploded and killed
them both. The first victim was Steve Christensen, who
was briefly aware of his injuries before he died. His

right thigh was torn open, one foot was nearly blown off, pipe shrapnel hollowed out his chest, and a sturdy nail flying off the bomb went through his eye and pierced his brain. Other nails pierced him elsewhere on his body.

The next victim was the wife of Christensen's former business partner, Gary Sheets. Her name was Kathleen and she had found a package intended for her husband sitting on the walkway between their house and garage. Picking it up, she set it in motion and the instant explosion blasted her into the air. It ripped out her stomach and right breast. A corner of the garage splintered and pieces of her ripped clothing were caught up in a tree. A neighbor found her lying faceup in the driveway and called it in. Gary Sheets feared that the anonymous killer was a disgruntled investor who'd lost money in his bankrupt corporation.

Yet the next afternoon, another man, Mark Hofmann, was wounded when a bomb detonated in his blue Toyota sports car. Since he was supposed to have met with Steve Christensen the day before, to close a deal on a rare Mormon document collection, it became clear that these victims were not chosen at random. Something connected them all, and mutual acquaintances who knew about the collection began to worry.

Hofmann was taken from his burning car to the hospital. He survived, but sustained a number of injuries and burns along his right side, including losing his kneecap and a finger. A forensic bomb expert examined the wreck and declared that the third "attack" had been an accident and that this victim was himself the bomber.

At first, no one believed it. Hofmann was an amiable guy, even a bit awkward and naive, who had built a thriving business dealing in rare documents. He had no criminal record and no apparent motive. To the contrary, he had a young family, had just purchased a nice home, and was in good standing with the Mormon church. In fact, his associates said, he'd been collecting controversial documents for the church to keep them out of the hands of anti-Mormon agents. Or so he had told them.

Hofmann had said a lot of things that turned out to be mostly lies, and in the end he did confess to both the forgeries and the bombings. In exchange for a life sentence instead of the death penalty, he entered a plea of guilty to several counts of murder and fraud and gave a full recounting of his crimes. At the age of thirty-two, he went into Utah State Prison on January 23, 1987. He was convinced that within seven years he would be out, but his transparently smug confession diminished any chance of parole.

While he'd talked extensively about how he had forged the documents that had fooled so many experts—including the FBI—he had offered few details on the way he'd constructed the bombs or chosen his victims, and investigators were still puzzled about several key elements. He'd also claimed, despite evidence to the contrary from his car and injuries, that he'd used the third bomb to try to kill himself. Since I was planning to interview inmates at this facility, I put Hofmann on my list. He'd been an educated man, said to be a genius, who'd been thriving for almost a decade strictly on fraud. He was at the high end of the continuum—enigmatic and complex, not at all a garden-variety convenience store stop-and-rob kind of guy. His ability to repeatedly dupe historians, document examiners, and the elders in the Mormon church increased both his appeal and the challenge for us.

Talking with those who commit certain types of crimes requires a strategy. First, we come in cold. They don't know we're coming. That way they can't turn us down ahead of time or get their attorneys involved. We make the appropriate arrangements in advance with the prison, but ask them not to tell the inmate.

Prior to an interview, it's important to know as much about the target individual as possible. Often they'll try to lie, so if we show them we know what they did, it alerts them to our preparation. It also flatters them. It feeds their narcissism and often makes them want to talk. Hofmann knew there had been books written about him, so I read *The Mormon Murders,* by Steven Naifeh and Gregory White Smith, *Salamander*, by Linda Sillitoe and Allen Roberts, and the newspaper clippings about his crimes and his month-long preliminary hearing. I was able to get a pretty good sense of who he was.

[2]

As a kid, Mark Hofmann had three passions: explosives, magic, and history. To pursue the latter, he'd go through stacks of coins to try to find rare ones that he knew were valuable. By age twelve, he had acquired an electroplate machine and eventually found a way to build up the mintmark—a *D*—on a Denver dime, because it made the otherwise ordinary coin worth thousands of dollars. He even found a coin dealer to authenticate it after the U.S. Treasury pronounced it genuine. In the years to come, Hofmann would view the authentication by those who ought to know as affirmation: By definition, his forgeries were now the real thing. He might know they were fakes, but the buyers did not, so what did it matter? He soon figured out how gullible people were. They saw what they wanted to see, and he enjoyed conning them. In fact, he admired Joseph Smith, the founder of the Mormon church, for *his* ability to dupe people, on a large scale, with only fantasy and fiction.

When he was thirteen, Hofmann began to collect Mormon memorabilia, and then to manufacture it on his own. As he learned how to trade these items, he grew obsessed with the church's history and went on, in Salt Lake City, to become a dealer in rare documents. At first he created and sold only fragments, but then he worked on longer pieces. He later explained how he had removed paper from nineteenth-century books, learned how to age ink, and then developed a way to forge someone's handwriting from other extant samples or from that person's signature. He immersed himself in the other person's perspective and trained himself to write without hesitation. So many documents came from him that when the FBI later used seventeen samples to authenticate one of his "historical signatures," Hofmann had done fourteen of them.

During his intense studies of church history in college, Hofmann had developed a fundamental distrust of the hierarchy in the Mormon church. One book I read attributed this to the fact that he had a shameful family secret—a polygamous marriage involving his grandmother that had taken place after the Mormon decree against plural arrangements. Yet the sustained nature of his calculated deception of the church seemed to me to be about something else. "The real reward of the whole business," he told one feature writer, "is being able to see things that no one else knows about." On the surface, that meant his "discoveries." In his own mind, it must have meant his duplicity. He had set out to deliberately prove that the church was a fraud, even as he told others he was protecting his heritage. In fact, as soon as he made an important "find" that he insisted must remain a secret, word somehow often leaked out and put the church in an awkward position. I think he was simply pleased with how much he was getting away with. It was a game, and he was good at it.

First he won the church's confidence by producing the "Anthon Transcript," a faith-enhancing document that supposedly affirmed an authentication, by an expert named Charles Anthon, of the Egyptian hieroglyphics on the golden plates on which the *Book of Mormon* was based. It had disappeared and Hofmann had "found" it. That got him access to the church archives, which gave him more fodder for deception.

Among his many significant religious forgeries was an important piece known as the "salamander letter," which told an alternate version of the story of Joseph Smith's discovery of the golden plates. Smith had claimed that when he was fourteen years old, an angel revealed their location to him, but this alternate version indicated that something else had happened, and it wasn't good.

In the Mormon church, there were fears that some document might turn up one day that would verify rumors that Smith had been an occultic "money-digger," i.e., that he had hired himself out to farmers to go over their land with a "seer stone" to try to locate buried treasure. This activity not only indicated fraud, which, of course, was illegal, but also tied Smith to magical activities. Apparently there was a record that *some* Joseph Smith had been arrested for money digging in 1826, but the elders insisted it was not *the* Joseph Smith. His many revelations had come from God, not the dark arts.

The salamander letter, supposedly written by Martin Harris, a close friend of Smith and the farmer who funded the *Book of Mormon*'s initial printing, was dated 1830. It indicated that Smith had indeed found the golden plates, but that a white salamander guarding them had transformed itself into an "old spirit" and struck Smith three times. The salamander did not want Smith to take the plates, but he did anyway. If this rendition of events was true, it undermined Smith's testimony as to what had occurred and also implicated him in something more nefarious. That meant that the entire foundation of the Mormon faith was at stake.

Hofmann "discovered" this letter, "authenticated" it with handwriting by the same person found in the back of an old prayer book—handwriting that he had also forged—and sold it to a collector who was to donate it to the church. The elders would keep it in the vault that was reserved for what many believed were the church's great secrets. To get the right "voice," Hofmann had read old newspaper accounts and letters from the time period. He made up the salamander, and he included in the letter references to some of the people who had "authored" his other forgeries. It was clever, painstaking, and certainly amusing for him.

Hofmann then "discovered" a cache of papers and diaries, potentially embarrassing to the church, known as the McLellin collection (William McLellin being a renegade Mormon apostle and a former friend of Joseph Smith), which Steve Christensen was going to help to authenticate for the Mormon church. These papers had been lost for almost a century and showed the early days of the Mormon church to be far different from the descriptions favored by the official church. A religion of some 12 million members worldwide and with assets of over $30 billion could hardly afford to have those papers out in the open for anti-Mormon factions to discover. A church-sanctioned, unsecured loan of $185,000 was on the line, paid to Hofmann for purchasing the collection, but once the transactions were finished, Christensen could turn over the papers and let the church decide what to do with them. The McLellin deal had been complicated, with Hofmann giving one story after another about why he couldn't deliver the papers when he'd said he would (the reason being that they didn't exist). The loan had come due, the papers were not there, and Christensen had had to vouch for Hofmann to bank officials.

Hofmann kept asking for time. He was showing a new discovery of Americana to the Library of Congress and expected to get at least $1 million for it, but the purchase had been delayed. He'd already sold an original letter from Daniel Boone that proved certain legends to be true, poetry by Emily Dickinson, and pieces from Mark Twain. Now he had "found" a document called *The Oath of a Freeman*. It was reputedly the first document ever to be printed on an American press, in Massachusetts in 1639. A copy of the text was available, but the original had long been lost. That is, until 1985 when it "came into" Hofmann's hands. (Actually, he had copied pages from a similar book from the same printer, using the characters to re-create the words from the *Oath*. Then he made a printing plate using a page from a book three centuries old. He also made ink by burning part of the leather binding from another antique book. He allowed the paper to grow moldy and then oxidized it to fade the ink. When he was satisfied, he got a collector to offer it to the Library of Congress.) He hoped that if the Library bought this, he could pay off the McLellin loan, along with another impending loan coming due to someone else, and then claim he was "unable to get" the nonexistent McLellin collection. He was gambling and it was soon becoming clear to him that he was losing. That's when he turned to another passion: explosives.

Since Hofmann was known in some circles as something of a double-dealer with a history of writing bad checks, the bank was nervous, but the church wanted that collection, so Christensen set up a meeting with everyone in his office for the morning of October 15. He expected Hofmann to be there, and in fact, Hofmann had come in around six-thirty A.M. Just after eight A.M., Christensen entered his office building, got on the elevator, and went to the sixth floor. A foot-square package addressed to him was propped against his door, so he picked it up. That movement detonated the bomb.

That afternoon, Hofmann met with church leaders and they assured him that Christensen could be replaced. They assumed, with the second bomb getting Kathy Sheets, that the violence was related to some business transaction unassociated with the church. That meant Hofmann still had to come up with the

McLellin collection, right away. In a dilemma, he made a third bomb, but this one got *him,* and that was the end of his career as a forger—or as anything. Since there were burned documents in the trunk of his car, it was assumed that he had expected to say it was the McLellin collection, now damaged beyond repair. However, as I've related, the entire scheme eventually unraveled. Nevertheless, with the successful forging of documents by 129 different people, and some 450 Mormon documents that deceived the elders and experts of one of the wealthiest and most powerful churches in the world, it was clear that Hofmann was something of a skilled genius.

Forensic document examiners worked hard to figure out how Hofmann had fooled so many experts and accumulated so much money from his forgeries. After repeated experiments with paper and ink, they found a copy of a book in his home by Charles Hamilton called *Great Forgers and Famous Fakes* and figured out the recipe and method he had used for making ink that defied tests for determining its age. They also noticed that, unique to all Hofmann-handled documents and to no others, there were two characteristics: ink that ran in a single direction and that cracked like alligator skin. The anomalies specific to many of the documents Hofmann had sold indicated forgery. In addition, the smudges he had made to duplicate the effects of Smith's left-handed writing style had failed.

While a wealth of experts—many of whom had invested in Hofmann's documents—were prepared to testify on his behalf, he eventually admitted his widespread deception. Many of his artistic creations were traceable to books he had read about early Mormon history. He'd also cheated associates by trading his fakes for some of their genuinely valuable documents, and then selling those documents to enrich himself. Nevertheless, collectors continued to buy and sell his work as if it were the real thing. Even as late as 1997, Hofmann forgeries were still showing up. A library in Amherst, Massachusetts, purchased a two-stanza poem, from Sotheby's for $24,150, that they believed Emily Dickinson had penned. There was a neat little inscription on the other side of the paper, "Aunt Emily," that seemed to have originated with a relative of the poet. It was only when someone decided to find out who might have written it that the fraud was exposed. Although the poem was written on the correct paper for the period, with the correct writing instrument and the right literary themes and style, it was nevertheless traced to Mark Hofmann. He had taken delight in seeing others enthusiastically appraise it as an undiscovered Dickinson work. Later he said that he thought that the "Aunt Emily" inscription had been a nice touch.

[3]

I once saw a cartoon that featured two men talking near a sign that read, "Please Don't Feed the Sharks." One man commented to the other, "This one works a whole lot better than the sign that said, 'No Jumping from the Bridge.' "

The point is that a "No Jumping from the Bridge" sign may deter some, but "Please Don't Feed the Sharks" appeals to everyone's self-interest, and self-interest is what psychopathy is all about. A psychopath often perceives a direct prohibition as a dare. He may never have considered jumping, but if it's clearly prohibited, he has to do it. As a career criminal once told me, "You make the rules; I'll break 'em."

I was aware that the intake psychiatrist who had evaluated Hofmann had said there was no evidence of psychopathy, but I wanted to make up my own mind about that. Psychopaths have a good record of deceiving even the experts. From my reading, it was clear that the professional who had evaluated him knew very little about his history: He'd been impulsive, cruel to animals, callous about how he harmed others, an easy liar, and quick to use every advantage for himself. At his hearing, he had said that he didn't care whether his bomb at the Sheets house found the right target—it made no difference to him whether he killed a dog or an innocent stranger. He'd also fooled a lot of sophisticated people; he was glib and showed no remorse for any of his deceptions or crimes. He had kissed his children after the murders, convincing himself that his plan was in *their* best interest. Those are all psychopathic traits.

One thing we see, which is different from what researchers see with psychopathic populations in prisons and hospitals, is the kind of behavior they exhibit in the wild, so to speak. They act out their fantasies more completely, the fantasies are more florid, and their behavior provides a much better measure of psychopathology than some of the tests used in a prison.

We once had a case of a man who urinated on the seats of women's cars and left notes for them to find that made them feel as if he knew them and had violated them. He would videotape them as they sat in the urine and found the notes, and his crude commentary, recorded on the tape, provided him with the illusion that he could enjoy over and over the idea that he was the one in control. In the meantime, he terrorized them. Sometimes he knew where they lived and indicated as much in the notes. So "in the wild," he was free to do this as long as he could get away with it, and we could learn things about his criminality from the notes and videotapes. In captivity, regardless of whether or not he talked about his crimes, clinicians and academicians would not get the same sense we did of what he was doing. So what we see would add a lot to a psychological evaluation in a prison or a hospital.

We look at not just the type of sexual acts a rapist might commit, for example, but also at the sequence. There's a difference between a guy who starts with oral sex and then vaginally or anally assaults a victim, and a guy who anally assaults and then forces the victim to perform oral sex. It can be the same sex acts, but the second sequence is more degrading and humiliating. Also, the verbal behavior is important, whether or not he scripts his victim to say things, such as we had seen with the Scarborough Rapist.

So I was going to base my judgment on what I knew about Hofmann and what I saw him do in front of me, rather than on in-house psychological evaluations. My partner, Larry, and I would decide how to make this interview work.

Generally, we go in with a specific protocol designed to meet our objectives. Our interviews are done from a law-enforcement perspective. We evaluate their level of criminal sophistication by analyzing the method and manner in which they committed their crimes and then by interviewing them. We want to know what, if anything, they did to avoid detection and apprehension and what, if anything, may have deterred them. We want to know how they weighed their risks, what precautions they took, their degree of planning and preparation, and how the victim was selected. If we can understand how they avoided detection and apprehension, we can use that information to do our job better in cutting short their criminal career.

Criminal motivations are as diverse as the criminals themselves and can vary even within the same type of crime. A man who kills his wife by carefully planning and staging the crime to look like an accident so he can collect her life insurance is motivated differently from the offender who kills his wife in a blind rage. Both are domestic homicides, but the motivations are dissimilar, which makes the method and manner of the homicides different.

For the first killer, the violence is instrumental in nature, a means to an end (the insurance money) and not an end in itself. For the second killer, the violence is affective or emotional in nature and the murder is an end in itself, rather than a means to an end. Such emotionally driven offenders usually show less concern for the consequences of their behavior and rarely have taken any advance precautions to avoid detection or apprehension. Those who are guilt ridden and ashamed may become suicidal. Other more psychopathic offenders, even though they killed in a rage, may attempt to stage the scene after the fact and engage in other post-offense behavior to avoid detection.

We gather as much information about the individual we're about to interview as possible, not just routine information, but behavioral issues, personality characteristics, or any evident disorders. Then through records we determine whether or not there's an indication of mental illness or psychopathic behavior. We're also interested in what seems to be important to him, to see if we can use it in the interview process.

[4]

The Utah State Correction Facility is built on a barren plain south of Salt Lake City. The buildings are concrete, with guard towers and high fences. We could see a mountain range from there, but it was a dusty, isolated place.

Once we were in the prison, we asked for access to Hofmann, but the prison officials insisted he'd never talk with us. He spent all his time alone in his cell, they said, twenty-three hours a day, and he spoke to no one. During his one allowed hour of exercise time, he just walked around the yard.

"He's the most uncommunicative guy we've had in here," one official told us. "He's totally isolated, so you'll be wasting your time to meet with him."

I asked that he be put in a room with us so he could tell us himself that he didn't want to talk.

"Well, you're wasting your time," the official said again.

"It would be a waste if I didn't take a run at him," I responded. "So if you don't mind, I'd appreciate the chance to talk with him."

We were taken into a small room, about ten by twelve, with cement walls, a steel door, and no windows except for the Plexiglas window on the door. Although it was protocol for a correction officer to be with us, we wanted to be alone with Hofmann, so the officer agreed to stay just outside the door.

There were three chairs in the room, and we arranged them facing one another and in such a way that Hofmann would sit next to the door. We wanted him to have the psychological message that he was free to go—we were not trapping him in the room. Our interview strategy is that two of us go in with the idea of giving the subject the chance to develop a rapport with one or the other of us. We'll both talk with him a little at first, but once we see whom he responds to, that person assumes the lead in the interview and the other agent fades slightly into the background and generally takes notes.

I chose the chair that put Larry to my right and the empty chair to my left.

"You want to place a small wager on this one?" Larry asked.

I brushed some debris off the seat before sitting down and said, "I think we've got a good shot. Being locked up in a single cell twenty-three hours a day for years and talking to nobody, he's like a dam ready to burst. We've just got to find a way to make it happen."

Larry pulled a pad of paper out of a small plastic briefcase. "This guy is nobody's fool. We've got to be careful not to shut him down."

Then the door slowly swung open and Hofmann was brought in.

[5]

He was of medium height, was wearing a beige prison outfit, and appeared to be neatly groomed. Although the books had indicated that he'd lost weight in prison, he looked somewhat pudgy, and I could see where his right hand was scarred from the bomb. It was also disabled from a suicide attempt he'd botched when his wife had filed for divorce. His face was round, his dark hair slicked back, and he was wearing glasses. He seemed a little nervous, a bit unsure about what was going on. Our first job was to allay those fears and calm him down.

We introduced ourselves as FBI agents, then let him know we were from the BSU. He stepped backward, toward the door, and said, "My attorneys told me I can't speak to any investigators."

"We're really not investigating any crimes," I said. "We'd like to speak with you, not about your case, but more about you so that we may better understand why these things happened."

Hofmann wasn't buying it. He looked back and forth at Larry and me and then down at the floor, shaking his head. "I told you, I can't speak to any investigators."

I said, "That's fine. We understand. You don't have to speak with us, but you can listen to us, can't you? We've come a long way to see you and we'd appreciate it if you would listen to us for a moment. Aren't you interested in what it is we have to say?"

The reality was that we were interested in him as a person with the underlying dynamics that had motivated him to commit the crimes. But we were also interested in his crimes, including all of his pre-offense and post-offense behavior. It just wasn't the right time to let him know that.

"Well, I guess I can listen," he said.

For a while, he remained standing near the door, as if ready to call the guard and leave. He was skittish and we had to think carefully. Precarious situations like this are not uncommon during these types of interviews. If we say or do something that offends our target, or makes him uncomfortable, it's over. It's a tenuous balancing act that requires watching, listening, patience, good judgment, and a little bit of luck. Paradoxically, while we want the details of the crimes, we have to avoid addressing them directly. We also have to watch our attitude: The minute they sense that we're judgmental or upset in some way with what they've done, the interview is over. We have to outwit them without their catching on. One way is to give them the impression that they're controlling the interview.

We'd had a situation similar to this one with a child killer in Virginia. He said he knew what we were there for and how we worked, and he insisted he didn't want to talk about what he'd done. We said fine, and it took about an hour to get him to talk with us about anything at all. We managed it by playing to his need to be in control. We'd say, "We'll only talk about what you want to talk about." For a lot of psychopaths, it's a matter of how well they can manipulate us. So by laying aside our protocol of questions, we let them think that's what they're doing. In that interview, I said to the child killer, "I understand you're the oldest of five children, is that right?"

"Yeah," he answered.

"Well, now that wasn't so hard, was it?"

"Well, no, we could talk about that."

So we went on and talked about his family and his upbringing. We reached the point of the murder, leaped over it, and talked about whether his family visited him in prison. So that made him feel comfortable and put us in a different place altogether than we'd been several hours earlier. He grew more willing to talk to us, and soon he laid the whole thing out: how he went to look for one kid he'd spotted before. That kid wasn't there that day, but another kid was, so he took him instead.

It's gamesmanship and it is often the only way to obtain the information we want. When I asked Hofmann to just listen, that gave him a sense that he had room to make decisions. He could decide whether or not he would respond. Now that he was beginning to listen, I shopped for a theme that would resonate with him. Many of these offenders view themselves as victims, so absolving them of responsibility for their actions by blaming other circumstances, things, or people is a typical interview tactic. All the while, we were reading Hofmann's nonverbal signals and we used those to guide us.

For example, if he listened but didn't really pay much attention, which I could see from the way his eyes roved around the room or how he moved in his seat, then I'd know I'd have to move on to another theme. It went on like that for a while, but he stayed in the room.

We always start discussing things that are remote from the crimes. While we're building rapport, we stay away from the more emotional or incriminating types of incidents.

I recalled that Hofmann had been in some financial difficulty before the bombings and thought that he had probably been afraid that someone would discover his fraud. "You must have been under a tremendous amount of stress before these things happened," I said.

His eyes met mine and he started to nod. He sat forward. Those nonverbal behaviors indicated that we had found a theme that resonated with him so I continued down that road.

"Mark," I continued, "I don't think everyone appreciates the pressure that you were under and we want to get everything right. You're the only one who can help us do that."

This increased his sense of self-importance and was an invitation for Hofmann not only to control the interview but to manipulate us as well. He couldn't lie without talking, and we wanted him to begin talking with us even if he was lying. We could deal with the lies later. Hofmann looked at me and began nodding. We were setting the hook and I could feel him tugging on the line, but it was far from a good catch. If we misjudged him or said the wrong thing, we could still lose him.

During these interviews, we know we're being consciously manipulative, just like the offenders have been, but it's not as if there's some fragile boundary between them and us that makes us more alike than different. Doing this kind of thing feels awkward. I have to make a conscious effort to do it because it's not a natural way to relate to people. It's a skill we have to develop to be able to do these interviews effectively. We know we're manipulating and that it's for a purpose—a good purpose, but it's not the way we are in our daily personal lives.

I tried to set the hook more firmly by expanding on the theme that these things wouldn't have happened to him if it hadn't been for all the stress. But I still kept my distance from the crimes. I said, "Mark, I've interviewed a lot of vicious bastards, but you're not one of them. You're different. I judge a man not so much by what he did but by why he did it. If I thought you were a callous thug who acted only in your own interest, I wouldn't waste my time talking to you. But you're not a callous thug. The amount of stress you were under was enough to drive anyone crazy, but you maintained your composure. I think you acted as you did not to help yourself, but to help your wife and children."

He maintained eye contact, indicating that he was listening, so I kept going. "A lot of people think that you did these things for yourself, but I don't think so. This is your chance to get the truth out. Can you help me understand the tremendous amount of stress that you were under?"

That question hung in the air for what seemed like an eternity. Hofmann dropped his head and shoulder slightly and said, "Well, okay, I guess I could talk to you about the stress." This was the first chink in the dam. He was talking.

It turned out that while Hofmann was arrogant about his cleverness, he wasn't as flagrantly narcissistic as many psychopaths are, so my line was harder to sell. Even so, everyone likes to have people say nice things. Narcissists are quicker to lock on to that, but to some degree everyone responds to flattering comments.

Hofmann seemed impressed with what we knew about his background. We said we understood the sophisticated, meticulous approach he used in creating the forged documents and the significance those documents held for the Mormon church. As we discussed his work with him, we took a measured, articulate approach, because even mirroring his own manner showed appreciation for how he did things.

Since he was intelligent, we had to be careful about being transparent, and frankly, I did admire his ability to pull this off for so many years and deceive a rather imposing religious organization.

And that was the other thing we knew about him: his dislike of the Mormon church. He thought the history and doctrines were all bullshit, but he had played the game. I used this to continue my basic theme: "The duplicity and hypocrisy of the church was a stress for you, and you had the courage to see it for what it was." I showed that I concurred and sided with him, which seemed to inspire in him more confidence and energy.

From that point on, the chink we'd driven into the dam widened, and his hesitant trickle of information became a flood. He started talking and went on for hours. It went on all day and into the night, until the guards finally had to throw us out.

We discussed his childhood and his initial doubts about his church. He'd held out hope for a time that he was wrong, but then he'd been baptized. That event had changed everything. He'd been under the impression that baptism was a life-altering ceremony and that afterward he'd see everything differently. So he was baptized, but to his disappointment, the world looked just the same. It then became his mission to prove the church's hypocrisy. He was already aware of the fact that he had a talent for deceiving people and he knew that most people are gullible. His childhood exploits had been thrilling, so he decided to make fraud and forgery his life's mission—and to make as much money at it as he could.

His distrust and paranoia about the church had grown along with his ability to forge. The more documents he got the church to acknowledge and then hide, the more vindicated he felt. It seemed natural to use his ability as a con man to prove how the church was conning people, too. They were getting back what they were giving. He had a thorough understanding of the history of the church and its legacy, and the potential problems these documents would create were they to surface. In his mind, the elders flunked every test he gave them. Thus, it seemed to him that he had the moral high ground, and that meant, in a twisted sort of way, that he wasn't doing anything wrong. In fact, he was engaging in this important undercover sting operation. He was uncovering wrongdoing.

Then things closed in, he said. The real pressure was on. "So to take the heat off, I started doing some bombings. I wanted to divert their attention."

Now we'd reached the point at which he himself brought up the crimes. He used the word "bombing," not us. He was willing to talk, so from his original position of wanting to just leave, to the one he'd now reached, hours later, he was revealing just about everything. For us, it had simply been a matter of developing rapport and constructing an interview based on the issues that were important to him.

Before he had finished, Hofmann had told us where he bought the parts for the bombs, how he made them, and where he put them. As he talked, he began to sweat. He became emotionally and possibly even sexually aroused as he described how he'd planned and carried out his murders, reliving the crimes in astonishing detail. It was then that he displayed clear psychopathic traits.

It was obvious to us that he didn't identify with his victims or show any awareness of the fact that he'd caused pain and suffering. He didn't seem to care that a bomb he'd intended for one person had killed another—

an innocent woman. The indignity of what had happened to her had no effect on him, and he seemed to think the results of the bombings were incidental. He might as well have been talking about butting a cigarette. He had no ability to connect with that at all. That was chilling. What mattered to him was that it hadn't worked according to his plan and he'd been forced to come up with another one. Everything he said was about "me, me, me." Psychopaths are easily unmasked by their inability to project empathy. They care only about their own suffering and pain.

I noticed that while Hofmann talked easily about a lot of the details, he persisted in saying that the third bomb had been meant for him. He said he'd had enough and wanted to kill himself, but the bomb had blown up too soon and only injured his arm and leg. I knew from the evidence of how the explosion had hit him that this was a lie. Yet I couldn't get him to change his story. My opinion was that he'd gotten out of the car, reached back in to get the bomb, dropped it or hit the switch, and it had gone off. If it was a suicide attempt, why not put the bomb on your lap and set it off? If he was trying to kill himself, how was it that only his arm and leg were injured? I felt sure that he had intended to kill someone else.

Even though he wouldn't admit the truth of that, we did manage to get quite a bit of information over the course of that day. I later talked with Jim Bell, one of the investigators who had worked the original case, and he was excited about how we were able to fill in holes. They'd had some ideas about where they thought Hofmann might have put the bombs together, and it turned out that what they had surmised was consistent with what he had said to us.

In interviews with violent felons, we are always sensitive to the potential for deception. Deception may take several different forms, everything from concealing something important to what psychologist Paul Ekman has called "duping delight," which is the sheer joy some offenders get from conning others, especially investigators who have a reputation for being difficult to fool. Sometimes deception is hard to detect. Other times, it's blatantly obvious.

[6]

I was once part of a satellite conference with John Wayne Gacy, who was in prison in Illinois. Here was a guy who had murdered thirty-three young men. He had twenty-eight bodies under his house, and he was saying, "Well, I might have done five." He was clearly lying, and he had to know we weren't stupid and that we had the facts, but he wasn't going to give it up. He was just going to tell the story he wanted to tell.

You can catch these guys, but they'll decide whether or not they'll give it up. They want something they can still control or they want the feeling that they've put one over on you. They may even try to wrest control from who's interviewing them. They think that if we buy the lie, that makes them smarter than we are.

Our approach often is to allow them to go ahead and believe that, which is using their own momentum to undermine them. In the meantime, we find a way to determine if they're lying and then get around it to discover the truth. Sometimes we don't know whether or not we've succeeded until we get back to the office. It works the same if they're manipulative: We manipulate them with their own behavior into thinking they're succeeding.

I generally assume two things: 1) they haven't told me everything, and 2) they've probably lied about something. It's impossible for us to know every detail of what someone has done, but if we go in informed about the crimes and can demonstrate that knowledge, then we may decrease the likelihood that they'll throw us a curve ball. It puts them on a short leash, and we can pull that leash up if we need to. But revealing what you know must be done carefully and an investigator should never reveal to the offender everything he knows about the case.

Despite what people commonly believe, there is no universal way to detect deception or a single type of behavior that is consistently associated with it. Gaze aversion, self-manipulations, and fidgeting or shifting positions are not necessarily good indicators. In fact, some current research indicates that deception is associated with a *decrease* in some of these types of movements. However, liars do tend to engage in certain verbal behaviors such as shorter responses, implausible answers—like Gacy's assertion that someone else buried twenty-three of the bodies in his basement—or generally evasive responses to questions.

The child killer I mentioned earlier would not admit to torturing his victim with a stun gun, but there were clearly marks on the boy's genitals. Even when confronted with irrefutable factual evidence, he would not confess to it. Sometimes offenders are uncomfortable with what they've done. They don't want to confess to something that's indefensible. Or else they might just want to hold something back.

In general, the best approach for detecting deception

in these situations is to start by being skeptical. It's a given that murderers, rapists, and other felons will lie. I generally start an interview by establishing an "honesty baseline," having them answer nonthreatening questions to which I already have the answers so that I can observe their behavior when they respond honestly, something like how a polygraph interview works. If their behavior changes later in the interview, especially when responding to more pertinent questions, it may be an indication of deception.

When I do encounter possible deception, I've found that it's best to ask more questions and drill down into that specific area. But it must be done without revealing everything that you know. If an offender knows the full extent of the interviewer's knowledge, then, combined with his own knowledge, he knows everything. That makes it easier for him to lie successfully. Investigators must use their knowledge of the case strategically during the interview.

I often go back to a troubling area later in the interview and ask the offender to repeat what he has said before. This is another good way to detect deception, because if the offender is lying, he will often have trouble remembering what he said previously.

And last, one of the best ways to detect deception is to be thoroughly and completely informed about the offender and the crimes that are to be the focus of the interview. The more details known, the more apparent the offender's lies will be.

With Hofmann, when he talked about the third bomb as a suicide attempt, his demeanor changed and the pitch of his voice got higher. He sat up in a defensive posture. Up to that point, he had been open, but he closed down then. That was a signal to us to avoid this material until we were almost ready to leave. We save potential confrontations until the end, because we don't want to risk terminating the session prematurely. When we've finished, then we can go back and revisit troubling areas. If the interview becomes confrontational at that point and the offender shuts down, at least we've gotten other information that we wanted.

Hofmann was defensive at one point but not upset. Talking about his crimes seemed cathartic for him, even exciting, and we left on good terms.

Afterward, I wrote him two letters, the first to thank him for his time, consideration, and truthfulness. I told him that the discussion had been helpful, and if the opportunity ever arose, I'd like to visit again. He didn't write back. I wrote a second letter to reiterate what I'd said in the first one. I never heard from him.

Studying cases in the field, along with the offender interviews, is the best way to gain insight into the offenders' minds and methods, manner, and motives for committing their crimes. We see what precautions they took and how accurate or inaccurate their concerns were. You can't generalize to all criminals from a single case or interview, but that's how we gained our knowledge, one offender at a time. You just build on that, like the accumulating layers of a pearl, and pretty soon you've got a database that's worthwhile.

In this particular interview with Mark Hofmann, we learned a lot that day about the machinations of a clever criminal, which was our original goal. The more information we can get from people like him, the better we can understand the criminal mind, and that information may someday help us to avoid a situation such as the one we had at Waco, Texas, in 1993. Mistakes were made and many people died because those in charge failed to understand the dynamics of a paranoid religious sect under the control of a cunning manipulator. Watching David Koresh in action, up close, from start to finish, taught me important things about the psychopath who believes he's God.

7: Negotiating with God

> Then the fire of the Lord fell [on Mount Carmel] and
> consumed the burnt offering and the wood and the
> stones and the dust . . .
>
> —1 Kings 18:38

[1]

Early on Sunday morning, February 28, 1993, around
seventy armed agents from the Bureau of Alcohol, To-
bacco, and Firearms (ATF) prepared to move. Their
object: a surprise raid on a group of buildings outside
the southwestern Texas town of Waco. Known as
Mount Carmel, the compound was occupied by more
than one hundred members of an apocalyptic religious
group known as the Branch Davidians. Their charismatic leader, David Koresh, claimed to be God. They
did their own gardening, survived on meager rations,
and believed that they had been specially chosen to
usher in the end of the world and the second coming of
Christ. As prophesied in the book of Revelation, they
anticipated violence.

The local newspaper was running a series of articles
about their activities, the second of which appeared
that morning. Defectors had denounced Koresh, alleging child abuse and polygamy, and had sent a detective

to snoop around, so it seemed likely that those being trained to guard the place would be watchful and edgy. Some had been posted all night on a tall watchtower that provided a good view of the flat seventy-seven acres.

Koresh had initially predicted that "the Apocalypse" would occur in Israel. Now that he was in Texas, he changed his mind and proclaimed that it would occur there, at Mount Carmel. He and his followers would await the attack by the government that would signal the end of the world.

In preparation, they had stockpiled .50-caliber sniper rifles that could pierce armor and kill at a thousand yards, as well as up to a hundred AR-15 assault rifles converted to full auto, night-vision equipment, improvised hand grenades, and large quantities of ammunition. Since possession of hand grenades and illegally converted guns were violations of federal law, that gave the ATF primary jurisdiction.

Anticipating positive press coverage, the ATF had given the local media notice of the planned raid. That was the first in a dizzying cascade of errors that led to the ultimate disaster. Armed with advance knowledge, a TV cameraman unwittingly compromised the raid that morning. He got lost trying to find the place, and when he spotted a postal worker making his rounds, he asked the man for directions to the Mount Carmel compound. He explained that it was to be raided that morning and that he was going to cover the story. The postal worker, David Jones, was not only a Branch Davidian but was also David Koresh's brother-in-law. He couldn't get to a telephone fast enough.

Robert Rodriguez, aka Robert Garcia, was among

the people inside the compound. Rodriguez was one of eight undercover ATF agents renting a house nearby. These agents were masquerading as students at Texas State Technical College who were interested in Koresh's Bible studies. However, the ATF had underestimated Koresh's paranoia. He thought these "students" seemed too old and their cars too expensive, so he'd run checks and found that three of the four cars were paid off. He now knew that they weren't students.

Rodriguez had arrived for another lesson the morning of the raid. In reality, he was there to ensure that everything was quiet at the compound before the raid. The Bible study proceeded normally until Perry Jones told Koresh he had an emergency phone call. Koresh took it, and, according to Rodriguez, returned badly shaken. Everyone wanted to know what was wrong. Rodriguez would later testify that Koresh looked at him and said that neither the ATF nor the government would ever bring him down. Rodriguez was stunned. He had to warn his fellow agents that their raid was compromised. He made an excuse to leave, and as he started for the door, Koresh shook his hand and said, "Good luck, Robert."

Aware that they had lost the element of surprise, ATF management considered their position and decided to go forward. That horrifically flawed decision was to cost many lives and initiate the longest standoff in United States history.

The agents got into a convoy of vehicles and drove out to the barren grounds to serve their warrants and seize the illegal items. A Blackhawk helicopter from the Texas National Guard accompanied them, along with two Apache helicopters.

At 9:30 A.M., as three teams formed to enter the building, an agent went to the compound's front door and knocked. They'd been preparing for this for eight months, and each team had a distinct assignment— protect the children, neutralize the military force, or seize the arms. They hoped for a quick resolution, before lunch.

Koresh, wearing a bulletproof vest, cracked open the door. As agents streamed toward the building, he yelled that there were women and children inside and that he wanted to talk, but agents continued to pour out of the vans, moving toward the compound according to plan. Koresh slammed the door. Gunfire immediately erupted. We heard later that Perry Jones, standing behind Koresh, was struck twice as bullets pierced the steel doors, and that Koresh was hit in the side.

Several agents were hit right away as well, and rounds were fired at the hovering choppers, forcing them to land. One ATF agent gained entry into the building, only to be shot in the head and killed. Several agents who had climbed to the roof rolled off when Davidians began firing through the ceiling. Bullets even pierced the reporters' cars, and then concussion grenades began exploding among the agents. The fire was returned full force, but the Davidians had the advantage of cover, concealment, and multiple points of fire, including the tactically advantageous position of firing from the tower.

When things calmed down, ATF Agent Jim Cavanaugh and Lieutenant Larry Lynch of the McLennan County Sheriff's Office negotiated a truce. It allowed the ATF to go in and remove their men. Four agents were dead and at least sixteen had been wounded or injured. These were transported to the nearest emergency facilities, twenty minutes away.

At the request of the ATF, FBI negotiators were dispatched to the site. The first one on the scene was Byron Sage, a seasoned agent. At 2:29 P.M., Koresh demanded that he be able to broadcast his religious teaching over the radio, otherwise, no one would come out of the compound. Sage agreed. The broadcast occurred at approximately 4:00 P.M. over Dallas radio station KRLD and the message was rebroadcast twice within the next hour. At approximately 4:55, three Davidians crossing a field near the compound ambushed several ATF agents. The agents returned the gunfire, killing one individual and capturing another. The third escaped.

Negotiations for a peaceful surrender continued, but Koresh responded with belligerent Scripture readings. He then participated in several live interviews with the media about how the ATF had endangered his flock. He emphasized the fact that a number of children lived in the compound and said that he'd been shot and was bleeding badly. He expected to die. Koresh called his mother and left a message on her answering machine. "Hello, Mama, it's your boy. They shot me and I'm dying, all right? But I'll be back real soon . . . I'll be merciful, okay? I'll see y'all in the skies."

By that time, the ATF was reinforced with more of its own, and with Texas Rangers, members of the FBI's Hostage Rescue Team (HRT), the FBI's Special Agent in Charge (SAC) from the San Antonio office, a bomb squad, and several U.S. Marshals. The media, too, began to pour in. Koresh released four children ranging in age from three to six, and everyone settled in for a long night.

It was the beginning of a confrontation—two group dynamics that were mutually resistant and typically incendiary would face each other. In short order, I was to become the BSU's sole representative on the scene.

[2]

The FBI has primary jurisdiction in cases involving the murder of federal agents, so the Bureau was tasked with bringing this chaos under control. The command switched hands. The ATF did not have the resources to set up the type of command post and operational support necessary for a sustained encounter of this magnitude. It all happened quickly, including my own involvement.

The World Trade Center had just been bombed that Friday, two days before, and I was watching CNN over the weekend to check on further details. New York City was in my region, and if suspects were not readily developed, I felt sure I would be drawn into that investigation. I would be assigned either to the Strategic Information and Operations Center (SIOC) at FBI headquarters or would be sent directly to New York. I watched the breaking news, waiting for word, only to see federal agents being killed in another place altogether, so I sat forward and listened. To my surprise, I saw footage in Waco, Texas, of tactical agents being shot, rolling off rooftops, and being evacuated. Some were clearly dead.

"What the hell is this disaster?" I asked.

Then my phone rang. It was John Douglas, the acting unit chief. I expected to be sent to New York.

"The Bureau is taking over the situation in Waco," he told me.

My focus abruptly switched from one scene of violence to another. "Are you kidding me?"

"No. You need to go up to SIOC."

"You mean first thing tomorrow morning, or—"

"Right now, and plan to work through the night. I'll find someone to relieve you tomorrow."

I drove to FBI headquarters to join a team of agents being assembled to oversee this operation. As I crossed the 14th Street Bridge into Washington early that Sunday evening, the few remaining tourists were heading out of town, leaving the Washington Monument and the Capitol quietly illuminated against the darkening sky. FBI headquarters seemed strangely still as I cleared security and proceeded to the command center. Once inside SIOC, it became obvious that the Bureau was orchestrating a quick and sizable response. Logistical considerations were ironed out as negotiators, hostage rescue team (HRT) operators, SWAT teams, Rapid Start, tech agents, FBI pilots, and support personnel from around the country collected their gear and made their way to Waco.

Our man there was Pete Smerick, who called us frequently and also sent written memos. It quickly became clear that the Special-Agent-in-Charge (SAC), Jeffrey Jamar, sent over from the nearest FBI office, was planning a tactical campaign in response to what the Hostage Rescue Team and the ATF agents were suggesting. Smerick thought this was the wrong approach and would get people killed. He was actively resisting it. Then people got upset about his written reports, because these would become part of the file, so the decision was made to stop putting our recommendations in writing.

My initial assignment at SIOC was to construct indirect personality assessments of David Koresh as an individual and the Branch Davidians as a group in order to develop a meaningful intervention strategy. The trouble was, we had no information about Koresh or the Branch Davidians. Strict attorney general guidelines barred the FBI from gathering intelligence about any individual or group unless they had committed a crime. That included even public source information, such as newspaper clippings. These guidelines had been set up in the aftermath of COINTELPRO, an acronym for counterintelligence-program. Its initial purpose was to identify those individuals or groups that might pose a threat to the security of the country. During the 1960s, that program had spawned some FBI excesses, resulting in stricter guidelines. In addition, FBI agents were being sued individually for alleged abuses. All of this had had a profoundly chilling effect on intelligence gathering. The Bureau was particularly hamstrung when it came to "religious" groups.

Freedom of religion cloaks even the most unorthodox and potentially threatening of groups with a constitutional protection against government intelligence gathering or intervention. This is a particularly vexing problem. While religious freedom must be vigorously protected, there has always been an odd cohesion between religion and violence. All major religions have prohibitions against suicide and homicide, yet ironically a great deal of violence is perpetrated in the name of religion. The Crusades, Belfast's Catholic/Protestant skirmishes, the Sikhs and Hindus in India, Aum Shinrikyo unleashing a deadly gas in the Tokyo subways, and, of course, the Taliban attacks are all clear examples, and each group offers a theological justification for violence. For law enforcement, the distinction between freedom of religion and religious violence is the distinction between belief and behavior. We are all free to believe whatever we wish, but our behavior must be in accord with the law. Murdering someone in the name of God is still murder.

However, our hands were tied, so during the early days of the standoff, we felt our way blindly with this group. Yet we did eventually put together a fair picture of what we were dealing with.

[3]

The Branch Davidians embodied a pattern that has been observed among other violent religious groups: They were unconventional, well-armed and xenophobic. David Koresh was a charismatic psychopathic leader with paranoid tendencies who taught his followers daily that they had been "specially chosen" for a transcendent mission of cosmic significance. He was the prophet, the sole source of truth, and they were its embodiment. All else was evil or in error, especially the secular government. As the Messiah he would lead his followers in the final clash between good and evil. He could easily point to the ATF raid as proof of his prophecies and of the beginning of the "end times." Thus, he could incite his followers to vanquish their enemy. Violence was a sacramental right, a divine duty. As Eric Hoffer, in *The True Believer*, observed, "... a true believer is apt to see himself as one of the chosen, the salt of the earth, the light of the world, a prince disguised in meekness who is destined to inherit this earth and the kingdom of heaven, too. He who is not of his faith is evil; he who will not listen shall perish."

The local authorities were first alerted in 1990 to illegal activities among cult members living at the religious center outside town known as Mount Carmel, and the McLennan County sheriff, Jack Harwell, set out to establish a liaison with them. He didn't want trouble and he thought it best to let them know in a friendly way that he was aware of them. Since he'd followed their activities, he turned out to be an important source of information for us.

The cult was led by Vernon J. Howell, a member of the Branch Davidian Seventh Day Adventist Church, who claimed he was the Son of God and the only true prophet. He'd changed his name to David Koresh because it exuded power. "David" referred to King David of the Bible and "Koresh" meant death.

Yet I had to go back further than that to trace his rise to power.

The Seventh Day Adventists advocated purity of the body as the temple in which the Holy Spirit resides, so their habits of eating, drinking, and any other form of ingestion were strict. They believed that the final battle between good and evil was imminent and that only a select number would witness the return of Jesus Christ and be saved.

Within this congregation during the early 1930s, Victor T. Houteff emphasized teachings about the coming Apocalypse. He saw himself as chosen by God to cleanse the church, and when his extremist dogmatism forced him out, he took a number of followers with him. In 1935, they purchased a plot of land outside Waco, and named it the Mount Carmel Center. Then Houteff renamed his sect the Davidian Seventh Day

Adventists, and when he died in 1955, his wife, Florence, succeeded him as leader. She predicted that the world would end on Easter Day in 1959, and many converts flocked to Waco in hopes of being ushered into heaven.

When the Kingdom of God didn't arrive as promised, many disillusioned people left the Davidians, but one man, Benjamin Roden, remained and attracted a group of about fifty followers. He called them Branch and they became the Branch Davidians. He believed he was King David's successor and was to live to usher in the second coming of Christ. When he died in 1978, Christ had yet to show, so Roden's wife, Lois, became the new prophet.

In 1983, an ambitious high school dropout named Vernon Howell joined the Branch Davidians. Howell was born in 1959, in Houston, the illegitimate son of Bonnie Haldleman. He grew up in the Dallas area and attended public schools, but he was a poor student, possibly dyslexic. By the ninth grade, he had left school altogether. Yet he was an avid reader of the Bible and played the guitar. At eighteen, he moved to Tyler, Texas, where he joined the Adventist Church. When church leaders were bothered by his long hair, casual dress, and challenges to their authority, Howell became disillusioned and moved to Waco to be with the Branch Davidians.

He was charismatic, easygoing, had the good looks of a rock star, and exhibited an encyclopedic knowledge of the Bible. He could take any verse and discuss it endlessly, which made him seem highly intelligent, even gifted—possibly inspired. By contrast, Lois Roden's influence on the group was fading; her proclamation that the Holy Spirit was feminine disturbed a number of followers, and her son George, the heir apparent, was not held in great esteem. Howell walked into this power vacuum and saw his opportunity. He challenged George for the leadership of the group.

As these two faced off, Howell found an effective way to grab power: He charmed the older Lois into inviting him into her bed. He claimed it was by God's divine command that they produce a child together. That didn't sit well with George, so he and Howell had a couple of fights and George began wearing a gun.

The two men gathered their respective supporters, each claiming exclusive access to God's revelation. Howell insisted that as God's "seventh messenger," it was he who would set off the chain of events that would bring on the Apocalypse.

When Lois died in 1986, power swung back to George, who forced Howell out. Howell and his small flock drifted for a while, going to California to get more disciples. He then returned to Texas, where he began to impregnate young women who had been "chosen to bear children for God." He also began a campaign to overthrow Roden by getting him arrested. To acquire proof of a legal misdeed, he and several other armed men invaded Mount Carmel. Roden came at them with an Uzi and they shot back. Surprisingly, no one was killed. Both men were brought up on charges, and during the trial Roden appeared to be the more fanatical and dangerous of the two—especially when he had a corpse brought into the courtroom to prove that the true Messiah could raise the dead. He couldn't. Howell was acquitted of all charges, and he pointed to this as a sign that God was protecting him, the true prophet. The whole courtroom drama was impressive enough to win many of the Branch Davidians over to him, so Roden left town in disgrace and humiliation and was later committed to a mental hospital.

Howell believed that he was a harbinger straight out of the Book of Revelations and that he alone could interpret the cryptic prophecies of the Seven Seals, which included the meaning of the four horsemen of the Apocalypse. In accordance with a sudden inspiration in 1989, which he called the "New Light," he divided husbands from wives in his drive to acquire a biblically sanctioned harem, and claimed the women as his own. It was important that, as God, he spread his seed and sire a divine army. Husbands and wives were separated from each other and made to live in single-sex quarters. Many happily married couples were shocked. Some, like Marc Breault, left the group.

Still, Koresh had managed to collect a band of several hundred disciples and those who remained were "true believers" over whom he had immense control. He dubbed his male followers Mighty Men, from the name given to the guards of King Solomon's bed. It was estimated that he'd claimed at least fifteen girls and women as his own, some as young as twelve, while the other men were to devote themselves to celibacy. Breaking up families was an effective way to gain power. Howell seemed to have an instinct for how to isolate and control.

In 1990, Howell changed his name to David Koresh and dictated stricter rules about what people should eat and how they should spend their days, changing those rules on a whim.

By 1992, Koresh had intensified his teachings about

martyrdom for the cause. At the same time, he was stockpiling food and collecting an arsenal to defend himself against any attacks, whether from defectors, or government agents (referred to as the Babylonians). The Davidians managed to stockpile enough canned goods, grain, and ready-to-eat meals to last a year.

Because he could recite extensive Bible passages from memory, Koresh could join disparate ideas in Scripture, which impressed his followers. They were also afraid of his unpredictable temperament. He might stay in bed all day or he might harangue his flock for sixteen hours straight. Whatever the others did was subject to his control, and because he was the "Lamb of God," they didn't dare think for themselves. To do so risked their future salvation. He was allowed to sin, but when he did, he said that he endangered salvation for them all.

He demanded to know from members of his group how far they were willing to go in defense of the true faith. The only way to serve God was to be willing to die. He even taught the children that suicide might one day be required and showed them how to do it with cyanide or a gun. Mount Carmel was renamed Ranch Apocalypse.

[4]

The days immediately following the failed raid were a blur of intense activity. Tactical personnel, technically trained agents, agent pilots, helicopters and fixed-wing aircraft, support personnel, managers, local law enforcement, consultants, and worldwide media descended on Waco, each intensifying the swirl of activity. Three SACs from other FBI offices assisted Jamar, and by five o'clock P.M. on the second day, they had a fully functioning command center.

The main command post (CP) out of which most of us worked was an airplane hangar at Southwest Technical College, about a mile from the Branch Davidian compound. A second CP was located in a recreational vehicle closer to the compound.

The Critical Incident Negotiation Team (CINT) worked in "cells." At first, they worked in two twelve-hour shifts, and then switched to three eight-hour shifts that often overlapped. Each shift had a team leader who coordinated with the SAC, a primary negotiator handling the phone, a secondary negotiator who acted as a strategy coach, a scribe historian who kept the daily log, and someone to prepare the situation reports.

There were two phone lines into and out of the compound. The day of the raid the initial communications occurred between ATF Special Agent James Cavanaugh and David Koresh. On the other line, Lieutenant Larry Lynch of the McLennan County sheriff's office was in contact with two of Koresh's trusted lieutenants, Steve Schneider and Wayne Martin (a Harvard-educated attorney), and a cease-fire was negotiated. After the Davidians had conducted their initial angry interviews with the media, the phone lines were rerouted so that those people inside could dial out only to the negotiators. During the second day, three negotiators kept up unceasing contact with fifteen different Davidians.

HRT set up their tactical operations center (TOC), and established an inner perimeter around the compound, as well as sniper observation posts that were designated Sierra One and Two. FBI SWAT teams formed an outer perimeter.

We learned that Koresh had two wounds. The most

significant was just above his left hip. The second was a superficial wound to his left wrist. He refused medical treatment for himself and initially refused our request for information about others inside who might be in need of medical assistance or might have been killed. Nonetheless, negotiations proceeded well, as ten more children were released that day, including a five-month-old baby.

With HRT agents driving Bradley fighting vehicles around his property, and unable to dial out to anyone except the FBI, Koresh became frustrated and angry. He threatened more violence, contradicting his earlier assurances. Negotiators defused his anger by getting him to refocus on his holy mission, i.e., he had a message to deliver to the world. Then they reached an agreement. He would provide an hour-long taped message to be played on the radio from coast to coast. Once that was done, everyone would come out. As a show of good faith, he sent out more children, for a total of sixteen so far.

The FBI made arrangements with Christian radio stations for this broadcast to be done during the afternoon of March 2. The tape arrived at eight A.M. with the release of two more children and two adults. At that point, Koresh said he was going to take a nap. On the tape, he declared: "I'm the anointed one . . . my father, my God who sits on the throne in heaven, has given me a book of seven seals . . . it's the fulfillment of prophecy."

As airtime approached, HRT dropped off a stretcher for Koresh, which two Davidians retrieved, at the front of the compound. As several Christian radio stations broadcast Koresh's message, negotiators worked out the surrender logistics. Koresh was to come out first, carried on the stretcher. Then every two minutes, Steve Schneider was to send someone else out. Vehicles were moved into place to pick them up, along with medical personnel. Criminalists and investigators waited to process the crime scene. Everyone was relieved that this thing, which could have been disastrous, appeared to be coming to a peaceable end.

Later that afternoon, Koresh spoke to negotiators and assured them that the plan was proceeding. Everyone inside was saying his or her good-byes and Koresh was going to lead them in prayer.

Then, at six P.M., everything changed. Koresh announced that God had instructed him to wait. There would be no surrender that day. Thereafter, all he offered were Bible readings and stubborn statements of resistance. At midnight, the Davidians went to sleep.

The FBI routinely relies on outside consultants for advice and this situation was certainly no different. Several psychological and psychiatric experts, including psycholinguists, were contacted and asked for their input. We would then take that information, evaluate it, and look for ways to implement it.

Among the experts who came to the command center quite early on was Dr. Park Dietz. I have worked many cases with Dr. Dietz over the years and consider him to be the most insightful forensic psychiatrist in the country, if not the world. He arrived in Waco on March 2 and spent several days monitoring negotiations and reading the hundreds of pages of material we had amassed on Koresh and his group. Dietz concluded that Koresh would probably not leave the compound and could be suicidal. In fact, based on the man's paranoid and controlling leadership style, he might have a suicide pact with his followers. Better to die than to lose power.

Later, just as predicted, we learned that despite what Koresh had said, he had actually formed a different plan for that day. He believed he was about to die from his wounds. Once dead, he wanted to be carried out on the FBI's stretcher. Members were to follow his stretcher out and then open fire on FBI agents, killing as many as possible.

Some Davidians were given hand grenades, and Koresh had instructed them to stand together in small groups and pull the pins. That way they could take as many of "the Beast" with them as possible. Women who were afraid to do this were to arrange to die at the hands of other members, but everyone was to die. Then, after saying good-bye and talking about meeting in the next world, they gathered in the dining room to pray and wait to be told to proceed. For them, being killed by return fire would not be a "suicide by cop" but would be martyrdom in the name of Christ. Some of the Davidians referred to their death and resurrection as a "translation."

During the 1994 criminal trial held later in San Antonio, Texas, Kathy Schroeder, a member of the Branch Davidians, testified about this plan. "After it [Koresh's message] was aired," she said, "we were all going to come out, David on a stretcher that the FBI had sent in, and fire and draw fire." She specified that this mass "firing" was to be at the agents, and if Koresh was not already dead by that time, they were to shoot him as well. She went on to testify that they had alternative plans that included her blowing up other females with a hand grenade. She reported that the mood was joyful. "Everybody was ready to be translated."

However, Koresh had assured the negotiators that everyone was going to come out peacefully.

"Okay," they said, "including you."

"Oh, I'm, I'm still here."

They asked him again if anyone was intent on committing suicide.

"No," he assured them, "I don't think anyone's going to commit suicide."

"Nobody's going to be coming out with guns so that somebody can shoot at them?"

"Nobody's going to be coming out playing John Wayne."

According to later reports, God apparently got in touch with Koresh again and advised him that he and the Davidians should not emerge at that time, because Koresh had sinned immediately after the raid by indulging in whiskey, cigarettes, and prohibited food. Should they die then, they would not be saved.

If he hadn't suddenly changed his mind that day—probably because he realized he was *not* about to die—many more people would have died.

Disappointed, we all settled in for the long haul. A quick resolution now seemed unlikely. Koresh was much more interested in talking about God and Scripture than in surrender. The next day, he reiterated that God was in control and speaking through him. He claimed he was "taking orders," because "my boss is making decisions on whether to pounce on you or not." If we failed to understand him, he added, God would punish us with "World War Three." Insisting that he was Christ, Koresh commanded the agents to study the Bible.

"You know who I am and who I claim I am," he said.

"You claim that you're the Lord," one negotiator patiently responded.

"I am Christ."

"Well, you didn't say that. You claimed to be the Lord."

For Koresh it was all the same. "Christ is the same as the Lord. King of kings and Lord of lords. The Prince of the kings of the earth. Yep. What can I say? Shall I lie? No, I will not lie."

Throughout his tedious, disjointed monologues, the negotiators remained conciliatory and stayed focused on getting more children out.

The next day we learned from a note pinned to a child who'd been released that once certain children were clear of the building, the adults would prepare to die. Koresh indicated that the "other" children would leave, but not his. That meant that if a suicide plan was in place, a number of children could die as well.

[5]

It was at this point that I left my post in D.C. and went to Waco. I was to replace Pete Smerick. During that first week, he and Mark Young, our field coordinator from the Bureau's Houston office, were concerned that the on-scene commanders viewed Koresh and the Davidians as common criminals and cop killers. They were moving too rapidly toward a tactical resolution. Smerick and Young suggested that if the armored personnel carriers did not back off, we'd have more blood on our hands. Koresh had psychopathic tendencies, they pointed out. He was narcissistic, manipulative, controlling, and without remorse. If provoked, he would act on impulse and his followers would do whatever he said.

"For years, Koresh has been brainwashing his followers in this battle between the church and the enemy," one of their memos read. "On February 28, his prophecy came true. Koresh is still able to convince his followers that the end is near, as he predicted. Their enemies will surround them and kill them.

"In traditional hostage situations, the strategy which has been successful has been negotiations coupled with ever increasing tactical presence. In this situation, however, it's believed that the strategies carried to excess could eventually be counterproductive and could result in loss of life. Every time his followers sense movement of tactical personnel, Koresh validates his prophetic warnings that an attack is forthcoming and they're going to have to defend themselves. According to his teachings, if they die defending their faith, they will be saved. . . ."

Smerick also noted that "it's been speculated that Koresh's religious beliefs are nothing more than a con in order to get money, women, and power, and that a strong show of force will crumble that resolve, causing him to surrender." Yet the wanton display of force by the FBI was ". . . making his prophecies come true. We're playing into his hands. Only backing off would show that he was wrong."

In other words, Smerick advised that the SAC was taking the wrong approach, and that a show of force would create a bunker mentality and significantly increase the potential for failure. He went on to say that a mass suicide could not be discounted since Koresh would realize that once outside the compound, his status as a divine leader would diminish considerably. A display of force to pressure him should be the very last option considered.

Smerick requested to be relieved and Jamar approved, so I was dispatched to Waco with the hope that I might see the situation differently. If not, I was encouraged to use a more diplomatic approach to the on-site commanders. Smerick had been too vinegary for their taste.

Armed with all this information and aware of the many sources of mounting tension, I arrived in Waco and reported to work at the old airport hangar where we had office space on the second floor. I knew that I was going into a tense situation in which the SAC did not take contradictory opinions well. He also didn't care for the behavioral science people and I was the only one there representing our unit. We hoped I could have some influence, but I wasn't about to write any reports. My job was to use what I had learned about the Davidians and Koresh to help with negotiations.

I worked closely with Gary Noesner from the Special Operations and Research Unit (SOARS). Tall, red-headed, and easygoing, Gary was the wisest, most experienced, and most successful negotiator in the FBI. He was in charge of negotiations at Waco and he had assembled a cadre of experienced people, including Byron Sage, the first negotiator on the scene and the last to leave.

The number of personnel involved over the fifty-one days was staggering. We had Jamar as the commanding SAC, with three subordinate SACs. There were also numerous Rapid Start staff members, plenty of HRT agents, a number of negotiators, over a hundred ATF agents, some U.S. Customs agents, and several SWAT teams. On any given shift, there were over two hundred people involved, along with around forty support personnel. In addition to that, we had people from the local police department, the county sheriff's office, the Texas Rangers, and the Texas Department of Public Safety. Even the army and the national guard had representatives there. By the time the incident was over, more than seven hundred people in law enforcement had played a part. There had never been an engagement of that magnitude in the history of law enforcement in the United States.

My primary mission in Waco was to continue to map the twisted topography of Koresh's mind, as well as the dynamics of the group itself. I would monitor the negotiations so I could get a sense of how they were behaving inside the compound. I'd also monitor the feedback from the microphones that we sent in so we knew what was being said among them once they hung up the phone. That was a valuable source of information because we could learn how sincere they were and whether they were making plans that were different from what they had told us.

I used the raw data to provide suggestions about what we were dealing with, whom we might target, and how we should do it. I had to pay attention to the nuances of what was being said, and note any inconsistencies or red flags. I was in there all day with the negotiators, taking notes on each person they talked to. I had to watch their behavior as individuals and I also had to look at the group collectively. Those are different areas of psychology, with separate but interrelated issues. I had to keep all of that straight and make quick decisions about how to guide the negotiators with logical recommendations. I was there from six in the morning until eight or nine at night, being in the sessions as well as calling into SIOC to give verbal reports.

In the meetings with Jamar and his team, we discussed the best strategy for getting the Davidians into custody without anyone else being injured or killed. Another ATF-style raid on the compound was ruled out as too risky. The older children might take up arms, and the last thing any of us wanted was a situation in which children and agents were confronting each other at gunpoint. So what were we to do? That's where the FBI became deeply divided.

Those who saw the Davidians as a pack of cop killers pushed for the use of force on the theory that the FBI could intimidate them into surrendering. That approach was evident in the early days of the standoff. The FBI responded to Koresh's threats by ratcheting up its show of force, which in turn provoked more threats. That inspired the FBI to bring in Abrams tanks. In other words, it was a strategy of limbic brain–based chest thumping that escalated the tension and resolved nothing.

Having been leader of an FBI SWAT team for a number of years, I know that there are times and places where force is necessary. We use force not because we can but because we must. Most violent criminals want to live to play again another day and they surrender when confronted by superior force, but this situation was qualitatively different. A blatant display of force was likely to be counterproductive.

Koresh and the Davidians were unquestionably dangerous, but their motivations were entirely different from those of garden-variety thugs. Their deeply held values and beliefs were under attack and they were not about to be coerced or bullied into abandoning them or surrendering to the "forces of evil." What anyone else thought about the rationality of their beliefs was irrelevant. It was their commitment that mattered. If the goal was to provoke them into a gun battle, that would be easy. Death wasn't their worst enemy, so getting them out without violence was going to be a far more daunting challenge. That's because their leader was so powerful.

Koresh was a cunning, manipulative megalomaniac with paranoid tendencies who had two relatively autonomous selves, one rational and one delusional. A megalomaniac considers himself to be deified, and Koresh's followers reinforced his megalomania daily. Koresh also exhibited the classic symptoms of paranoia, which include both persecutory and grandiose delusions.

His primary grandiose delusion revolved around his self-proclaimed religious identity, but even that was not simple. He couldn't seem to decide exactly who he was. Sometimes he called himself Jesus Christ; sometimes the Lamb of God, destined to open the Seventh Seal and usher in the end of the world; at other times he was the second messiah. Koresh referred to "the bizarrity of my presence" and implied, among other things, that during a trip to Israel he had ascended via celestial flying saucers to Orion, where certain mysteries were revealed to him. But he wasn't completely delusional either. He could be rational, logical, cunning, and manipulative. He also had earthbound concerns. During the standoff, he even expressed interest in a book deal and demanded that copies of *Newsweek* and *Time* be provided so he could see how they had portrayed him.

Koresh engaged in what some psychologists refer to as "aggression immersion," i.e., the repetitive, intentional exposure to violent material in order to validate violence as a behavioral norm. He repeatedly played to his group videos about the Vietnam War, such as *Full Metal Jacket, Hamburger Hill*, and *Platoon*. He also had them prepare through weight training, military-style drills, firearms training, and obstacle course drills. The governmental forces of Babylon were going to descend upon them, according to him, and they had to be ready. Yet in reality, the federal government had no interest in Koresh or the Davidians *until* they began stockpiling illegal weapons and explosives. Their paranoid beliefs became a self-fulfilling prophecy.

Now the dead and wounded lay on both sides of the doors of Ranch Apocalypse, giving Koresh's prophesies a horrific validation. Any vestige of skepticism that might have existed before the attack was killed as well. If he was right about the government coming to attack, then he must be right about everything else. Or so they reasoned.

[6]

Jamar's mind-set resonated with that of the HRT leader, Dick Rogers. First, neither suffered contradictory opinions gladly. Second, both perceived the standoff as primarily a tactical problem that called for a tactical resolution. They believed that the Davidians could be pressured into surrendering. Coming off a successful raid at the Talledega Alabama Prison, HRT was feeling very strong and confident about their ability to resolve any problem tactically. They had little tolerance for a more measured approach.

The HRT mind-set at Waco is accurately set forth in the book *Cold Zero*, written by former HRT sniper

Christopher Whitcomb, who was at Waco. In describing life as an HRT agent, Whitcomb states, "You spend the vast majority of your time enduring peace, hoping in the back of your mind for trouble," and that "fifty alpha males caged in a highly secure compound tend to itch. That itch turns to scratch, and soon becomes aggression." At Waco he justified HRT's "tightening the perimeter" approach from a behavioral perspective. "The closer we got to the building, the less Koresh felt sovereign over his property. We worked like a crawling weed, climbing into his sense of domain, choking off his personal space. I imagined him watching through the windows, locked rigid in frustration as we closed in, his self-proclaimed deity fading in the diesel exhaust."

Whitcomb was exactly wrong. Tightening the perimeter validated Koresh's deification, which intensified and strengthened the group's solidarity and cohesiveness. Koresh had prophesied about the enemy coming in "chariots of fire," as found in the Book of Kings. The Bradley fighting vehicles, Abrams tanks, and other military vehicles driving across their sacred land were those chariots of fire.

Whitcomb wrote that, "Every one of us sat there in that shithole for almost two months, hanging on the outside chance that some spineless pukes back at Headquarters would give us the chance to do good." But constant encroachment and harassment wasn't the best approach. Smerick had been right. HRT needed to back off. We needed a less aggressive posture. As Sun Tzu observed in *The Art of War,* "Even though you are competent, appear to be incompetent. Though effective, appear to be ineffective. . . . Draw them in with the prospect of gain, take them by confusion."

What I could see happening was a phenomenon known as "groupthink," a maladaptive form of group decision making. Irving L. Janis, a Yale scholar, coined the term after studying the way decisions were made during the Bay of Pigs invasion and the escalation of the Vietnam War, and he has written extensively about it. Applying his ideas to the Waco situation, I believe that both sides thought of themselves as the "good" people who were morally right, so therefore whatever happened was not their fault. It was that "other group" that was wrong and was committing evil acts. The more the "other" side did, the more the "good" side felt justified in defending themselves, and neither side was ever likely to change its position.

Groupthink creates an insular perspective and exaggerates the stress from external threats. The group leader implies that there is no better solution than his and he pressures the others for agreement. Anyone who questions or argues with the leader and his prevailing theory is vilified and mocked. This was obviously the case both inside the Davidian compound and in the FBI command post. Koresh was God and Jamar was the infallible SAC.

For example, Jamar supported the use of tactical force and pressure. Those who suggested that this strategy was counterproductive were treated with derision, and even replaced. Some tactical agents even referred to their fellow dissenting agents as "Davidians." I have no doubt that people inside the compound who questioned Koresh got tagged with similar labels.

When groupthink dominates decision making, there is a low probability of a successful outcome. When *both* groups are ensnared in this dynamic, disaster is within reach.

That siege was the longest fifty-one days of my life. It was enormously stressful. It was like a nightmare you couldn't wake up from, or like watching two trains on the same track running full steam ahead at each other. You know what's going to happen but there's nothing you can do. Catastrophe is inevitable and the tension of waiting for it is high.

We were up at five in the morning, going into the motel diner to get breakfast. The HRT guys would be coming off their night shift and they'd see us. They'd have heard rumors of some kind during the night about what we were doing and they'd confront us. "Hey, we heard you were sending steaks in to these people. What the hell are you doing?"

"We sent orange juice in," we'd explain, "with a mike planted in the box."

The day started like that with attacks from our own people and usually went downhill from there. We were seen as the guys dragging the anchor, as an obstacle to a hard-ass tactical resolution. We were creating problems. By the end of each day, I was just emotionally gutted.

[7]

In the hangar, the negotiators had two adjoining rooms. The outside room was used for meetings and strategizing, but the actual negotiations occurred in the inner room. The furnishings were spare, no more than what was needed—a table, some chairs, and a phone. One agent would conduct the negotiations while others would monitor the situation and slip their written suggestions to him. It was a tried-and-true system.

Yet as frustration from both sides grew over the

weeks, cartoons got taped onto the door and walls to provide some comic relief. One depicted a Viking seated at a table slapping a spiked mace in the palm of his hand while talking to a second Viking at the table. A third Viking, looking cross-eyed and blowing bubble gum, is entering the room. The cartoon was labeled. The Viking slapping the mace in the palm of his hand was the HRT leader, the second Viking was Jamar, and the clueless, cross-eyed, bubble gum-blowing Viking was chief negotiator Gary Noesner. In the cartoon, the HRT leader is slapping the mace in the palm of his hand while saying to Jamar, "Look, boss, we've been out there for twenty-four days already and I think . . ."

Another cartoon depicted four cavemen inside a cave. Two cavemen (labeled HRT) are threatening a third (labeled Noesner) with a spear and a club as a fourth takes notes. The Noesner character is saying, "Look, guys, I'm just the negotiator. I'm not making the decisions."

And we were not alone in the search for some humor. At one point, when Koresh felt closed in, from a window he hung a banner that said, "God help us. We want the press." Some clever media people were quick to respond from their encampment. Their banner read: "God help us. We *are* the press."

Over the next six weeks, we talked with Koresh and fifty-three of his followers. During the first week, we had appealed to Koresh's rational side and that strategy had resulted in the release of twenty-one children and four adults.

However, by March, Koresh was emphasizing his deity. "It's true I am the Christ," he insisted. "I am the Lord . . . but it's better to be called the son. I am the Son of God . . . the anointed one. I teach the seven seals. It's the fulfillment of prophecy . . . If you reject the seven seals, you're rejecting me. If you reject me, you reject my father and then judgment cannot be diverted. You will be punished. And your great nation, the United States of America . . . the lamblike beast of Revelation thirteen is going to be made an example of above all nations and it's all going to come to an end in one hour. This is what Revelation is talking about—the fall of Babylon."

He played this to his advantage as he released only those who were of no value to him: older people, children not his own, and a couple of young males because they were drinking his whiskey. We would take them regardless of who they were and negotiate for more.

In the meantime, we were coming up with more tactics. One was to undermine the group's solidarity. We appealed to the parents to protect their children, and had the children who were already released speak on tape to ask their parents to join them. We reassured the parents that if they came out, they would be reunited with their children and would not be harmed. We scheduled press conferences, which we knew the Davidians watched, to express our legitimate concern for their safety and to clarify inaccurate speculations. However, the mind-set that stymied our efforts was best revealed by Davidian Wayne Martin, the Harvard-educated attorney, who quoted from the gospel of Matthew 10:37: "He that loveth father or mother more than me is not worthy of me; and he that loveth son or daughter more than me is not worthy of me." And so it was for the Davidians.

Another tactic was to undermine the Davidians' trust in Koresh. We knew that he was being duplicitous. He would tell our negotiators one thing and then tell his flock another. We recorded him on the phone, and when his words undermined his preaching, we'd broadcast that over a loudspeaker for everyone inside to hear, hoping to enlighten at least a few of them.

A primary goal that crystalized as I assessed their backgrounds and behavior was to drive a wedge between Koresh and Steve Schneider, his chief lieutenant. If the negotiators could get Schneider to reconsider his allegiance to Koresh and come out, we thought it would be a huge break in the group solidarity. Toward this end, they spoke with Schneider for well over a hundred hours.

We knew a few things about him that shaped our strategy. He had a degree in religion from the University of Hawaii. He had attempted to start his own church, but that had failed. After a severe disappointment in the Seventh Day Adventist Church, he'd become Koresh's principal evangelist. He and his wife, Judy, then moved to Texas from Hawaii, and Judy became a leading female figure in Koresh's drive for discipleship, while Schneider became one of Koresh's confidants. At one point, during his "New Light" campaign, Koresh had claimed Judy as his own wife. Schneider had been disappointed, because they'd been trying for several years to have a child together. She quickly became pregnant by Koresh, which had to be yet another blow. We hoped that we could use that to inflame some anger. Working on him, we urged him to think about the situation:

"Steve," we'd say, "just look at yourself. You're on a spiritual quest, which is noble and honorable, and we respect that. But just step back and look at where you are. You've been in a deadly gun battle with federal agents. Meanwhile, some other guy has told you that you can't have sex with your wife, but he can. The Bible takes a pretty clear position on adultery, doesn't it, Steve? How did you get into this situation? You didn't really want your spiritual quest to come to this, did you?"

And he'd say, "Well, no."

"Then reclaim your life. Get your wife and daughter and come on out."

Yet even as we softened his resolve, we knew we had to get over some major hurdles. The first was getting Schneider to admit to himself that he had made a mistake in following Koresh. After all, he had given Koresh all of his worldly possessions and his wife. To admit this was all a mistake would be a hell of a step. Second, if he came to that conclusion, he would have to be willing to do something about it. The negotiators had him seriously rethinking his situation, but once off the phone, he would again come under the spell of Koresh. It was a clear case of cognitive dissonance. The options are there, but the one that   the most will inevitably negate the other. Koresh carried more weight with Schneider than did the FBI.

To deal directly with Koresh, we tried several different strategies. One was to appeal to tangible things that he coveted, i.e., power, control, and the ability to have sex with lots of women, all within the context of being a divine prophet. I spoke about this with Dr. Park Dietz several times while he was in Waco and he added an insightful theological dimension. Koresh, he said, seemed to have assumed the identity of the biblical "Cyrus," which is "Koresh" (death) in Hebrew. Cyrus was to have 140 wives and to deliver the message of the seven seals. So we decided we would try to get Koresh to "discover" that he had not yet had all of his 140 wives and wouldn't be getting any more while inside the compound. It was a sound approach, as it validated rather than undermined his self-image as a prophet.

We also relied on a strategy of drawing a distinction between ourselves and the ATF, and with the concurrence of those agents, casting them as the dark, demonic force of evil. In that context, we offered Koresh a face-saving scenario that took the responsibility off him. "You didn't know who it was," we'd say, "you didn't know that there were arrest and search warrants or even that it was a government agency. It was just a bunch of guys in ninja gear pointing guns. Of course you were right to defend yourself. When you found out who it was, you called 911 and tried to stop the shooting. There's the evidence. David, you need to render unto Caesar what is Caesar's and unto God what is God's. This must be resolved, at least partially, in Caesar's court and you've got a good chance of winning there as well. The last time you were in court you defended yourself and you won. Now you'll be in a federal court, commanding worldwide attention, probably with live coverage. The courtroom will give you months of coverage. It will be a continuation of your message throughout the world. You need to emerge as a successful prophet, not a dead one."

He loved that. He was already on the covers of national magazines, and this possibility resonated with him. However, he also remained painfully aware of the negative consequences of coming out.

He understood that there were four dead ATF agents. That wasn't going away. He was also worried about other charges. He had persuaded all of his followers that, among other things, his seed was divine and therefore only he could procreate. He was impregnating girls fourteen years old, perhaps younger. Whether that was consistent with "God's law" was apparently debatable among the Davidians, but as far as man's law was concerned, there wasn't any debate. Sexually abusing children is a crime. So as much as Koresh craved celebrity, he remained keenly aware of the consequences for murdering law-enforcement officers and molesting children.

[8]

One morning I drew a cup of coffee from the aluminum urn in the negotiator's ready room, geared up for more tension, and turned around to find Gary Noesner putting on his jacket. Round shouldered and a bit rumpled at times, he looked as tired as I felt. Although with a good sense of humor he usually kept things light, his expression could be intense, as it was that morning. Gary nodded toward the door and said, "Let's take a walk."

I knew something was up. This was not for the other guys to hear. "Sure," I said. "Let's go."

We climbed down the stairs to the main hangar where an unmarked Boeing 747 was being serviced. Standing over sixty feet tall, the plane dwarfed us as we walked under its nose and toward the outside door.

The morning sun was cold and brilliant. We walked away from the hangar, along the barbed-wire fence that paralleled the runway. That fence may have kept out curious kids, but the strong, steady wind cutting across the prairie was undeterred. Gary turned his head slightly toward me and said, "I'm having a problem getting Jamar and the Bureau to separate from the ATF. Whatever inroads we've made during negotiations get negated every day in the joint press briefings. The Davidians are watching, and there we are, standing shoulder to shoulder with the ATF. We're sending them a mixed message."

He was clearly right. We were trying to convince the Davidians that we believed the ATF was in the wrong and then we showed up on national television, holding hands with them. "Mixed message, my ass," I said. "We look hypocritical, incompetent, or both. Have you suggested having separate press conferences? Or at least having a distinct separation between the Bureau and ATF during the same conference?"

"Several times, but there's a real disconnect. Headquarters wants to present a unified FBI/ATF front to the media and the public—you know, we're all law enforcement and we are all in this thing together. I'm not even sure the people making those decisions at headquarters realize what we're trying to accomplish down here. Jamar has heard this from me and has obviously dismissed it. I was thinking that if you and your unit back at Quantico could make a pitch at headquarters, explaining how this joint media approach is undermining our strategy, it couldn't hurt."

I considered that. "For the most part," I pointed out, "headquarters is giving Jamar his head on this thing, so he'll be a hard sell. And headquarters also wants the PR value of having us all united. Even if Jamar sees the wisdom of what you're saying, I don't think he'll go for it. I think he'll view it as some sort of pussified cop-out, like we're becoming Davidians. Bottom line, it's the right thing to do and I'll give it a try, but I'm afraid we're pissing into the wind."

I'm sorry to say that my instincts were right. Despite my calls back to SIOC, the joint FBI/ATF press briefings continued unabated. We began to wonder if anything we believed about the situation mattered.

Meanwhile the Title III intercepts, or "bugs," we were sending into the compound continued to provide us with some invaluable insight into the mind-set of Koresh and the Davidians. Koresh's animosity toward the government was evident in many of the conversations we picked up. For example, on March 13, he appeared to be giving some of his followers a pep talk when he said, "Christ is gonna win. No one's gonna stop it. That's what I want you to think about day and night. . . . What they've done to us will be done to them tenfold. They come jumping on us; they should have no complaints when God comes jumping on them. . . . See how they feel when their dicks are cut off . . ."

As things seemed to deteriorate, we had to rethink our position. Traditional negotiation strategy avoids face-to-face negotiation, but with fewer people coming out and Koresh remaining unrepentant, we broke with tradition and arranged a face-to-face meeting with Davidian representatives.

On March 15, in the rain, negotiator Byron Sage and Sheriff Jack Harwell had an hour-long meeting with Steve Schneider and Harvey Martin on a driveway about fifty yards from the compound. Harwell corralled Martin, leaving Byron to concentrate on Schneider. It was an amicable discussion and they agreed to talk again two days later. However, Koresh canceled that meeting. It seemed that Schneider and Martin were afraid they were being set up. Nonetheless, in a few days, there was an upswing in the situation.

On March 21, negotiators got seven people out. Once released, they called back in and advised that everything was fine, and the general tone of the messages from inside was that others would be coming out soon. That night, agents began blasting loud music into the compound, from Buddhist chants to obnoxious songs like "These Boots Are Made for Walking." Several times during the night, people inside asked that it be turned off. Finally, at 11:35 P.M. Schneider angrily relayed a defiant message from Koresh: "Because of the loud music, nobody is coming out." The next morning he spoke with negotiators for half an hour. Everybody inside remained angry.

That afternoon, a number of key people met at the command post to discuss this. Gary said, "Jeff, after getting seven people out yesterday, the night crew then blasted loud music into the compound. Now they're pissed and no one is coming out. What's going on?"

"It needed to be done," Jamar insisted, "because only seven people came out. That's not enough. If they don't like it, they can send out more people and then we'll knock off the noise. That's how it works."

"That's not how it works. We reward the behavior we want and punish the behavior that we don't want, not the other way around. It's trickle, flow, gush. Start with a trickle of people coming out, reward the trickle until it becomes a flow, and then reward the flow until it becomes a gush. Last night we punished the behavior that we want."

"You're missing the point, Gary," Jamar said angrily. "I *am* punishing the behavior I don't want. I don't want seven people coming out. I want them all coming out."

Dick Rogers, from the HRT, jumped in. "We can get those people out in thirty minutes," he said. "My men are trained, capable and ready to go. We've been screwing around for damn near a month now. It's clear that the negotiators can't get those people out, but we can."

Jamar agreed with him, accusing the negotiators of doing a poor job.

I was surprised by how angry and condescending he was with Gary and his team, and I grew increasingly concerned about the lack of coordination among all of us.

"Jeff," I said, "we're getting away from our fundamentals. Tactical maneuvers and negotiation strategy have to be coordinated if we are going to have even the slightest chance of talking these people out. Right now we have no coordinated strategy and your tactics are undermining negotiations."

Jamar looked at me and asked, "Do you *really* think we can negotiate everybody out of there?"

"I am confident that we can get more people out if we ease the tactical pressure," I assured him. "Whether we can get Koresh out is another question. If we can convince him that he's leading his people to safety but not diminish his status as a prophet, we've got a good chance."

The tension eased and we started to get back to work. It took into that evening to finalize another strategy, and at ten P.M. an offer signed by Jeff Jamar and Sheriff Jack Harwell was delivered to the compound. We weren't terribly optimistic, but if nothing else, it made Koresh deal with the issue. In effect, addressing Koresh, it said:

> In order to resolve the current situation peacefully, we are making you the following offer. Upon the departure of all people remaining in the Mount Carmel camp, we agree that:

1. You will be able to continue to communicate with any members of your congregation who will be with you at McLennan County Sheriff's Department if their attorney concurs. This will include your ability to hold worship services and will not interfere with your religious practices. ·

2. You will be afforded the opportunity to appear live on *American Talk* on the Christian Broadcast Network, hosted by Craig Smith. This offer is contingent upon all persons remaining in the Mount Carmel camp departing the premises beginning at ten A.M. and completing departure by twelve noon on March 23. The television crew at CBN headquarters in Virginia Beach, Virginia, will be available to arrange a live worldwide satellite broadcast from Waco. This is an extraordinary opportunity for you.

This met demands Koresh had previously made, plus added live media coverage of their exit—an attempt to offset paranoia about being "set up." It also appealed to his grandiosity. At 2:55 A.M., Koresh rejected the offer.

[9]

Among my responsibilities was consulting with child psychologist Dr. Bruce Perry, from Baylor University, who had evaluated the kids released from the compound.

He had learned a lot about their social and religious lives. Apparently, everything revolved around Koresh. The children all called him their father and referred to their natural parents as "dogs." Those children fathered by other men were "bastards." By age twelve, the children were usually split off from their mothers. The fathers, of course, were not allowed to live with their wives or children. The children did not understand the notion of a family unit, but they did know about the "whipping room," where Koresh wielded a paddle known as "the helper" to physically punish sin or disobedience. It left circular lesions an inch across on the children's buttocks. Dr. Perry would visit the Methodist home where the released Davidian children were housed. At one point, he was holding a five-month-old infant when a small girl approached him and asked, "Did you come here to kill the baby?"

The information Dr. Perry developed was consistent with everything else that we learned. All of the essential elements of a harmful apocalyptical group were present. Such groups are usually centered around a dominant charismatic leader, often uneducated, who is powerfully persuasive and verbally compulsive. The leader has an exaggerated need to control others, and his needs are central. The group is considered the sole and exclusively enlightened arbiter of truth; everything else is evil or in error. They believe that they have a transcendent mission to convert the world; therefore their role in history is of cosmic importance. They isolate themselves from the rest of the world, and their "specialness" is often reinforced through rituals, unique diets, or special clothing.

Such leaders and their followers may also use mental and physical degradation, especially with children, to maintain control. The group's tight structure reinforces conformity and members are not allowed to think for themselves. Those who need such structure are most vulnerable to its debilitating and cohesive effect. Despite the values with which they might have been raised, in their eyes, it is the group and their leader who decide what is right.

While we factored in advice from our psychological consultants, we declined to work with many of the religious consultants who were calling us with advice, and we were later criticized for that. In my opinion, the input of the religious scholars had some value, but it was limited. The fundamental question in that area was, what is this group's religion? My answer to that was Koreshianism. There was only one expert in that and he made it up as he went along. If the Koreshians had a doctrine, it was whatever David told them, and that changed from day to day, hour to hour, and sometimes minute to minute. He was the prophet, the chosen one, the sole arbiter of all truth. The primary issue wasn't interpreting a religious doctrine but understanding Koresh's psychopathology.

Yet we had endless offers. Besides several people who thought they were God and wanted to go in to set Koresh straight, we had religious scholars and others who were faxing in so much material that we experienced fax meltdown. On the secular end, a rock band said they could help by playing music known to have a demoralizing effect. We didn't accept their offer either. Even with these constant diversions, we were aware that nearly a month had passed and fewer people were emerging. Things did not look good.

[10]

On March 25, the negotiators reluctantly complied with Jamar's demand for new strategies. Rather than yield to Koresh's demands, they now made their own. They wanted a minimum of twenty people out by the end of the afternoon. We didn't hold out much hope that it would work, but with the pressure on, we wanted to ensure that by the time this went tactical no stone was left unturned. When no one emerged, HRT removed motorcycles and other vehicles from the compound. It had to be clear to Koresh that we were closing in for some purpose.

Two days later, Schneider denied Koresh's self-professed divinity and hinted to a negotiator that the FBI might burn the building to get them out. Then several days were taken up with meetings between Koresh, Schneider, and two lawyers. Once that was completed, Koresh decided that he wanted to spend Passover in the compound, but it turned out that he wasn't sure when Passover was, exactly. We had no choice but to wait. Then as that religious period neared an end, he announced that he would observe it for seven more days. Passover was officially at an end, but who could argue with God?

Koresh sent out four letters between April 10 and April 14. The April 10 letter was typical.

> I offer to you my wisdom. I offer to you my sealed secrets. How dare you turn away My invitations of mercy . . . Who are you fighting against? The law is Mine, the Truth is Mine . . . I AM your God and you will bow under my feet . . . I AM your life & your death. I AM the Spirit of the prophets and the Author of their testimonies. Look and see, you fools, you will not proceed much further. Do you think you have power to stop My will? . . . My seven thunders are to be revealed . . . Fear Me, for I have you in My

snare . . . I forewarn you, the Lake Waco area of Old
Mount Carmel will be terribly shaken.

On that same day, discussions about tear gas were resumed between FBI headquarters personnel and the
newly sworn attorney general, Janet Reno. There were
intermittent conversations with Koresh, who offered
only defiant ramblings, and meaningful talks appeared
to be stalled. He said that he needed time to write a
manuscript on the Seven Seals, and he was at work on
that now. We viewed this as just one more stalling tactic.

On April 17, the FBI received approval from Reno
to end the fifty-one-day standoff with nonlethal tear
gas. No one was coming out, and the sanitary conditions in the compound were deteriorating. The operation was getting expensive, and had no foreseeable
end. Tear gas was uncomfortable, but it would not
harm anyone. The HRT was instructed to use CS gas
over a period of forty-eight hours and then be ready to
capture people as they emerged. Arrest warrants were
obtained for every adult known to be inside, and search
warrants for the compound were in hand.

Tanks continued to remove vehicles from the front
of the compound. Tension was high, and it was clear
that Koresh was upset, especially when they moved his
black Camaro. He called the command center and said,
"If you don't stop what you're doing, this could be the
worst day in law-enforcement history."

A sniper with a good view of the compound reported
that someone from inside had hung a sign on a window
that read, "Flames await." It was an ominous message.

In the predawn hours of April 19, Texas state troopers went door-to-door at the houses near the compound, telling people to remain inside, and warned that

there might be some noise. Then just after dawn on Monday morning, April 19, Byron Sage phoned the compound and demanded one last time that Koresh and his followers surrender peacefully. They refused. At six A.M., Sage called again and warned those inside. Tear gas was going to be inserted into the building. It was not an assault; no agents would enter the building and no one should fire a weapon. The Davidians threw the telephone outside—a sign to us that all negotiations were over. At that point, Sage began broadcasting the following message from a prepared script.

"We are in the process of placing tear gas into the building. This is not an assault. We are not entering the building. This is not an assault. Do not fire your weapons. If you fire, fire will be returned. Do not shoot. This is not an assault. The gas you smell is non-lethal tear gas. The gas will temporarily render the building uninhabitable. Exit the compound now and follow instructions. You are not to have anyone in the tower. The tower is off limits. No one is to be in the tower. Anyone observed to be in the tower will be considered to be an act of aggression and will be dealt with accordingly. If you come out now, you will not be harmed. Follow all instructions. Come out with your hands up. Carry nothing. Come out of the building and walk up the driveway toward the Double-E Ranch Road. Walk toward the large Red Cross flag. Follow all instructions of the FBI agents in the Bradleys. Follow all instructions. You are under arrest. This standoff is over. We do not want anyone hurt. Follow all instructions. This is not an assault. Do not fire any weapons. We do not want anyone hurt. Gas will continue to be delivered until everyone is out of the building."

As Sage made this announcement, two combat engineering vehicles (CEVs) approached the buildings, and probing the fragile walls with their long metal booms, they began to spray tear gas through nozzles into the compound. Noncombustible carbon dioxide propelled the gas to avoid the possibility of fire. Nearby sat an Abrams tank and nine Bradley vehicles. Everyone was under orders that if children were in any apparent danger, the mission was to be aborted.

The moment agents began pumping in tear gas, the Davidians began to fire, and right then the scope and pace of the operation changed. The initial plan was for this to be an incremental operation taking as long as two to three days. Now everything escalated. While under fire, the CEVs kept inserting gas. Sage continued to cry over the loudspeakers, "This is not an assault. Do not shoot. We are not entering your compound."

The local hospital, Hillcrest Baptist Medical Center, was on alert, and about a mile away ambulances stood by. No one was supposed to get hurt. It looked as if it was going to be a long morning for us all. The wind was fierce and we knew that couldn't be good for the tactical teams. Byron continued to implore Koresh to lead everyone to safety. "Don't do this to your people. Be a messiah. Lead them out." Koresh stalked around in the compound, yelling, "Get your gas masks on."

By noon, the CEVs had made a total of six gas deliveries, and all the while, Sage kept saying, "David, you have the capability right now, *right now,* of calling an end to it. Do not subject yourself or your children to any more discomfort. You have some precious kids in there and we do not intend to, nor do we want to inflict any injury on those kids. The same applies to you and your followers. Please, David. It is time to bring this to an end."

There was only silence from the compound.

Shortly after noon, one of our sniper/observer teams reported seeing a man who was wearing a gas mask and who appeared to be lighting something. Shortly after that, they saw a small fire in that area. Sage got back on the loudspeakers. "Don't do this to those people. This is not the way to end it."

At 12:10 P.M., smoke was seen coming from the second floor, on the right side of the building, as well as from the back, near the kitchen. Because of the dry wind and fragile wood, the fire raced through the building like a wind tunnel. Bob Ricks, one of the subordinate SACs, cried out, "Oh my God, they're killing themselves!"

Agents close to the buildings heard gunfire, and they assumed that the people inside had decided to end it. A loud explosion rocked the building and a giant plume of black smoke filled the sky. Helicopters and fixed-wing aircraft flew back and forth, recording what they could, but no one knew how dangerous it might be to get close. Byron continued to plead with those inside, "If you can't see, walk toward the loudspeaker, follow the voice." Another explosion erupted and we saw the Davidians' ammunition bunker blow up.

Ruth Riddle, one of the Davidians, was upstairs in her room with her gas mask on, holding her Bible. She made her way to a hole in the wall and jumped. An HRT agent spotted her, left his armored vehicle, and ran into the smoke and flames to rescue her. She seemed to be turning around to go back in when he grabbed her, yelling, "Where are the kids? What did you do with them?" She refused to speak, and she fought with him as he dragged her to safety.

Another Davidian, Renos Avraam, was on the roof of the front of the building. Agents drove a Bradley vehicle up to offer him a way to escape, but Avraam waved them off. He then jumped off the roof and walked toward one of the Bradleys with his hands raised. Four other Davidians left through the front right of the building. All refused to disclose the whereabouts of the children.

But there was one last hope. We had heard that buried on the property was a school bus that the Davidians had planned to use as a bunker. We thought that perhaps the children had been ushered there to avoid the flames. Sixteen HRT members made their way around the fire and into an underground concrete pit that led to the buried bus. They told us later that it was pitch black and they had to activate the flashlights mounted on the barrel of their rifles. Rats swam around them as they pushed past the human waste and body parts that floated in the thigh-deep water. They feared that the door to the tunnel might be booby-trapped, but crashed through it anyway. The air inside the tunnel was cool and free of gas. They rushed down the tunnel to the bus. To their disappointment, it was empty. That meant the children were still in the building and were probably dead.

Firefighters arrived but had to keep their distance due to gunfire and the possibility of more explosions. Around twelve forty-five, they entered the building and found numerous incinerated bodies. Most were well beyond immediate identification.

By the end of that horrifically painful day, while nine Davidians survived, at least seventy-four died, including twenty children under the age of fourteen, with the majority of children under the age of seven. While rumors spread that Koresh had gotten away through underground tunnels, his body was later identified by dental records. He'd been shot in the head at very close range. Agents found his body, along with that of Steve Schneider, in the area of the communications room. Schneider had also been head-shot and the medical examiner determined that the muzzle of a gun was inside his mouth when it was fired. The deaths of Koresh and Schneider were ruled to be either suicide or consensual execution (suicide by proxy). Many of the other victims had died from gunshot wounds and one child had been stabbed to death. Over 100 firearms and 400,000 rounds of ammunition were eventually recovered from the scene.

[11]

There were reasonable questions asked afterward. Why did the ATF go forward with the initial raid knowing that they had lost the element of surprise? Why were alternative plans dismissed, such as luring Koresh out of the compound where he could be detained while the search warrant was executed? How did the ATF acquire such faulty information? It turned out that the guns were not secured, as they had believed, but were readily available—and thus more dangerous. Prior to the raid, the ATF had conducted no surveillance of the compound, but the raid planners did not know this. These same planners also believed that only 75 people lived in the compound. In fact, there were closer to 125 people present on February 28.

As for the main event, accusations were flung from

both sides that the other had started the fire, but there's clear evidence that the Davidians did it. When the matter came to court later, we produced audiotapes of people inside the compound joking the day before the explosion about "catching on fire," and Schneider had stated that another Davidian had always wanted to be a "charcoal briquette." On the actual day, there were recorded conversations, which once they were professionally enhanced, provided clear evidence that the Davidians had poured fuel early in the morning of April 19 and then burned down their own compound.

Our Title III intercepts recorded the following statements:

"David said pour it, right?"

"Did you pour it yet?"

"David said we have to get the fuel on."

"Have you got the fuel . . . the fuel ready?"

"So we only light it first when they come in with the tank, right?"

"I want a fire on the front . . . you two can go."

"Keep that fire going . . . keep it."

A subsequent independent arson investigation showed that the fire was deliberately set from inside the compound. Three separate points of origin were identified and all three flamed up. In addition, Davidians who survived the fire have acknowledged that other Davidians started it. Graeme Craddock stated that he observed other Davidians pouring fuel in the chapel area of the complex on April 19, 1993, and that another group member, Mark Wendel, yelled, "Light the fire!" Davidian Clive Doyle told the Texas rangers on April 20 that Davidians had spread Coleman fuel in designated locations throughout the complex, although he declined to name names.

There were congressional hearings, the FBI conducted its own internal evaluation, and independent experts reviewed the incident and made recommendations. All of this resulted in a number of positive changes.

Some structural changes occurred within the FBI, such as combining HRT, negotiations, and the operational arm of the Behavioral Science Unit into one group, called the Critical Incident Response Group (CIRG). Command is no longer determined by geography, but by training and experience. Certain SACs have received advanced training in handling such matters, and they will assume control regardless of field division placement. Negotiators and behavioral science agents will have more involvement in the decision-making process and more responsibility for developing and maintaining contact with outside experts in various fields.

However, the real take-home message from what happened is *prevention*. The primary lesson of Waco is to avoid getting into a similar situation in the future. Once people have been killed, no one wins, regardless of the final outcome. To avoid triggering this type of violence, it's important to understand how imperative boundary control is to a paranoid group, especially to its leader.

Boundaries separate and distinguish the group from the rest of the world. Good boundary control allows a group to screen out "dangerous" outsiders and their ideas. This increased isolation translates for the leader into more power, influence, and control over the group. Isolation cultivates the malignant growth of paranoia, intensifying the group's need to protect itself from the threat of the outside world. It comes as no surprise, then, that violence often erupts at that boundary. I think that neither the ATF nor the FBI fully appreciated the significance of boundaries as trip wires for violence.

We also need to understand those groups that need no such triggers to become violent. The first known successful use of a biological weapon in the United States occurred in 1984 when a group led by Bhagwan Shree Rajneesh used *Salmonella typhimurium* to poison over 750 residents of Wasco County, Oregon. In 1995, the religious group Aum Shinrikyo simultaneously attacked five different trains with sarin gas as they converged on the center of Tokyo. Thousands of people were poisoned and twelve died. Groups such as Heaven's Gate and the Order of the Solar Temple have turned their violence inward, committing mass suicide. And then, of course, Al Qaeda and other Islamic terrorists have carried out numerous attacks in the name of Allah.

While most religious groups, including new and unconventional movements, are nonviolent, the threat of religiously oriented violence has been frequent and severe enough that it cannot be ignored. The threat can be from individuals or groups, large or small, homegrown or from the far corners of the earth. Predatory parasites and religious terrorists emerge from virtually all religious backgrounds, twisting and contorting traditional religions into grotesque instruments of intolerance, repression, and apocalyptic violence.

If law enforcement waits for actual violence before intervening, it's too late. There should be a more effective approach. I believe that adapting the public health model, with its emphasis on primary prevention, is the best way to minimize the risk for violence in many contexts.

Primary prevention begins with good intelligence

and a benevolent, nonconfrontational approach by law enforcement. This is especially important with groups that are prone to paranoia and mistrust. This softer, smarter approach can diffuse some paranoia and allow mutual trust to develop over time. It also allows for early detection of any antecedent risk markers for violence. This is not a radical approach, but simply a variation on standard community policing programs being used throughout the country. When officers and the people in the community they serve (including religious groups) get to know one another in the normal course of daily routines, then stereotypes can be overcome, concerns addressed, and a mutually beneficial relationship built on trust and understanding can develop. Everyone has a stake in the safety and security of their community.

Making contact with a group while their boundaries are still permeable is wisdom in action and provides the best chance to avert violence. Sheriff Harwell had achieved that relationship with Koresh and the Davidians, but unfortunately, the ATF failed to appreciate his potential function for reducing the risk of violence. Had the ATF asked, it's likely that Sheriff Harwell could have persuaded Koresh to meet him away from the compound prior to the raid. Koresh could then have been detained while the search warrants were executed, or the ATF could have returned to the compound with Koresh to conduct their search. In either case, the chance for violence would have been reduced and perhaps eliminated.

But even the best violence-prevention efforts will not be 100 percent effective. We must accept the fact that there will be standoffs between unconventional groups and law enforcement. One of the self-inflicted failures for the FBI at Waco was the departure from its traditional methods for handling such situations. There was no unified strategy in place. Tactical decisions were not coordinated with negotiation strategy, and, in fact, they were often at odds.

At the beginning, we got thirty-five people out with tried-and-true negotiation methods. Initially, we threatened force a little but not too much, and we were getting people out. The HRT people were frustrated because it was slow work. Koresh was playing his games, and Jamar was impatient. So when we were pressured to abandon what was working to step up the program, people stopped coming out. It wasn't that we didn't know how to handle the group. We just stopped doing it the way we normally would have.

After much external and internal probing, some appropriate administrative changes were made and the FBI saw the wisdom of returning to what works. It did so in 1996, in its next major standoff.

The longest standoff in law-enforcement history occurred between the FBI and the Freemen, a well-armed, paranoid, right-wing Christian-identity group in Montana. In this case, the FBI did not establish an armed perimeter around the Freemen during the standoff, nor did they use any military assault–type tactics or equipment. Instead they developed and followed a unified plan that coordinated tactical and negotiation strategy. During what turned out to be the standoff's last few days, the power to the Freemen's compound was cut, but that was done in support of negotiations rather than in spite of them. After eighty-one days, the Freemen, who had threatened to kill FBI agents and other law-enforcement officers, surrendered quietly, leaving over 100 guns inside their compound. Not a shot was fired, and no one was injured. By coordinating carefully chosen and mutually supportive techniques and strategies, violence was averted.

[12]

Approximately one year after the standoff in Waco began, eleven Davidians were tried on murder and conspiracy charges in a U.S. district courtroom in San Antonio. On February 26, 1994, the jury acquitted all defendants of the conspiracy and murder counts, but convicted five for aiding and abetting manslaughter and three others on weapons charges. The remaining three Davidians were acquitted of all charges. Some surviving Davidians and relatives of the deceased filed a wrongful death civil suit against the federal government. Yet on July 14, 2000, after a four-week trial, the jury returned a verdict for the defendants, the U.S. government. They found no evidence that government agents had fired indiscriminately or without provocation and no evidence that the government started the fire on April 19, 1993.

We do need to understand that in these situations, it's not about being bigger or stronger, or having more authority or firepower. Having 100 victories in 100 conflicts is not the highest skill. Defeating your opponent without a fight—that is the highest skill. Mature martial artists and sage leaders alike know this simple truth.

Even as I assisted the negotiators in Waco, I awaited word on the court date of one of the most interesting serial killers I've ever come across. The local investigators had consulted with me about six months before the siege at Waco, and eventually that case came to trial. In many ways, this offender was the opposite of Koresh, although both shared clear psychopathic qualities. He was the classic Hannibal Lecter—smooth, smart, secretive, and shockingly brutal. The rise and fall of this killer is a case I'll never forget.

8: The Poet's Shadow

> A bestial and violent man will go so far as to kill because
> he is under the influence of drink, exasperated, or
> driven by rage and alcohol. He is paltry. He does not
> know the pleasure of killing, the charity of bestowing
> death like a caress, of linking it with the play of the no-
> ble wild beasts: every cat, every tiger, embraces its prey
> and licks it even while it destroys it.
>
> —Colette

[1]

Blanka Bockova finished working at the butcher shop
in Prague, Czechoslovakia, on Tuesday, September 14,
1990, and headed to Wenceslas Square for a drink. The
square was originally a horse market, but now one
could see the BMWs, Mercedeses, and occasional
Lamborghini that had taken it over. With a series of
gaudy galleries, bars, cafes, shops, pricey hotels, and
greedy cabbies along the half-mile boulevard, it was
the place in Prague to see and be seen. Police sometimes played cat and mouse with the pimps and prostitutes there, and other times they turned a blind eye.
That made it a natural hangout for Blanka Bockova,
who enjoyed socializing and meeting new people. She
certainly wasn't a prostitute but might trade sex for fa-

vors or have sex with men whom she found charming. Her friends finished their drinks in a bar that Tuesday night around eleven forty-five P.M. and decided to head home, but Blanka wanted to stay. She said she would find her own way home. When they left, she was talking to a well-dressed man around forty years of age. That was not unusual, but what followed was.

The next morning, Blanka's body was found about seven-thirty A.M. on the forested bank of the Vlitava River, not far from her home. She was on her back, with her gray stockings knotted around her neck. She had been strangled, stabbed and beaten. While she still had on her gold ring, her clothing was missing, and she was covered in earth, leaves, and grass. There was no identification on her—it was later discovered in the river, along with her clothes—and the body had been left with its legs purposefully pulled apart, but there was no sign of rape. A tampon was still in place and investigators found no semen or other biological traces of the killer. Yet fresh bruises bore witness to her resistance. She had fought hard. The Prague authorities were stumped. They had no other cases like this, and other than the suave stranger her friends described to them, no leads.

About five weeks later and 470 kilometers south of Prague, in Graz, Austria, a street prostitute named Brunhilde Masser vanished. She had last been seen on October 26, 1990.

Then in Bregenz, Austria, a tourist city that borders Switzerland and Germany, Heidemarie Hammerer disappeared on December 5, 1990. She had worked as a prostitute for about ten years and was fairly streetwise. Twenty-six days later, on New Year's Eve, hikers discovered Hammerer's fully clothed body outside Bregenz, in a forested area. On closer examination, it appeared that she had been redressed after she was killed and then dragged through the woods. The cold weather had helped to preserve the remains, so the pathologist could determine that she had been strangled with a pair of panty hose, presumably hers. Also, her wrists were bruised from some kind of restraints, and while no sexual discharge was present, investigators did pick up quite a few red fibers on her that were inconsistent with her clothing. Her stomach was covered with leaves and she also still wore her jewelry. Her slip had been cut with a sharp instrument and used as a gag. She had bruising on her buttocks and elsewhere on her body. Her cause of death was listed as asphyxiation caused by suffocation and strangulation. The regional office of the Austrian Federal Police began an immediate investigation.

Then, five days after Hammerer's body was discovered in Bregenz, hikers stumbled across Brunhilde Masser's badly decomposed body in an isolated forest north of Graz. She lay prone in a streambed, naked, stabbed, and covered with leaves. She had probably been strangled with her panty hose, but the advanced state of decomposition made that difficult to determine with absolute certainty. Her buttocks had been partially eaten by animals and her clothing, handbag, and other personal property were missing. But she still had on her jewelry. The Austrian Federal Police assigned to the Styrian region took up this investigation.

These crimes were unusual for Austria, where prostitution is legal and sexual homicides are virtually nonexistent. Austria is generally noted for its decidedly positive attributes. Woven into the fabric of Austria's culture is a rich history of artistic and intellectual accomplishment. From Mozart in Salzburg to Strauss in Vienna; from Beethoven to Gustav Mahler; from the art of Gustav Klimt to the psychiatry of Sigmund Freud, Austrians have enriched the world immeasurably through their contributions. And so, even as an imperceptibly small but growing darkness began to spread across the landscape, there were new cultural accomplishments to be acknowledged and celebrated.

An artistic and literary icon was in the making in Vienna. The literati there had lionized a debonair novelist and award-winning playwright named Jack Unterweger. He was a self-made intellectual. Born to a prostitute, he had overcome his impoverished, illiterate background to become the darling of Viennese cafe intellectuals. He was much in demand, attending book launches, literary soirées, and opening nights. His book *Fegefeur* (*Purgatory*) was a bestseller and had been made into a highly acclaimed movie, and he was a frequent guest on television and radio talk shows. A traveling theater troupe presented his plays, and he sometimes attended their openings. A suave and stylish figure given to wearing white suits, red bow ties, silk shirts, and gold chains, he drove different cars but always with the same license plate: "JACK 1." Thriving on his celebrity, this single, talented, good-looking, gregarious author frequented the trendiest champagne bars and nightclubs in Vienna, where women fawned over him.

"Their panties would hit the floor when Jack walked in," one of his acquaintances said. "He was screwing all of Austria." Life was good to Herr Unterweger, but for others it was far less charitable.

Elfriede Schrempf vanished from her usual corner in Graz on March 7, 1991. Two days later, an unknown male made a series of harassing phone calls to an unlisted number that was written in Schrempf's private notebook. The caller made menacing remarks, mentioned Elfriede's name, and hung up.

In the five-month period from October 1990 through March 1991, one woman was murdered in Graz, one in Bregenz, and now a third was missing from Graz. The Austrian Federal Police, who knew nothing of Blanka Bockova's murder in Prague, were concerned, but it was far from clear that these events were related. The two in Graz might be connected, but what about the murder in Bregenz? How many offenders were there? Could there be one offender in Graz and another in Bregenz, or separate offenders in Graz and one in Bregenz or could a lone offender be good for all three? And maybe Elfriede Schrempf's disappearance wasn't a crime at all. Maybe she'd just run away. At this point, all anyone knew for sure was that she was missing.

If somehow all three cases were the work of the same offender, where should you begin to look for him? Was he an Austrian or could he have come from nearby Switzerland or Germany? There were no real leads, and just as the investigation had begun to fade, Ms. Schrempf's body was discovered October 5, 1991, when hikers found her skeletonized remains in a forested area outside Graz. She was covered by leaves, and wearing only a pair of socks. The investigation picked up.

Then, in less than a month, Silvia Zagler, Sabine

Moitzi, Regina Prem, and Karin Ergolu each vanished without a trace from the streets of Vienna. For these four cases, there were no crime scenes to process, no autopsies, no causes of death, no rape kits, and no physical evidence. It was disturbing. Austria averaged only one prostitute murder a year, and now in Vienna alone authorities were aware that there might have been four in less than a month. For streetwalkers, fear and foreboding permeated the atmosphere, while frustration dominated the Siecherheits Bureau at police headquarters. Modern Austria had never experienced a serial killer, but speculation about that possibility was running rampant.

The public's lust for information triggered an orgy of media coverage. This was not lost on Herr Unterweger, who saw the darkness at Vienna's doorstep as an opportunity to enhance his celebrity. By using his street smarts, charm, and intellect, he could obtain information unavailable to others. He would rocket above the rest of the press pack and might even uncover information that eluded the police. But first he had to know what the hookers knew and what the cops knew. So, with a tape recorder in hand, he hit the streets, interviewing hookers and investigators. As he published what he learned, the public's worst fears concerning the missing women were confirmed.

Sabine Moitzi's body was discovered on May 20 and Karin Ergolu's on May 23. Both had been dumped in forested areas outside Vienna, lying prone, and both had been strangled with an article of their own clothing. Ergolu's body was naked except for her jewelry and Moitzi wore only a jersey, pulled up. Moitzi's money was missing, but her clothing and handbag were found scattered within several yards of the body.

Ergolu had been subjected to blunt-force trauma on the face. Her handbag and clothing were missing, except for her shoes and the body stocking that the killer had forced down her throat. No more speculating about what might have happened to them. The darkness was tangible. With the recovery of these bodies, the storm of media coverage intensified and Unterweger was in its eye. He prepared a feature for an Austrian television program that often used his interviews with law-enforcement personnel and prostitutes on the street. People were impressed by his coverage and by his stated desire to give a voice to the dispossessed, caught in the underbelly of society as he once had been. Jack was in his glory. This unfolding story of unprecedented murder had the attention of virtually all of Austria— including a retired detective from Salzburg.

At that time, August Schenner had been retired for five years, but of course there really is no such thing as a "retired detective." That's an oxymoron. Sure, detectives turn in their badges and guns and have retirement parties and all of that, but that's just for show. Being a detective isn't just a job, it's a way of life, and as long as they're drawing breath, they're detectives. Schenner had been following the media coverage of the crimes in Vienna, Graz, and Bregenz, and when connections began to click, he picked up the phone and arranged to meet with his successors. He told them that he believed their quarry was hiding right under their noses in the person of the famous journalist and writer, Johann Jack Unterweger.

They were incredulous, so Schenner took them back to two murders that had occurred nearly two decades earlier. In 1974, one woman had been strangled with her undergarments and dumped in the woods, while the other, a prostitute, had been strangled with her stockings and a necktie. Adhesive tape had been applied to her mouth and her body had been thrown into a lake, near Salzburg. Schenner carefully laid out the investigations, pointed to the similarities among the crimes, and stated that Unterweger had been convicted of the first murder, but was not charged in the second one, primarily because he'd already been given a life sentence. Schenner had actually interviewed him for seven hours in the prison, and he had been uncooperative. So were the authorities, who saw no point in pursuing the second case. In fact, Schenner had gotten the impression that Unterweger was running the prison, and he thought it was important to note that just four months before the recent string of murders had begun, Herr Unterweger, acclaimed writer, had been paroled.

The investigators listened carefully and then conducted their own thorough background investigation on Jack Unterweger. Just who was he and exactly what had he done?

[2]

Born to an Austrian prostitute, Theresia Unterweger, on August 16, 1952, Jack was immediately abandoned. In fact, his mother had been behind bars while pregnant with him, as if showing him his own fate before he was even born. He never knew who his father was, although it was rumored that an American soldier had fathered him. For seven years, Jack lived with his alcoholic, womanizing grandfather under conditions of neglect and abuse. Then he was shuttled between foster situations. His first arrest for assault, at age sixteen, involved an attack on a prostitute, and between the ages of sixteen and twenty-five, he had committed fifteen separate offenses, including burglary, car theft, receiving stolen property, and abduction of a minor female. He had also forced a young woman into acts of prostitution and taken the money she had earned. During those years, he was in and out of prison, and by the age of twenty-four, he went in for murder.

The victim was Margaret Schaefer, eighteen, who was a friend of Barbara Scholz, a prostitute Jack knew. Together they robbed Schaefer's house and then lured her into a car and took her into the woods. With a belt from her coat, Jack tied her hands behind her back, beat her, removed her clothes, and demanded certain sexual acts that would gratify him. She refused, so he hit her in the head with a steel pipe. Then he used her bra to strangle her to death, leaving her nude body faceup in the forest, covered with leaves.

Scholz later gave the police a complete statement about the crime. When they questioned Jack, they had all the details, so he broke down and confessed. In a Salzburg court, he admitted to the murder, saying in his defense, "I envisioned my mother in front of me and I killed her."

The forensic psychologist who examined him, Dr. Klaus Jarosch, pronounced him an emotionally impoverished, sexually sadistic psychopath with narcissistic and histrionic tendencies. "He tends to sudden fits of rage and anger," Jarosch wrote. "His physical activities are enormously aggressive, with sexually sadistic perversion . . . He is an incorrigible perpetrator." If ever released, the doctor added, this man would certainly kill again.

In 1976, Unterweger was convicted of murder and sentenced to life in prison.

That's when things took an unusual twist. While he went into prison illiterate, he used the time there to learn to read and then to write. Eventually he was writing poems, short stories, and plays that got some attention in the outside world. In 1984, his prison autobiography, *Fegefeur,* was a bestseller and his rage-filled tale, "Endstation Zuchthaus" ("Terminus Prison") won a prestigious literary prize.

"I wielded my steel rod among prostitutes in Hamburg, Munich, and Marseilles," he wrote. "I had enemies and I conquered them through my inner hatred."

His memoir, which detailed his life since childhood, was a bit more literary in places. It begins in despair: "My sweaty hands were bound behind my back, with steel chains snapped around my wrists. The hard pressure on my legs and back makes me realize that my only escape is to end it. I lay awake, removed from the liberating unconsciousness of the sheep. Bathed in shit, trembling. My miserable small dreams are a daily reminder. Anxiously I stare into the unknown darkness of the still night outside. There's security in darkness. I try to divert my thoughts from wondering about the time. I ask only for the immediate moment, for in that lies my strength. It's still night, already late into the night, getting closer to morning."

Later in the piece, he says about himself, "I was no knave, but a beast, a devil, an ungrateful child who was happy to be bad. I had no remorse." He spoke of his hatred "internally burning," and yet the literary critics who so admired him failed to see that he had not been cured at all. He was a cauldron of pent-up rage.

Jack painted himself as a tragic victim. In one passage, he talked about his lonely sex life, how he thought endlessly about anonymous naked women and how he longed to have them. To him, they were meant for his pleasure. He felt most sorry for himself on his birthday, as he performed clandestine self-comforting activities under the blanket, out of the guard's sight. To him it was all "the feeling of a despised emptiness."

Critics, other writers, and prison reformers embraced him for his brutal honesty and the way he'd confronted his past. For some reason, they found his egocentric complaints to be insightful and they suggested that he was a good example of how art could redeem a criminal. Journalists began to contact him in prison, and in one interview in 1989, he revealed his duplicitous nature when he said he felt that prostitutes were of better character than secretaries who went on business trips with their married bosses. "For me, the prostitute is an honest woman," he said. "And one must be conscious of the social role that she plays."

Eventually the public and press demanded that Jack's life sentence be commuted. He was a citizen, they said, who could make a contribution. On May 23, 1990, after serving only fifteen years, he won parole, and was determined never to go back.

This latest series of crimes had begun a few months after he was released. This didn't prove that Jack was a killer, but investigators thought it was worth a look. Jack was beginning to stand out from the rest of the press pack, but not for the reasons he had anticipated. He had gone from being just another talking head to being a serious suspect.

The police then instituted a discreet surveillance on him to see exactly what he was doing. To their disappointment, he did nothing suspicious. He went about his business, meeting literary colleagues and dining with various women. Then, on June 11, three days into the surveillance, he flew to Los Angeles to write freelance articles for some Austrian magazines about crime in that city. He was now beyond their surveillance.

[3]

During the five weeks that Jack was in Los Angeles, the prostitute murders in Austria stopped. Dr. Ernst Geiger, the most experienced detective on the force and the number two man in the Austrian Federal Police, took charge of the investigation. Jack was a suspect and they needed to investigate him further, either to eliminate him or to tighten their case. They had to tread lightly but purposefully. The last thing Geiger or the investigators wanted was to be accused of targeting Unterweger simply because of his past transgressions. Through his credit-card receipts at hotels, restaurants, and rental-car agencies, they began to piece together Jack's movements.

Over the next several months, the authorities determined that Jack had been in Graz in October when Brunhilde Masser was murdered and again in March when Elfriede Schrempf was murdered. He was in Bregenz in December when Heidemarie Hammerer was murdered and a witness identified Unterweger as the man Ms. Hammerer had last been seen with right before she disappeared. On that night, this witness said, the man had worn a brown leather jacket and a red scarf. Red fibers had been found on her body.

They also determined that Unterweger had been in Prague the previous September. When they contacted authorities there, they learned that Jack's visit had coincided with the unsolved murder of Blanka Bockova. When the four women had been abducted and murdered in Vienna, Jack was there. The darkness was revealing its face. While it was difficult to believe that all of this could be just coincidence, probable cause for arrest was lacking and proof beyond a reasonable doubt was a long way off. But there was enough evidence to warrant an interview with Jack.

On October 22, 1991, officers of the Criminal Investigation Bureau in Vienna questioned Unterweger about the Austrian murders. Interestingly, the lead interviewer already knew his suspect: Earlier that summer, Unterweger had questioned *him* for an article about the series of murders. The investigators hoped that their interest in him might pressure him and trigger a confession—a technique that had worked with him before. Jack admitted that he consorted with hookers for his writing and for sex, but when they mentioned the names of the victims, he denied knowing any of them. He insisted that since he had no driver's license, he did not drive his car but had friends drive for him. The police knew this was a lie, but it didn't move them any closer to solving the murders. He had no real alibis, but investigators had nothing else to go on. Their evidence was circumstantial at best, so for the time being they had to give it up.

Yet now Jack knew he was a suspect, as did his friends in the media, and they could not understand why. He wrote more articles about the mishandling of the investigation and many of his colleagues took his side. Most of them jumped on his bandwagon with the idea that, "The chance of me knowing a serial killer is one in a hundred million, so the chance of Jack Unter-weger being a serial killer is zero." They had a vested interest in their original opinion that Jack was "cured." Those who fought for his freedom decried his "perse-cution," complicating matters for the investigators.

The murders had stopped, but the radar screen wasn't completely blank. Regina Prem, who had disap-peared at the end of April 1991, was still missing. The following October—around the time Jack was being interrogated—Prem's husband and son, who had un-listed numbers, received telephone calls from a man who claimed to be her killer. He accurately described what she'd been wearing the night she disappeared. He was her executioner, he said, and God had ordered him to do it. She had been left in "a place of sacrifice" with her face "turned toward hell." He also said, "I gave eleven of them the punishment they deserved." Three months later, in January 1992, her husband found five empty cigarette packs of the brand that Regina pre-ferred rolled up in his mailbox. Among those packs was a passport photo of her son that Regina had carried with her in her purse.

Ernst Geiger went around questioning Austrian prostitutes, who knew Jack and described him as a reg-ular customer who insisted they wear handcuffs during sex. That was consistent with the man who had mur-dered the victims. They would continue to watch him. Geiger then tracked down the BMW Jack had driven when he was released from prison. He'd sold it, buying a VW Passat. They didn't think they'd find evidence but, surprisingly, they did find a hair fragment. Al-though it was a long shot, they sent it for analysis.

Manfred Hochmeister, at the Institut fur Rechtsmedi-

zin in Berne, Switzerland, looked at the hair and found
that there was sufficient skin on the root to perform a
successful DNA analysis with the PCR technique. They
compared it to the DNA of each of the victims and
found that it matched the first victim, Blanka Bockova
from Prague. That placed the strangled woman with
Jack Unterweger, since he'd driven the car at the time,
but it only meant that she'd gotten into the car. Still, this
match was helpful in getting a warrant to search his
apartment in Vienna.

When investigators arrived, Jack was not at home,
but police found a menu and receipts from a seafood
restaurant in Malibu, California, and photographs of
Unterweger posing with female members of the Los
Angeles Police Department. They also found a brown
leather jacket and a red scarf, which they seized from
the apartment.

On a hunch, Geiger contacted the LAPD. He asked
about unsolved murders there and discovered that the
authorities in L.A. were investigating three seemingly
linked prostitute killings. Comparing dates with detectives Jim Harper and Fred Miller, Geiger realized that
all three had occurred when Unterweger was in town.
Looking further into the matter and using the recovered receipts, he learned that the places where each
victim had last been seen alive were all near one of the
seedy hotels in which Unterweger had stayed.

Now, for the first time, the LAPD had a viable suspect. The detectives did some digging and discovered
that Jack had shown up at the Los Angeles Police Department and introduced himself as a European author
studying crime. He convinced them that he should be
afforded the courtesy of a "ride-along." The patrol offi-

cers chauffeured him around L.A. to show him the areas where streetwalkers plied their trade. He paid close attention, charming his hosts and even having a souvenir picture taken with several female officers. He actually did write some articles, which concentrated heavily on prostitution. In one he wrote, "Real life in L.A. is dominated by a tough struggle for survival, by the broken dreams of thousands who come to the city and an equal number who leave, sometimes dead."

The detectives were bemused. This guy had actually gotten the police to show him where to find potential victims. If he was the killer they were seeking, he was brazen.

Back in Switzerland, analysts at the University of Berne had finished their examination of the leather jacket and red scarf that had been removed from Unterweger's apartment. Fibers from these items were consistent with those found on the body of Heidemarie Hammerer. As far as the probable cause needed for an arrest warrant was concerned, that put them over the top.

In February 1992, a judge signed the warrant. Just in case there was trouble, a SWAT team went to Jack's residence to help pick him up, but he was already gone. In fact, he had cleaned the place out. Geiger quickly checked all ports of exit—the train stations and airports—but there was no sign of the elusive writer.

They went around Vienna, interviewing Jack's friends and associates. Piecing the stories together, they learned that Jack had gone on a vacation with his girlfriend, Bianca Mrak.

[4]

Mrak, eighteen, was a tall, slender, and pretty girl who had met Jack the December before in a wine bar where she worked as a waitress. She was flattered by the attention of this good-looking celebrity and quickly moved in with him. He told her he might leave the country to get away from all the pressure and publicity. She agreed to go with him wherever he went and asked her mother to help them with cash.

They went to Switzerland for a few weeks, and Jack was about to return to Vienna when a former girlfriend warned him that the police were closing in. The newspapers had announced his imminent arrest. He told Bianca about it and they went to the railroad station in Zurich, where Jack made calls to the Austrian papers to proclaim his innocence and insist that he was being framed. Then he and Bianca drove to Paris.

The authorities learned that Bianca's mother was sending them money via wire transfers. They went to her, and she agreed that if she heard from Jack and Bianca again, she would contact the authorities.

From Paris, Jack continued to call friends in journalism and television to convince them of his innocence. Then he laid out a deal: He promised to return and answer questions, but only if the arrest warrants were withdrawn. Despite his appearances in various media, police had no idea where he was hiding.

He left his VW Passat in Paris, removed the "JACK-1" plates, and tossed out his handgun and car phone. He thought about going to Africa or Sweden, but Bianca preferred America, specifically Miami, because she was a fan of Don Johnson and the 1980s television show *Miami Vice*. With the authorities closing in, they booked tickets via New York, arriving on February 10, but Jack made a fatal error when he failed to report on his application for a tourist visa his 1976 murder conviction. The two fugitives went right to Miami, where they booked themselves into a hotel. Then, on Miami Beach, they found an apartment to rent by the week. On an old typewriter he found there, Jack wrote a letter in his defense to Austrian officials.

"My flight was and is no confession. It is a different type of despair." He went on to point out that there was no way to prove anything against him concerning the murders because there was no evidence. "I was doing well," he wrote, "perhaps too good—and fate decided to punish me once more for my debt from the past. But in the moment, I still have something to say. If a fair, neutral official of justice is invited to determine that the warrant against me is unjust, I am ready to place myself at this person's disposal."

He made several calls to try to get this letter published, as well as to collect money from magazines for articles that he'd written. One magazine, *Erfolg,* offered him a fee for the exclusive story of his escape. He agreed to do it and gave them an address. He also requested some medication for thyroid disease. One interviewer asked if he was forcing Mrak to go with him, so he handed the phone over and let her speak for herself. She said that she was traveling with Jack of her own free will and that they were having a wonderful time.

To everyone, his story was the same. He had an alibi for this or that murder. For example, he said that there were twenty different people who would swear that he was at a reading on the night one woman had disappeared. With another, he was not even in the city, and with three others, he was home alone; but there was no evidence to support any of these claims. What was being said about him, he insisted, was a "controlled history" that originated in Graz; in other words, the police were making things up. They had singled him out as a scapegoat for their investigation only because they were angry that he'd been paroled and were intent on sending him back. If they had to, they wouldn't stop at framing him. He claimed that he had reported to the police every week since his release and reiterated that he was not going back to prison. Until he could get a fair hearing, and not one that framed him, he would stay on the run. When they went through the proper procedures, he said, he would have no concern because he had not committed these murders.

Then Bianca's mother got a call from Miami—a request to wire some cash—and she informed the police. They conveyed this to Interpol agents, who alerted U.S. officials. This was the beginning of the end for Jack.

Three deputy U.S. Marshals and an agent from the ATF surveilled a Western Union office on Collins Avenue, in South Beach, Miami, on February 27. They had a faded photograph of Jack and a general description of both Jack and Bianca. Because Jack had lied when he came into New York, and thus had entered illegally, they were directed to follow him and find out where he was staying.

The agents were enjoying the South Beach scenery when they spotted a couple walking down the street late that morning. They were dressed in casual clothing typical of a beach town—shorts and T-shirts—but the male's tight outfit had a distinctly European flair. He also had colorful tattoos all down his arms—the kind common to men who have served time in prison. It had to be he, the agents realized, but they were surprised that he was such a small, frail-looking man. This little guy was a serial killer wanted in several countries? Nonetheless, they had a job to do.

Bianca went to get the money while Jack waited outside. He seemed vigilant and restless. When she came out of the office, they continued up Collins Avenue and the marshals quickly followed.

But Jack was on the lookout for this and when he spotted them, he gave the word to Bianca to split up. She went one way and he another, going onto Sixth Street a block inland.

One agent went after the girl and grabbed her. Another went to his car and the other two followed Jack. Trying to avoid the inevitable, Jack ran into a restaurant and crashed through the kitchen, slamming into waiters and cooks, knocking pots off the stove and dishes out of the waiters' hands before making it out the back. The agents followed right behind, maneuvering around the food on the floor and the chaos in the kitchen to get through the back door. They soon cornered their man in an open-air parking structure. With guns drawn they ordered, "Freeze! Federal marshals!"

Jack saw that he didn't have a chance, so he gave up and let them cuff him. From reports afterward, it seems he was convinced that even if he went to jail, the police would be unable to hold him.

In the car on the way to the federal courthouse in downtown Miami, they told him that he'd entered the country illegally. Apparently, he thought that was all they had on him, so he became quite talkative, telling them in broken English how much he liked their car and that he'd put them in his next book.

Finally they mentioned that he was wanted for several murders in Austria and he immediately broke down and began to sob. To their minds, that was as good as a confession. He realized he'd been caught.

Bianca had given up the address of the place they were renting. She told the agents that she'd made money dancing at a topless club, Pure Platinum, and she'd always handed the money over to Jack. A search of their rented rooms turned up a thick travel journal, along with more of Jack's writings, and it was clear to those who translated it that he had every intention of eventually killing his girlfriend. Bianca had just escaped with her life.

The journal was confiscated as potential evidence for putting Jack at just the right times in the places where the murders had occurred.

He was kept in the Metropolitan Correctional Center, southwest of Miami, to await extradition, but both California and Austria wanted to prosecute him. It was a dilemma.

The LAPD detectives proceeded as if they were going to extradite him to California. They got a search warrant for tissue samples, and then drew Jack's blood, also taking hair samples and swabs of saliva for DNA testing. His DNA matched that found in semen from Shannon Exley's body, one of the L.A. victims, but she had semen from six other men as well and unfortunately there had been no discharge in the other two prostitutes. The rest of their evidence consisted of receipts for hotels near where the murdered women had last been seen.

To assist, Austrian authorities went to L.A. and gave the detectives whatever they needed to make a case, including crime scene photos and information on Jack. However, they pointed out that, unlike the legal system in America, if Austrian citizens commit crimes in other countries, they can be tried for them in Austria. That meant that if Jack were turned over to Austria, he could be prosecuted in one court for all eleven murders. Since it was clear that the criminal patterns were stronger when seen in all of the crime scenes together, Austria would have a better chance of putting him away. They also had physical evidence in two cases. With the L.A. murders, they now had three. The officers agreed that Jack should be tried where he would have to pay for what he had done. Austria seemed the best venue.

Jack realized this. When the United States gave clearance to return him to Austria, he tried to delay the procedure by fighting extradition. Detectives Miller and Harper went to see him and assured him that they could bring him to California, where he might face the gas chamber. He quickly agreed to be deported, apparently in the belief that with all the public opinion on his side in Austria, he could persuade a jury that he was innocent. He was also taking no chances with the gas chamber. While waiting to make his court appearance before a federal magistrate regarding his extradition, Jack rocked nonchalantly in his chair and joked with other inmates.

He was sent overseas on May 28, and even as he got off the plane, he had a self-satisfied smirk on his face, as if he knew he could still manipulate the system. He had sworn he would never go back to prison and he intended to keep that promise to himself.

Then, while in custody awaiting trial, he continued

to do things that would delay the trial date, all the while giving interviews. He claimed that he had been fully rehabilitated, and in *Profil,* in October, he asked, "Would I be so stupid and so mad that during the luckiest phase of my life, in which I've done theater productions, played a role onstage, organized a tour, and made many wonderful female friends, I would go kill someone each week in between?"

He also kept a journal of his thoughts and his poetry about the time he'd been free, and wrote letters to the press insisting on his innocence. He could prove it, he said, although he offered nothing that would do so. He kept saying that his only hope was that the real killer would be found.

Then, a year after her disappearance, late that spring, parts of a skeleton were found that were identified as the remains of Regina Prem, the woman whose husband had received those frightening phone calls. She had been left in the woods, which was consistent with the other murders, but no clothing or jewelry was found, and her manner of death could not be determined.

Upon learning about this, Jack took the opportunity to say that perhaps they would now find evidence that would divert the investigation onto its rightful track.

[5]

I knew about virtually none of this when my phone rang one day in Quantico during the summer of 1992.

"Hello, Gregg," said the caller, "this is Bob Farmer in Vienna."

I knew that Bob was the FBI's legal attaché assigned to the U.S. Embassy in Vienna, Austria. Because Vienna is one of the Bureau's more sought-after overseas

postings, I was about to engage in some routine harassment about keeping the Austrian ski slopes safe for the
free world, but before I began, I heard a sense of ur-
gency in his voice that stopped me.

"I've got some work for you," Bob said.

"Really?" I inquired, unsure where this conversation
was headed.

"It looks like we have our first serial killer here," he
continued. "This is big news in Europe and there's a lot
of pressure on the Austrian authorities. They've made
an arrest and are sure that they've got the right guy, but
because of his celebrity status and some other issues,
they're afraid they might lose him at trial. They want to
tap into your collective experience at Quantico on serial murder. This is their first time out of the box in a
case like this and they don't want to blow it."

I was ready to act. "You know we'll be glad to assist
in any way that we can. I'll need to know more about
what they have and how they're dealing with it, but either I have to go there or they need to come here. We
won't be able to do it with just reports. I need to talk to
the people involved."

"They'd like you to profile the case."

That comment told me that they weren't altogether
sure what they wanted, so I cleared that up right away.
"If they've got the right guy, they don't need a profile.
A signature crime analysis might be more helpful to
them, but I won't really know how I can assist until I
get through the cases."

He said he would relay this to the Austrians and he
soon called back to let me know that the chief investigators were willing to come to Quantico.

"That's good," I said. "But before they do, have
them separate the victim files from the suspect infor-

mation, because we don't want to know anything about this person, not even a name."

As objective as we think we can be, we still might spin or interpret the cases to fit. Even in routine cases, I ask investigators to put suspect information in a separate sealed envelope. We put that aside and don't compare it until we've gone through the case and come to our own opinion. But I wanted a lot of information about the victims—the method and manner of their respective deaths, family history, occupation, the crime scene photos, and the full autopsy reports. I would start without any presupposition that these cases were linked and if I came to the conclusion that they were, I would tell the investigators the kind of person who was most likely to commit the crimes in question. Afterward, they could compare those characteristics with their suspect.

The two most logical officials for me to meet made plans to come to the states: Ernst Geiger, who was in charge of the investigation, and Thomas Muller, chief of the Criminal Psychology Service in the Federal Ministry of the Interior. They told me when they expected to arrive and I blocked out my calendar for two weeks during August. This would allow us to go through every case slowly, methodically, and thoroughly. I needed to start from ground zero.

We had rooms ready for them at the Jefferson dorm at the FBI Academy. They said they were bringing twelve boxes of reports, so I commandeered the downstairs conference room for the duration of their visit.

They arrived late one humid afternoon, and clearly they were under a lot of pressure. Ernst Geiger, thirty-eight, was around five feet nine, of medium build, with cropped brown hair and brown eyes. As he shook hands with me, he was cordial but deliberate and reserved, wearing an expression of perpetual concern. That was understandable, since this was the largest serial murder case in Austrian history. He had come into it a bit late and now shouldered the full responsibility for solving it and bringing it to a successful resolution in court.

Thomas Muller, around thirty, was a native of Innsbruck and a former ski instructor. He had a sturdy German build, but was taller, more casual, and more vigorous than Geiger. He spoke better English than Geiger, so he took the lead in their introductions and translations. At that time, he told me, there was no program in Austria for criminal profiling, and they did not have a clear understanding of the idea of a "signature" that linked crime scenes. They sensed it could be important and, in fact, it was to become a central feature of the impending trial.

We got started right away, laying out the victim files on the oval Formica table in the conference room. It was a basement room, so there were no windows, but at least the chairs were padded here and we could get fresh coffee.

I took a quick scan of the files of the eleven victims they believed were linked to the same offender: seven in Austria, one in Czechoslovakia, and three in the United States. Killers who travel outside their realm of familiarity, I thought, are rare. In particular, while they may cross into bordering countries, such as from Austria into neighboring Czechoslovakia, we almost never see them actually fly overseas to look for new victims. However, each individual killer sets his own pattern, and the point of Criminal Investigative Analysis is to remain open to the facts and not be unduly constrained by theories or statistics.

Once again, as with the Shawcross victims, I wanted to see the cases in the order of how he had killed them rather than the order in which they were found, but it soon became clear that there had been some "linkage blindness" in these cases. The Austrian Federal Police had divided the country into regions, and there wasn't always free-flowing communication between the different regions. There was even less with police in a different country, such as Czechoslovakia. We had a harder job than usual ahead of us to get consistent details across cases. There was nothing to do at that point but just dig in.

We worked for the entire two weeks, straight through, with total immersion. Examining one victim at a time, we looked at the way each had been killed, the manner of body disposal, the type of items left at the scene and the type removed.

One thing I had to factor in to my analysis was a significant cultural difference. In our country, where prostitution is illegal and even viewed as immoral, certain killers target these women to punish them for sinful behavior. However, in Austria, prostitution is legal. The women are registered and acknowledged by the state. It's more accepted, so there are no puritanical attitudes about it, or any sense that it's criminal behavior that must be stopped. It's also not infested with drug abuse. For the most part, these women are clean, healthy, and well dressed. They have a specified area where they work, and there's little violence, such as pimps beating them up, attached to the profession.

As I looked through the cases and asked questions, I

took extensive notes to try to distill the significant factors that would help to create a timeline and a means for comparing one case to another. In particular, I was looking for an escalation of certain behaviors. I also examined the terrain and type of geography at the disposal sites and their relationship to the cities of Prague, Graz, and Vienna. The bodies had all been placed in wooded areas on the city outskirts, often near water.

I quickly saw a pattern developing. We had a similar victimology and manner of disposal. Most of these women had been prostitutes and were left outside, with tree branches or other foliage placed over them. We had no semen left on or in those bodies. The cause of death for those on which we could tell was strangulation, but some bodies were too decomposed to make a determination. Most had restraint bruises on their arms and wrists. No one had seen them getting into a car, so this offender had been careful. There was an absence of any indication of sexual assault. The trace evidence was next to none as well, and he appeared to have a calculated MO. He was smart and he was organized.

I believed that this killer acted violently, probably out of impotence, similar to what Shawcross had done. He was insecure about his masculinity and when he could not perform after being stimulated, he struck out in anger and blamed the women for shaming him, so he left their bodies in humiliating positions. The violence itself had become erotic to him.

We went to the FBI's violent crime database, called VICAP. At that time, we had ten to twelve thousand solved and unsolved homicide cases on file, so we put key words in to narrow down the search field. Keeping translation difficulties in mind, I had put together a report about the signature analysis in this case. I wanted to keep it as simple as possible, so I used a minimum number of variables: age group in the victimology, the fact that they were prostitutes, the ligature strangulation, the outdoor disposal sites, how they had been left mostly or partly nude, and that they had retained their jewelry. We ordered a multidimensional ad-hoc search with fifteen cross-referenced criteria.

I thought we'd still come up with a large number of close matches, but after two days, aside from these eight cases, we had four in California. They included the three cases Geiger had in his files and one other, but the man responsible for that one was in prison. That was a convincing statistic—just using those variables, we excluded thousands of other cases in the database. The eleven thought to be in the series were the eleven linked by the computer. In other words, it would be highly unusual to have more than one guy engaging in this specific type of behavior during this same time period. Even more significant, this offender had committed all these murders in less than a year.

Now that we had a solid understanding of the murders and agreed that they were all linked, it was time to open the envelope that contained the suspect information. Ernst, Thomas, and I spent hours examining the details of Unterweger's life, from being born to a prostitute, through his juvenile crimes, culminating in the murder of Margaret Schaefer and then his rebirth as an artist. Finally, we looked over the critically important timeline from September 1991 through July 1992. We could put him at the location of each murder. Forensically, we could match fibers from Jack's clothing to fibers on Heidemarie Hammerer's body, and hair from Blanka Bockova was in the BMW he was driving at the time she was murdered.

When we overlaid the Margaret Schaefer homicide from 1974 for which Jack had been convicted, we had an astonishingly clear pattern. We had a suspect whose movements correlated with the homicides and whose first homicide bore striking similarities to them. He was either the unluckiest man in the world to have been in all those places at the wrong time or he was an excellent suspect. And then there were the knots.

The killer tied each ligature used to strangle his victims with the same unique knot. Los Angeles criminalist Lynn Herold, an expert in ligatures used for strangulation, first analyzed the knots from the three Los Angeles victims and described how they had been done: The bra had to be dismantled first, with the band stripped from the elastic, always on the left side, and then tied in an identical complex manner. She said that if three people went out randomly and strangled three other people, it was extremely unlikely that all three would have come up with this same sequence. In addition to that, it was the same knot that had been used to strangle the European victims.

As it became clear to me that Jack was the killer, I was amazed by how similar this situation was to the Jack Abbott fiasco here in the United States. Abbott had become something of a celebrity in prison from his book *In the Belly of the Beast,* which became a best-seller and garnered numerous positive critical reviews. It had developed from a series of letters he had written to Norman Mailer during the 1970s, and Mailer had helped him to get the collection published. Mailer then went before Abbott's parole board and championed his release, with the assurance that Abbott was a "powerful and important writer." Abbott got out of prison in 1981, and was immediately invited to dinner parties with New York writers. He also appeared on television shows like *Good Morning America*. Similar to Unterweger, he was celebrated as a reformed man.

Apparently, Mailer had failed to understand the meaning of Abbott's dedication to Carl Panzram, a killer who was first arrested at the age of eight and who had described himself as the "spirit of meanness personified." Panzram had remorselessly committed twenty-one murders and multiple rapes. This was the person whom Abbott admired, and Abbott, too, seemed unfazed by murder. He'd fatally stabbed an inmate in prison and then, six weeks after his release, he stabbed Richard Adnan, a twenty-two-year-old waiter, to death. So much for the redemptive power of the arts. The parallels between Jack Abbott and Jack Unterweger were obvious.

The reality is that once you educate a psychopath, all you get is an educated psychopath, making him much more dangerous.

[6]

The trial began in June 1994, in Graz, Austria, and I was immediately struck by the first in a number of differences between the Austrian criminal justice system and ours. Under Austrian law, Austrian citizens are accountable to the Austrian courts for their behavior, regardless of where it was exhibited. Being an Austrian citizen, Jack Unterweger was being tried in Austria for the three murders in Los Angeles, the one in Prague, and the seven in Austria. Apparently, they don't have a lot of heartburn over venue.

However, Jack's indictments did little to diminish his public support—at least initially. He was being interviewed more than ever, and he continued to tell the press that he was being framed. Many of his former associates believed him, and not surprisingly, one female journalist even collected notes for a book in his defense.

The news covered his story from every angle, so the prosecution team knew they would have to present as convincing a case as possible. Since the physical evidence was minimal, they were going to rely heavily on the linkage analysis and the way the Los Angeles murders tied in with those in Europe. They would also show the jury Jack's many faces: In addition to his charming and talented side, he had a diabolical side, which could be seen in the gruesome prison tattoos that covered his upper body.

As I was preparing to travel to Graz to testify, I sent a teletype to the Legat in Vienna asking them to arrange a time for me to meet with the prosecutor to go over my testimony before I took the stand. I wanted to make sure that we were all on the same page. I received a teletype back from Vienna informing me that I could not meet with the prosecutor or any attorney prior to testifying. In Austria, unlike America, all examination of expert witnesses takes place inside the courtroom. No one would get a crack at me until I was actually on the witness stand. That meant that I couldn't predict the kinds of questions either side might ask me. That put the Austrian attorneys in a position that American attorneys always try to avoid, i.e., asking questions to which they don't know the answer. This made the courtroom more of a minefield, where one wrong question, one misstep, could be disastrous.

Detective Jim Harper was going over from Los Angeles as a fact witness to lay out the Los Angeles cases, and criminalist Lynn Herold from the crime lab there was going to testify about the knots.

I arrived in Vienna two days early. I wanted to adjust to the time zone changes and have some breathing room, without interruptions, to finalize my trial preparations. The day before I was to testify, I then drove from Vienna to Graz.

Graz is a beautifully maintained old European city. A river flows gently through the city center and a clock tower rises above the red-tiled roofscapes. Street musicians play along the narrow, winding cobblestone streets. As I walked through the main area of Graz, I was surprised to see that a local newspaper had my picture on the front page. I realized that this was a big case in Europe, with massive coverage, and the media were eager for comments, but I had turned down all requests for interviews. The next morning, Thomas Muller met me at my hotel and drove me to the courthouse.

I was amazed by the good-size crowd standing outside the building. A machine gun–toting officer met us and escorted me into the courthouse through a rear entrance and down a couple of hallways to a sequestered area for witnesses. There I sat on a bench outside the courtroom, waiting to be called. Shortly after nine A.M., the door to the courtroom swung open and a bailiff called my name. He motioned for me to enter.

The courtroom in Graz was different from any others I've been in before. With its overhanging balcony along the back, it looked more like a theater. There were three judges and one alternate, who sat on an elevated platform at the front of the room, wearing black robes with red and purple sashes. The dark wood of their bench made a severe contrast with the light walls, and I sensed an air of formality in the large room, emphasized by the Austrian flag and court seal on the front wall. The witnesses sat in the center of the courtroom. Both the prosecuting and defense attorneys sat to the left, at separate tables, and the jury sat to the right.

It was a significant moment. After two years of coming to know Jack through his crimes and life history, I was now about to see him for the first time. I scanned the packed courtroom, and there he was.

There was no mistaking Jack Unterweger for anyone else in the place: slight of build and immaculately dressed in a double-breasted blue suit, a neatly pressed white shirt, and a red patterned tie. He looked right at me, and the moment our eyes met, everything moved in slow motion. Despite his small stature, this guy was larger than life. He was a *presence*. Jack was a malevolent thoroughbred. His smile was gracious and disarming, his gaze penetrating. He clearly loved the limelight, and his abundant charm filled the room. He was the center of everyone's attention.

I broke eye contact and turned to take my seat at the witness table. Yet he'd affected me in ways that other criminals had not. I could understand why he'd managed to manipulate so many. He dominated the place, and he was so charming he hardly seemed as if he could be a killer. I understood now why the prosecution team was worried.

Seated to my immediate left was a young and visibly nervous interpreter. She told me that she was very concerned about being able to accurately translate the questions to me, as well as my answers. I touched her hand lightly and told her to take a few deep breaths and relax; everything was going to be fine.

The press corps sat directly behind me and curious onlookers filled the rest of the seats on the main floor and in the balcony.

The Austrian judicial system is inquisitional rather than adversarial like ours. The adversarial procedure invites the parties to present their cases to an impartial judge or jury, while the inquisitorial system involves the judge more fully in the investigative process. The lawyers are certainly advocates, so there's a minor adversarial dynamic, but without the same type of theatrical flair of many American courtrooms. The nine-member jury needed only a majority vote, but the judges could concur or disagree.

The court was run in an orderly manner, but the circus atmosphere just outside the doors seemed to please Jack no end. He appeared confident that he was going to be free very soon. His attorneys had picked up on the theme that he was being framed and that the police were railroading him. Since there was little physical evidence against him, Jack and his team would play that for all it was worth.

What the prosecution relied on was:

1. A psychiatric report about Unterweger's incurable and sadistic criminal nature, narcissistic and excitable personality, and the lack of any evidence of insanity.

2. That Blanka Bockova's hair was recovered from the car that Jack had owned at the time of her death.

3. Around 100 red fibers from Brunhilde Masser's body that matched fibers from Jack's red scarf.

4. Character-witness testimony from former associates and girlfriends, one of whom he had allegedly

extorted money from (which had never even been proved but was allowed in this court).

5. The FBI VICAP analysis and the signature crime analysis.

6. The identical knots in the ligatures used to strangle the victims.

My job was twofold. First, I had to educate the jury about the signature aspect of crime analysis in general, and second, get specific with these crimes. I laid out my documents and prepared myself for questions of any sort.

Unlike the American system of jurisprudence, the questioning here began with the judges. They asked me who I was and what involvement I had in the matter being litigated before them. I identified myself as an FBI agent and gave them a brief overview of my role in the case. The judges then turned the questioning over to the prosecutor. He wisely asked the open-ended question, "Would you please tell the court and the jury exactly what you did in this case and what conclusions, if any, you have drawn regarding these homicides?" That gave me a lot of running room.

I explained the methodology used in analyzing the cases and how the VICAP check had linked these eleven homicides while simultaneously eliminating thousands of others. The statistics were clearly impressive. I then went on to discuss how this constellation of behaviors formed a unique "personality print," much like the way the constellation of ridges, loops, and whorls of a finger form a unique fingerprint. But unlike a fingerprint, this type of personality print couldn't identify who had committed crimes, only that it was highly probable that the same individual was responsible for all the homicides. The geography was an issue, as the murders spanned two continents, but I concluded that if we were to know who committed one of these crimes, and if that individual was in the same area at the same time the other murders were committed, it was highly probable that this one perpetrator had committed all eleven homicides.

The judges ordered a morning break around ten thirty. We all stood as the jury was dismissed and then I bent over to collect my notes and place them in my briefcase. I didn't know until I looked up that Jack had come out of his chair and was walking with purpose right over to me. The police officers and his attorneys ordered him to stop, but he wasn't listening to them. This was Jack, after all, the one who would introduce himself to the local police *before* he murdered; the one who would interview unwitting investigators about the progress of their investigation into *his* murders; the one who charmed and manipulated the Viennese literati into springing him from prison. Of course he would approach me without any hesitation. He was even smiling.

I shouldn't have been surprised, but I was. And yet this was the moment for which I had trained for so many years, the moment when I was to assess without thinking the type of energy my opponent directed toward me, and use it against him. I quickly centered myself and waited until he was within two feet of me, where he stopped. In broken but understandable English, he said, "The first murder was not a sexual homicide."

I realized he was referring to the 1974 killing of Margaret Shaefer. He was correcting me, but I knew that he was also attempting to charm me. His was a manipulative energy, and he knew I was a strong witness against him. Thinking fast, I replied, "Is that right?" Then, with the force of his own cunning, I added, "But the others were?"

At that point, his attorneys and a police officer grabbed Jack and pulled him back toward his seat, but I saw the light in his eyes. He shook his head, smiled, and responded, "A clever question." I sensed that he appreciated my wit, but he'd easily sidestepped the small verbal trap I had laid for him. Yet in that brief moment, we had been caught in a zone of two minds engaged in silent combat. I would never forget it.

Shortly after the break, Jack's attorneys, Drs. George Zanger and Hans Lehofer, began to cross-examine me. They asked if I knew of Jack's accomplishments, his status as a poet and prize-winning author who had many friends and girlfriends.

"Yes," I said, "I was aware of that."

They implied that after the success he'd known, he would have no reason to risk going back to prison. They then tried to attack my analysis by pointing out what they perceived as inconsistencies. The three women in the United States had been strangled with their bras, but no one in Europe had been strangled with a bra. My answer was that the best evidence I had was that the European women weren't wearing bras. The offender strangled each victim with her own underwear. He may have preferred a bra, but if none was available, he used whatever piece of underwear there was. I couldn't testify to the fact that he had used a bra on his first victim, the murder for which he had been convicted in 1976, but the prosecutor would later hammer that point home in his closing arguments.

Jack's attorneys mentioned that Bockova and the others had been left on their backs, and Masser on her side, so how could we link these crimes when the victims were found in different positions?

I noted that of all of the serial murder cases I was familiar with, I had never seen two crimes that were exactly the same. This was a distinction without a real difference. The salient aspect of these crimes was the fact that similarities linked them all to one another but distinguished them from the thousands of other cases we had checked.

The lawyers took another tack and pointed out that Jack had affairs with fifty or so women. Did it make any sense that a man having frequent consensual sex would be involved with prostitutes? Did I ever know of a man murdering prostitutes while having consensual sex?

This was one of those questions that they didn't know the answer to and probably wished they hadn't asked. Fresh on my mind was the Shawcross case. Like Jack, he had been in jail for fifteen years for murder, had gotten out, and then had murdered eleven women. He'd had a wife and a girlfriend, and yet he was out having sex with some prostitutes and murdering others at nearly the same rate as Jack. I offered a few other examples, and they quickly abandoned that line of questioning.

They were good lawyers, but it appeared to me that they really weren't sure what to do. They had no experience in dealing with the type of testimony I was offering, or with someone like me. Ernst Geiger told me later that I was the first FBI agent to offer expert testimony in an Austrian court.

I was still on the stand when we broke for lunch. Then, afterward, just before I entered the courtroom, I encountered one of Jack's attorneys, Dr. Lehofer. Dr. Zanger was clearly the lead attorney, with Lehofer as second chair. Of the two, he was more open. He stopped me outside and asked me in English if I might know his good friend, an attorney in New York. He gave me a name.

"No," I said, "I'm afraid I don't."

We had a short but pleasant conversation, and as we were parting, he surprised me when he said, "I tell Zanger, no more questions for you, but I think he will have more questions this afternoon and that is a mistake."

Lehofer was right. Zanger questioned me throughout the afternoon. I stuck to my assessment, and it was clear that they did not know how to take it apart. Another feature of Austrian courtroom procedure is that the defendant is allowed to question any witness directly, not just through his attorney. I was the only witness Jack declined to question.

Lynn Herold, from the Los Angeles crime lab, followed me and testified about the knots tied on the dead prostitutes in the American cases, and how they were extraordinarily similar to the ones tied in Europe. When a pair of panty hose was used, she pointed out, one leg was doubled back on itself and the other leg used as the third segment for the braiding, in a manner extremely similar to two of the bra cases, where two pieces of elastic were torn to form two segments, and the left strap was pulled through as the third leg of the braid. The chances were remote, she said, that more than one person would be using the same type of knot for murder.

In his own defense, Jack sidestepped the physical evidence and signature analysis, arguing to the jury that they should not judge him for his way of life. That was not a sufficient reason to deprive him of his freedom. He admitted that he did not understand the DNA analysis and therefore wouldn't address it. "My brain developed gene bums when I was studying," he said. He then exploited the same strategy that had won him his freedom before: He talked about what a "rat" he once had been, "a primitive criminal who grunted rather than talked and an inveterate liar." He "consumed women, rather than loved them." But he had changed. He had been rehabilitated. He was no longer that person.

"I'm counting on your acquittal," he said, "because I am not the culprit. Your decision will affect not only me but the real killer, who is laughing up his sleeve."

[7]

Altogether, this trial lasted two and a half months. The growing consensus in the press was that it was fair, even though the evidence was mostly circumstantial. As more facts came out, a lot of Jack's support atrophied away. People who had championed him were no longer so certain of his reform. As time went on, many of his allies realized that they were wrong. In the end, Jack, the clever psychopath, was pretty much alone with his lawyers and a few staunch girlfriends—but not Bianca Mrak, who had wised up long before.

On June 28, 1994, the day the verdict came in, a

bomb was detonated outside the courthouse. No one was injured, but there was damage to the building. Yet that did not delay the verdict: Jack Unterweger was found guilty of nine counts of murder—the Prague victim, all three Los Angeles victims, and five in Austria. The jury reasoned that the remaining two Austrian victims had been too decomposed to establish a definite cause of death, so on these they gave him a pass.

This verdict was personally gratifying to me. By convicting Jack of nine of these murders, it meant that the jury had understood the significance of my signature crime analysis.

There was no presentence investigation or separate sentencing hearing. The court immediately sentenced Jack to life in prison. He appeared stunned. That was it for him; with his prior murder conviction, he was done for. No one would let him out again. I think he was genuinely surprised.

This is an example of the way another facet of Criminal Investigative Analysis was applied. It wasn't about developing a profile, but was about working closely with the crime scene information and the data that we already had about sadistic killers to show how crime scenes can be persuasively linked. Ultimately, the job was done because the jury did return a verdict of guilty in those nine murders that were clearly linked. The investigators were lacking in forensic evidence, but the behavioral evidence made up for that.

Yet this case wasn't yet over.

I had mentioned to Geiger that suicide was a possibility, so they should watch Jack carefully. Not that he would be ashamed or remorseful enough to kill himself, but he could be motivated by the need for control. If he spent the rest of his life in prison, then society would have won. But Jack would never subjugate himself to the rule and law of a civilized people. Suicide could be his last defiant act, his last great "Fuck you!"

But the guards failed to watch him. True to his personality, within six hours of his conviction, Jack hanged himself in his prison cell by tying the drawstring of his jumpsuit around his neck with the same ligature he had used on many of his victims and leaning his weight forward and into it. It was ironic. In fact, one person observed, "It was his best murder."

The rebirth of Jack Unterweger, literary hero and Renaissance man, turned out to be the cruelest of fictions, and his situation raises a number of questions. What does it say about society's collective desire to believe in rehabilitation, its need to see the seeds of redemption in even the most barren soil? Are the hands—and consciences—of Unterweger's supporters now stained with his victims' blood, or are they guilty of nothing more than looking for the best in their fellow man? In looking for a ray of good, can one become blind to a torrent of evil? At the very least, I think it's fair to say that those who supported him were humiliated. An article in *Die Presse,* in August 1994, noted that, "For a while it was *chic* to listen to the convicted murderer who had turned good. But not many of those who supported him then like to talk about it now."

Never in my career as an FBI agent did I encounter a serial killer quite like Jack Unterweger. The next year, in 1995, I retired and went on to consult independently for a while with another firm and then on my own. But that didn't signal an end to murder and madness. In fact, it afforded me the rare opportunity to become deeply involved in the final chapter and ultimate solution of what has been referred to as "the murder mystery of the century."

9: The Preponderance of Evidence

Truth is incontrovertible. Panic may resent it, ignorance
may deride it, malice may destroy it, but it is still there.
——Winston Churchill

[1]

Who murdered Marilyn Sheppard? Was it a "bushy-
haired stranger," as many people believe, or perhaps a
pair of killers? Did she bite her attacker? Did her killer
bleed at the scene? Was she raped or just posed to
make the police think so? Was it a drug crime, a burglary that broke bad, or an affair that went sour?

These are among the questions and controversies
swirling around one of America's most enduring murder mysteries—one in which I was to become totally
immersed, playing an entirely different role.

The FBI does not get involved in civil cases, but
once retired, I was able to do that. Sometimes, in the
context of a civil trial, you have a homicide or rape
case, and the Sheppard trial was actually a homicide
trial in a civil-suit venue. The defendants, a team of
prosecutors representing the state of Ohio, had called
the Bureau to get someone to take a look, but the
agents there said they couldn't testify, so they referred
the prosecutor to me.

As a retired FBI agent from the BSU, I now talk with groups of prosecutors and law-enforcement officers, as well as consult on crimes, make parole recommendations, teach university courses, and serve as an expert witness. I also offer a threat-assessment program. With Park Dietz's Threat Assessment Group, I worked with many of the Fortune 500 companies on workplace violence.

So one day in November 1999, the phone rang.

"Behavioral Criminology International," I responded. "Gregg McCrary speaking."

"Good morning," said the caller. "This is Dean Boland, with the Cuyahoga County Prosecutor's Office in Cleveland, and we're reviewing an old homicide case here. We were wondering if you'd be interested in taking a look at it. You might have heard of it: the Sam Sheppard case?"

Like almost everyone in this country, I'd certainly heard of it, and also like many other Americans, my awareness had been shaped by the media. In fact, I'd seen some recent documentary programs on the case that were produced by *Dateline* and *Nova*. Even as I heard the name, I had flashbacks to the 1960s when, as a kid, I had watched the TV show *The Fugitive,* starring David Janssen as Dr. Richard Kimble. More recently, I'd seen the movie of the same name, starring Harrison Ford. The Sheppard case had inspired both. Their shared premise was that a doctor, falsely accused and convicted of the murder of his wife, goes on the lam to track down the real killer, known only as "the one-armed man."

Dean Boland brought me back to reality. "We're defending a civil suit filed by Sheppard's son, Sam Reese

Sheppard," he said. "We think you might be able to shed some light on it."

"Dean," I responded, "I'd be happy to look at the case, but isn't there DNA evidence that points to an intruder?"

"I don't want to influence you one way or the other," he said. "We'd just like your objective read on the crime and crime scene. You'll have all the material available to review and there's a ton of it: transcripts from both of the criminal trials and the appeals, hundreds of crime scene and autopsy photographs, along with all the results of the subsequent investigations, including the forensic lab work. Once you've been through it, we want your unbiased opinion, regardless of whether it hurts or helps us."

That sounded fair—and intriguing, so I told him, "I'll be happy to have a look."

A couple of weeks later, I walked from my hotel room in Cleveland, Ohio, through a raw, blustery November morning to the Justice Center to meet with the prosecutor's team. The office of the prosecutor is in this building, which also houses the sheriff's department, the Cleveland police headquarters, the county jail, and courtrooms. It takes up a city block. In the lobby, I located the correct bank of elevators and rode up to the ninth floor. I had arrived a few minutes early for my appointment with Bill Mason, the prosecuting attorney for Cuyahoga County, but was ushered in immediately.

I found Bill to be a soft-spoken, husky and solid man, around six feet tall, with a quick smile and a firm handshake. With his short blond hair and blue eyes, he had a clean-cut appearance. After we introduced ourselves, Bill asked his secretary to have Steve Dever, his chief trial attorney, join us.

Steve arrived shortly thereafter. He was shorter than Bill, with medium brown hair, friendly but businesslike. Together Bill and Steve explained the importance of the case. Sam Sheppard's son, known as Sam R, to set him apart from his father, was suing the state of Ohio for the wrongful imprisonment of his father. Were the state to lose the case, Ohio's wrongful imprisonment statute could result in a damage award to Sam Sheppard's estate of $25,000 for each of the ten years his father had been deprived of income, along with some amount of punitive damages, which put the figure at around two million.

However, they insisted, this case wasn't about the money. The prosecutor's office could have settled it, but they wanted justice for the victim, Marilyn Sheppard. They were also intent on protecting the integrity and reputations of those who had previously investigated and prosecuted this case. It was clear to me that Bill and Steve were convinced that Sam Sheppard had murdered Marilyn. I listened to them but kept my options open, as I had yet to review the case materials.

Finally Steve said, "We've set up a war room and have all of the materials there."

"Is it in the basement?" I asked.

He looked mildly surprised and responded, "Yes, that's right. How did you know?"

I thought about giving him my "death finds its way to the basement" observations. Instead I just shrugged and said, "Let's go down and get started."

In the war room, I met Dean Boland, the man who had initially called me, as well as Marilyn Cassidy, Andy Nichol, and several other members of the team.

This basement conference room housed a large rectangular table surrounded by a dozen chairs. Waist-high shelves lined the walls on two sides of the room, with filing cabinets against the third wall and a blackboard/screen on the fourth. The place was crowded, without a free inch of space anywhere. Boxes and binders of material sat stacked up on the shelves or were jammed into the filing cabinets. Still more case materials were spread over the table. Everything was there, from the initial 1954 police report to the latest trial motion, and Dean had been right: There was a ton of material. In fact, it was nearly overwhelming.

Just the transcript from the first trial alone was 6,000 pages long, and the second trial transcript was 1,500 pages. I looked these over and then noted that the records from the Bay Village Police Department's investigation filled seven five-inch-thick binders and ran to 2,100 pages. Then there were the photographs. I learned that there were 1,600 images from the coroner's office, including Marilyn's autopsy, the crime scene, and the later exhumations of both Sam and Marilyn Sheppard. In addition to that, there was a 400-page transcript of the coroner's inquest and seven books devoted exclusively to the Sheppard case. They had also collected every relevant documentary, fictionalized movie, and newsmagazine show. That was a lot of material, but once I saw how it was all organized, I realized that there was order in this chaos. Starting in one place and moving clockwise, I could work through the case chronologically.

"Where do you want to begin?" Steve asked.

I pointed to the far corner of the room and said, "Let me start over there. I want to begin with the initial police reports and crime scene photos, then Marilyn's autopsy, and work out from there. I'm going to need to know everything there is to know about Marilyn and Sam Sheppard, as well as any prior similar crimes in or around Bay Village, Ohio, at that time. I don't want any suspect information at this point, as it might taint my objectivity, even unconsciously. I just want to learn as much as I can about the victim and her circumstances."

Steve nodded and said, "We'll leave you alone to work, but if you'd like, we'll come get you when we break for lunch."

"That'd be great," I said. "Thanks."

They then left the room and I got to work.

First I needed to understand how we had gotten to this point. I had a lot of questions. Who was Sam Sheppard? Why had he been convicted in the first trial but found not guilty in the second? Was he truly innocent? Had he been wrongfully imprisoned or did his second attorney simply find some legal snake hole through which he could slither? And why would anyone want to murder Marilyn Reese Sheppard? The answers, I believed, were in the ocean of material that lay in front of me, so I dove in. Once I had a general sense of the case from records and reports, I knew I could dig down and examine in detail the underlying facts. But first the overview.

[2]

At the time of the infamous murder, in 1954, Samuel Holmes Sheppard was a thirty-year-old prominent osteopath working in Bay Village, Ohio. He came from a family of physicians and together with his father and two brothers, Richard and Stephen, ran the Bay View Hospital. Sam and Marilyn Reese had been high school sweethearts who had married. They had a seven-year-old son, Sam Reese Sheppard, known as Chip or Junior, and they seemed a typical affluent Midwestern family with a home overlooking Lake Erie, nice cars, and a fast boat. Then it all ended.

In the early morning hours of Sunday, July 4, 1954, someone bludgeoned Marilyn Sheppard to death in her bedroom. The police arrested Sam Sheppard and charged him with the murder. His trial started October 18, 1954, and concluded on December 22 that same year with a verdict of not guilty of first-degree murder, but the jury was not entirely persuaded of his innocence. His account had a few holes, and after 100 hours of deliberation, the jury convicted Sam of second-degree murder.

For motive, the prosecution pointed to Sam's extramarital affairs and strained marriage. Sam testified on his own behalf, but was caught lying under oath about a specific affair. Telling the story of the murder, he insisted that a "bushy-haired stranger" (later changed to the fictional one-armed man for the popular *The Fugitive* TV series) had killed Marilyn and attacked him twice—once in the second-floor bedroom and then again on the beach.

The judge sentenced him to life in prison.

However, this is where the story completely diverges from the popular conception of it. Sam was never a fugitive. He appealed his conviction, claiming insufficient evidence. The courts disagreed and he stayed in prison. Then Sam recruited a brand-new attorney, F. Lee Bailey, who filed a motion with the federal district court and managed to get the conviction overturned—not for lack of evidence but by claiming that prejudicial publicity had denied Sam a fair trial. Sam was immediately released, but was required to post a bond pending the state of Ohio's appeal of the ruling. The appellate court disagreed, but let Sam remain free pending his appeal to the U.S. Supreme Court, so in June 1966, the case wound up there.

Those justices ruled that the "circus atmosphere" generated by the press had the potential to influence the jury, which could have denied Sheppard a fair trial. No court has ever ruled that the jury was *actually* influenced by any publicity, only that the potential for it was present. Nonetheless, Bailey's argument prevailed and Sheppard's conviction was overturned. The state of Ohio either had to retry him within a reasonable amount of time or leave him alone. Firmly convinced that Sam had murdered his wife, the prosecutors prepared for a second trial.

It began in November 1966, and I began to read this transcript. I noted with interest that it was only a fourth the size of the transcript from the first trial. That told me that this jury had not heard much of the evidence that the first jury had heard, and my read of the transcript confirmed this. There was neither testimony from Sam in this trial nor any testimony regarding Sam's extramarital affairs. The jury was not even offered a motive that would explain why Sam might have brutally bludgeoned his wife. But the defense provided jurors with a new theory about who had killed Marilyn and some testimony to support it.

Bailey turned the Sheppards' marriage on its head by alleging that it was Marilyn who was having an affair. He also suggested that there were two killers—a husband-and-wife team. The "bushy-haired stranger" was out this time around, and the Sheppards' neighbors, Spencer and Esther Houk, were in. Bailey alleged that Marilyn had been having an affair with Spencer Houk, the part-time mayor and a full-time butcher in Bay Village. Ironically, it was Spencer, rather than the police, whom Sam had called first to report the murder. Spencer and his wife, Esther, immediately went over to the Sheppards' house and called the police from there.

During the trial, Bailey, in an accusatory manner, cross-examined Houk. He asked why Houk had not called the police before going to the Sheppard home, why he had taken his wife into a potentially dangerous situation, and why they had burned something that morning in their fireplace when the outside temperature that day never went below sixty-nine degrees. He gave the impression that the Houks knew there was no murderer in the house because *they* were the murderers. Bailey then offered some alleged "scientific" evidence to back up his claim.

He called Dr. Paul Kirk, who had done extensive analyses of the blood and the autopsy photos. Dr. Kirk testified that the killer had been left-handed, which would exclude the right-handed Sam. He also testified that the apparent blood spatter on Sam's watch was a transfer or contact stain resulting from incidental contact with Marilyn's body while trying to find her pulse, and that there was a spot of blood in the bedroom, where the murder had taken place, from someone other than Sam and Marilyn. It was type O, the same as Marilyn's, but with a different composition, which eliminated her as its source. To determine this, Dr. Kirk had performed an unprecedented test (used by no one today, including his protégé and Sheppard team expert witness Bart Epstein), claiming that in some testing that he did, one of the stains reacted slightly more slowly than the other. That implied it had a different source of origin. This result enabled him to conclude that the slow-reacting stain was type O blood from a source other than Marilyn. But there was a problem: Unlike true science, which demands repeatable experiments and replicable results to validate new procedures and novel discoveries, neither Dr. Kirk nor anyone else was ever able to repeat this alleged test.

The important point for Bailey was that Sam was type A, not type O, and therefore could not have been the source of what he and Kirk were now calling "the killer's blood." Bailey wrapped it up by claiming that the motive was jealousy, and without naming any names, provided a portrait of a very different murderer—a left-handed woman who had struck Marilyn "lightly" but repeatedly and was bitten during the attack, resulting in the blood trail throughout the house. It is undisputed that Sam had no open wounds, cuts, or scrapes of any kind on his body when the police arrived the morning of the murder. Perhaps the best decision Bailey made during this second trial was to keep Sam off the stand. That way the jury wouldn't hear about a lone "bushy-haired stranger" or any of the other things that Sam had testified to originally that weren't convenient for this new theory.

Clearly, the story had changed in a number of ways during the time period between trial one and trial two. Originally, there was one killer, now there were two. They were big; they were small. They hit hard; they didn't hit hard. They were left-handed; they were right-handed; it was a male, it was a female; it was a stranger, it was his friend.

After an afternoon's deliberation, the jury returned a verdict of Not Guilty. Sam Sheppard was free to go. He commented that he always knew there were "murderers." If that was true, why hadn't he said so during the first trial?

Interestingly, within the first few days after his release, Sam had married a wealthy German divorcée named Ariane Tebbenjohanns, with whom he had struck up a pen-pal relationship while imprisoned. Ariane was a stunningly attractive blonde who captivated the media. But when the press dug into her background, they discovered that her half-sister, Magda, had been married to Joseph Goebbels, Hitler's minister of propaganda. Because of this, Sam Sheppard's public image suffered and his life took a turn for the worse. In 1967, Ariane recounted to the media that Sam had a gun "and he threatened me . . . I'm deadly afraid of him right now . . . I don't even go near my house without a policeman." She filed for divorce that same year, repeating this charge, and asked for a restraining order against Sam. She indicated that he had taken up with a younger woman.

By 1969, Sam had become a professional wrestler, using the name Killer Sheppard. He married for a third time, this time in Mexico. By 1970, at the age of forty-six, he was dead from liver damage brought on by a serious alcohol-and-drug addiction. It was a sad and sordid story, but it still wasn't over. Now there was to be a third trial, set into motion by Sam Reese Sheppard and his attorney, Terry Gilbert.

The theory they floated was a variation on the "bushy-haired stranger" theme but this time they claimed that they had solved the murder and knew with certainty the killer's identity. It was a former "window washer" named Richard Eberling who had cleaned windows at the Sheppard house in the weeks prior to the murder. He had been arrested in 1959 for theft, and found in his possession were some of Marilyn's rings. Although it turned out that he'd stolen them from the home of Richard Sheppard, Sam's brother, and not from Marilyn, he did offer that he'd been in the house on July 2. He was fixing a storm window and had cut himself and dripped blood down the basement steps. Yet one of his employees denied this tale.

In 1987, Richard Eberling was convicted of murdering Ethel Durkin, an elderly woman in his care. He'd faked a will naming him as her beneficiary and then pushed her down a flight of stairs. At the time of his arrest, Eberling was living with his life-long partner, Oscar Buford Henderson, in a mansion in Lookout Mountain, Tennessee. Eberling had utilized the services of another woman to help in the forgery, and a money dispute with her had resulted in her providing information to law enforcement, which caused Coroner Balraj to exhume Durkin's body and reclassify her cause of death from accidental to homicide. From prison one day, Eberling wrote to Sam R, now an adult, and said he knew the whole story of his mother's murder. He regurgitated the Houk theory, claiming that Esther Houk had killed Marilyn in a jealous rage, but now said that Sam, along with Spencer, had staged a cover-up.

True or not, it was sufficient to ignite a fire in Sam Reese about setting the record straight once and for all regarding his father. Sam R didn't actually buy this variation on the Houk theory, but rather considered Eberling himself to be a viable suspect. There was as much as two to three million dollars to be gained if his lawyer could convince a jury that the state of Ohio had maliciously prosecuted and wrongfully imprisoned Sam Sheppard. Thus, when I considered all of this from my reading of the materials, I saw that we had several theories from the past to work through, along with the Eberling theory being offered now by Sam Reese's team.

They proposed that Eberling had two primary motives: unbridled sexual lust for Marilyn and a virulent hatred for Sam. Based on tool marks on a cellar door mentioned in a Cleveland police report, they theorized that he had entered the house through the outside cellar doors, made his way upstairs, raped and murdered Marilyn, and then assaulted Sam. They also theorized that Marilyn bit her attacker and that he bled at the scene. Finally, they made the spectacular claim of having used modern DNA analysis to identify Eberling's blood at the crime scene. Obviously, that type of forensic evidence would be extraordinarily compelling. But was it all that it seemed?

[3]

I wasn't interested in theories, only facts. Any meaningful analysis of violent crime begins with victimology, i.e., what elevated this person's potential for becoming the victim of violence? Very often, by just answering this question, investigators can identify a motive, which can then lead to the offender.

Did Marilyn Sheppard have a "high-risk" lifestyle? Was she involved in criminal activity—drug dealing or prostitution—or other lifestyle choices that would have elevated her potential for becoming the victim of violence? No. She was a doctor's wife and a stay-at-home mom who in 1954 lived in Bay Village, Ohio, a virtually crime-free environment. Prior to Marilyn's murder, I learned, there had been only one other murder in

Bay Village's history as both a village and a city. Yet she was murdered in her own home, in her bed, while her husband allegedly napped downstairs. In addition to lifestyle choices and situational variables, we examine a victim's personal relationships, especially marital or other intimate relationships, as a strained relationship is the most common precursor to violence. How were she and Sam getting along?

Letters found after the murder indicated that Marilyn had considered divorcing Sam, but that Sam's brother Steve had urged her to make the marriage work "even if it kills you both (which it won't)." Her decision might have been associated with Sam's infidelity. A police report indicated an interview with a Dr. Robert Bailey (no relation to F. Lee) who worked at Sheppard's Bay View Hospital, and his wife, who recounted a tearful Marilyn clutching a picture of one of Sam's girlfriends and vowing to "divorce him, ruin him financially and drag his name through the mud." The date of Marilyn's threat was just six weeks before her murder. (Dr. Bailey, now a retired physician living in Nevada, stood by that account as a potential witness for the upcoming trial.)

One of Sam's more enduring flings had been with Susan Hayes, an employee at his hospital. They had been intimate for about three years. But in February 1954, apparently realizing that this affair was going nowhere, Ms. Hayes left Sam and Cleveland behind, moving to California. In March, Sam and Marilyn drove to California. While there, Marilyn stayed at the residence of a Dr. and Mrs. Chapman. Sam did not. He stayed at the residence of a Dr. and Mrs. Miller. With Susan Hayes. While in California, Sam attended a wedding with Ms. Hayes as his date; he took her with him when he traded in his car; he even took her to a cocktail party attended by other doctors and their wives, including Dr. and Mrs. Chapman, with whom Marilyn was staying. Sam showered Ms. Hayes with gifts. Mrs. Miller was furious with Sam for having put them in this awkward social situation, but seemingly Sam could not have cared less. He was having a good time.

It was at this time, when Sam was shacked up with Susan Hayes, that Marilyn Sheppard became pregnant. Was this a desperate attempt to shore up a failing marriage? Or if Sam and Marilyn were not intimate, would Sam have been forced to consider the possibility that Marilyn was having an affair? How happy might that have made him?

When looking at the relevant victimology, the one variable that elevated Marilyn's potential for becoming a victim was her troubled relationship with Sam, and his take on this during the first trial was noteworthy. When he was questioned about whether he'd had an affair with Susan Hayes, he said, "I wouldn't call it an affair. We've been good friends for some time." Regarding his general pattern of philandering, he testified that, "During and following my wife's pregnancy, up to approximately two years, my wife became quite jealous. This was consistent with the termination of my didactic schoolwork and the initiation of my work as a physician, which included contact with many women, both patients and fellow workers. This jealous reaction improved steadily until she became seemingly much more tolerant than I would have considered the average female to be."

I read this comment and thought that Sam was incredibly arrogant, as well as obtuse, but did that make him a murderer?

I next examined reports about the crime and the crime scene, along with all of the evidence, to see how it added up. As my colleagues at Scotland Yard like to say, "First you have to clear the ground under your feet." In other words, we must eliminate the obvious suspects, such as people who were at the scene of the crime when it occurred, before moving on to others.

It is an undisputed fact that Sam Sheppard was in the house when Marilyn was murdered. Any other suspect, such as Richard Eberling, *might* have been in the house, but because Sam was at the crime scene when the crime was committed, his statements are especially significant. To establish credibility, they must be analyzed first on their own merit, and then, more important, analyzed within the context of all the available evidence. Of course, seven-year-old Chip was at the crime scene as well, but he apparently slept through the night and had no information of value. From this point forward, there were two primary sources of information as to what had happened: Sam Sheppard and the crime scene. Each would tell an intriguing tale, so I looked to see what the first responders to the scene had found.

As I sat down in the conference room to fully immerse myself in these records, I opened the black binder that contained the initial report from the Bay Village, Ohio, police department, dated July 4, 1954. I wasn't expecting much from a small town PD that didn't have any real homicide experience, but I was impressed with what I found. The report of the first officer on the scene, Fred Drenkhan, a twenty-seven-year-old patrolman, was thorough, articulate, and vividly descriptive.

Drenkhan and his partner were working the midnight to eight A.M. shift. They had passed the Sheppard home five or six times during that night and noticed no unusual activity at the house, on the road, or in the neighborhood. It was another quiet July night in Bay Village, Ohio. They were at the fire station on Cahoon Road when the dispatcher contacted them. It was 5:57 A.M. There was a problem at the home of Dr. Sam Sheppard. Somewhat surprised, the two officers proceeded to the scene, followed by firemen in an ambulance. They arrived at 6:02 A.M. There they found Sam, along with Spencer and Esther Houk, who directed Officer Drenkhan upstairs, where he noted that Marilyn had been severely beaten about the head but saw no evidence of a struggle in the room.

Going back downstairs, Drenkhan carefully noted that Dr. Sheppard's medical bag was "set on end." He would later testify that, "The contents were spilled out. There is a compartment on either wing and neither one of those was open or the contents spilled out. The contents from the center of the bag were spilled."

Sam told Drenkhan that he had been dozing on the daybed when he awoke to hear Marilyn yelling, "Sam, Sam!" He had run up to investigate and "saw a form with a light garment." He'd heard moans and little gurgling noises from Marilyn and then was struck from behind and knocked unconscious. When Cleveland police detectives questioned him later at the hospital, Sam recalled seeing his auxilliary police badge on the floor, noticing the glint of it and "reflexively" putting it back into his pocket. He'd gotten up and found Marilyn covered in blood and checked her pulse, but couldn't find one. He then had heard someone rummaging around downstairs and had gone down to investigate. Sam said he had chased a "bushy-haired stranger" from the house, down the wooden stairway to the beach, where he'd struggled with this figure a second time and was choked unconscious. He'd regained consciousness on the beach and returned to the house, where he'd checked Marilyn's pulse again. By his own account, he was unsure of what to do, but eventually went downstairs and called the Houks.

That was Sam's story, but how did it compare with the crime scene evidence?

[4]

Crime scene analysis is based in part on the transfer theory (Locard Exchange Principle), which postulates that any two surfaces coming into contact leave trace evidence on both. This is especially true with wet blood, which is incredibly adhesive. Everyone agrees that in this case, the hail of blood flying from Marilyn as the killer stood over her and repeatedly bludgeoned her would have soaked him (or her). In addition, if the killer was also bleeding, as the plaintiff now alleged, he would have been a continuing source of fresh blood. Sam swore that he had grappled with this blood-covered killer in the bedroom and later on a six-foot stretch of beach. Yet there were no signs of a struggle either in the bedroom or on the beach. Other than a small, diluted stain on the knee of his pants, Sam had no blood on him.

He claimed that the killer took his wallet out of his pants and took some of the money, but left behind a twenty-dollar bill. There was no blood on the wallet or around the pocket from which the bloody-handed killer would have removed the wallet. This money-hungry killer also overlooked $200 in cash in the den as he was removing a number of drawers. Sam claimed that he checked Marilyn's pulse two or three times at her blood-soaked neck, but he had no blood on his hands and swore that at no point had he washed or otherwise cleaned up. Downstairs at the scene of the alleged burglary, one would expect this blood-soaked and supposedly bleeding killer to have transferred some blood on or around the desks he touched, or on the drawer handles and drawers that he removed and neatly stacked, or on Sam's medical bag, or on the trophies that the offender broke, or on the doors that he opened as he fled to the beach. Curiously, there wasn't a drop of blood on any of them. There also wasn't any evidence of the killer using any sink or other source of water to "clean up" prior to ransacking the house.

I considered the possibility that the intruder plundered the house *before* the murder. That would explain the complete lack of blood, but it posed other problems. One would have to believe that 1) not only was the offender willing to risk immediate detection by rummaging through the house with Sam downstairs and squarely in the middle of this chaos, but also that 2) Sam, Marilyn, young Chip, and Koko, the dog, slept contentedly as a stranger ransacked their small home, breaking trophies, pulling out drawers, dumping them and Sam's medical bag on the floor. Not a likely scenario.

And then there was the problem of blood being where it shouldn't have been, assuming that Sam was being truthful: It was on Sam's watch. Tiny elliptical dots of blood were clearly visible on its face. There was also some apparent blood smearing on the watchband, but the cast-off blood on the face of Sam's watch was distinctly different. The coroner's medical technologist correctly noted that blood in motion from several successive sprays had made these two-millimeter dots, forming a spatter pattern. Blood drops that small don't travel far, so Sam's watch had been close to Marilyn as she was being bludgeoned.

Another thing that jumped out at me was the disparity of injuries between Marilyn and Sam. When the individual who poses the greatest threat to an offender sustains nonlethal injuries or none at all, while the person who presents the least threat to the offender sustains lethal injuries, one must consider the possibility of staging. The killer beat Marilyn about the head and face repeatedly with a blunt object. Over twenty of the thirty-five blows she sustained could have been fatal. Her autopsy listed the cause of death as multiple impacts to the head and face, with comminuted fractures of the skull and the separation of frontal suture, bilateral subdural hemorrhages, diffuse bilateral subarachnoid hemorrhages, and contusions of the brain. This offender was in a homicidal rage, had a heavy blunt object, and was repeatedly and brutally bludgeoning Marilyn. To buy Sam's version, we have to believe that the offender's homicidal rage immediately subsided when Sam appeared, and that he dropped the weapon and just hit Sam with his fist. The only undisputed injuries to Sam Sheppard were a bruise under his eye and a chipped tooth. There was a report at the time that he had sustained a fractured vertebra, but the validity of that injury was in dispute.

Sam clearly posed the greatest threat to the killer, not only at the scene but as an eyewitness to murder. Why would the killer spare him, especially after he had twice overpowered and knocked Sam out? This is especially troubling if the killer had been either Eberling or Houk, as Sam knew them personally and could have set the police on their trail within minutes of awakening. It only made sense if the killer's freedom was dependent upon Sam's survival. But how does Sam's testimony stand on its own? During the first trial he testified as follows:

Q: What did you do immediately upon hearing [Marilyn's] cry?

A: I can't tell you, sir. It awakened me, and I initialized the attempt to gather enough sense to navigate up the stairs.

Q: And how far into the room did you get?

A: I couldn't say.

Q: Well, did something happen?

A: Yes, sir, it did.

Q: What happened?

A: I was engaged or grappled and hit from behind.

Q: Did you see anyone in the room?

A: As I stated the other day, I saw a light top form.

Q: Now will you tell us what you mean by a light top form, Doctor?

A: Well, I saw a light garment.

Q: Yes.

A: It had the appearance of having someone inside of it, shoulders. That's about all.

Q: Did you see a head?

A: I can't say that I did.

Q: All you saw then is something light, which you figured was on a body, is that right?

A: I can't say that I figured that at the time, but as I look back, I felt that.

Q: And what was this object doing there?

A: I don't know, sir . . .

Q: Did you grapple with anything?

A: Yes, sir, I did.

Q: What did you grapple with?

A: Something in front of me.

Q: Well, was it that form that you have told us about?

A: I have the feeling that it was . . .

Q: And what part of this something did you grapple?

A: I can't say, again, definitely. I would say the upper part.

Sam also testified that, ". . . I felt that I could visualize a form . . . a being . . . a biped. . . ."

To be uncomfortable with this testimony, one doesn't have to know that deceptive persons are approximately six times more likely to provide evasive answers than are truthful persons.

[5]

Next, I examined the crime scene photographs. I saw how the drawers had been pulled out in what Sam had described as an attempt at burglary, and his medical bag spilled over onto the floor, as Officer Drenkhan had described it. I examined the photographs of the beach and the reports of the investigators. There was no sign of a struggle on the beach, and since the lake was inland, the smooth sand could not be explained away as tidal movement.

The photographs of Marilyn told their own story. She lay faceup on the bed closest to the door, and she had been pulled down toward the bottom of the bed, with her legs spread apart slightly. They were underneath a wooden bar that ran across the foot of the bed, bent at the knees, with her feet dangling a few inches above the floor. She lay in blood, her pajama top pushed up to her neck. The bottoms had been pulled off one leg and were bunched up around her foot. Deep gashes marked her forehead and scalp, and her blood-covered face was angled slightly toward the doorway. Although her breasts were fully exposed, a blanket had been draped over her waist. These photographs also supported Officer Drenkhan's observation that there were no signs of a struggle. There were odd blood splotches and patterns of blood on the bed, but these had come from pooling, not spatter. I wanted to look at them more closely.

Some investigators had said they couldn't tell whether or not the body had been moved. But it was obvious to me that it had. In the crime scene photograph, her body lay facing up, with her left hand positioned horizontally across her stomach. There is a concentrated pool of blood on the sheet, above her head, and a hand-print pattern in blood on the side of the bed. There are dried rivulets of blood on her left wrist that appear to defy gravity, as they run horizontally toward her fingers.

Physical evidence cannot suspend the laws of nature. The blood on the sheet, the handprint on the side of the bed, and the rivulets of blood running down toward her fingers can all be explained by the simple displacement of the body. The most logical explanation is that Marilyn's body had been lying facedown farther up on the bed, with her left hand over the side of the bed for a period of time. This would account for the concentrated area of blood on the sheet, the handprint, and the rivulets of blood running down toward her fingers as her hand was suspended over the edge of the bed. She was in that position long enough for the rivulets to dry, then rolled onto her back and pulled farther down on the bed. This meant that the killer was at the crime scene for some time before he moved the body.

In addition, an isolated blood smear on her ankle was consistent with a bloody-handed killer pulling her, by her ankles, down the bed. The crosspiece over her hips posed a real logistical problem for a sexual assault. If the killer didn't move her into the position shown in the photographs, then one must believe two things: 1) that Marilyn decided to sleep halfway down the bed, with her legs dangling off the end; and 2) that blood can defy gravity.

I was already aware of what the other side had to say on the matter. The Sheppard team had retained Emmanuel Tanay, a forensic psychiatrist from Detroit, and he had offered the following opinion: Marilyn was the victim of a sexually sadistic, torture type of killing, because the bottoms of her pajamas were removed, exposing her genitals. This, he said, is not consistent with killing by a husband. In contrast, the life history of Richard Eberling, convicted of the murder of an elderly woman by pushing her down a flight of stairs, is consistent with a person who would engage in sexually sadistic homicidal behavior. He also pointed out that a reliance on Dr. Sheppard's extramarital sexual behavior as a motive, even if true, was scientifically unreasonable.

He went on to say that spousal homicide is a distinct variety of homicidal behaviors, all of which can be reliably differentiated. Any psychologist or psychiatrist knowledgeable about homicidal behavior, he claimed, would probably conclude, even from limited information, that the killing of Marilyn was unlikely to be a spousal homicide. She was brutally assaulted while lying in her bed and in all likelihood was sleeping. Among the hundreds of men he had evaluated who have killed wives or girlfriends, he had never encountered a case of a man perpetrating a homicide in this manner. The crime scene and wounds were consistent with a rage assault perpetrated by a person who had sadistic personality features, lacked compassion, and had what he called a defective superego. Those features were inconsistent with what was known about the personality of Sam Sheppard. The physical evidence, he pointed out, contradicted a quarrel as a precipitant for what appeared to have been a sudden rage response, yet it was consistent with a sadistic sexual assault. There was no reason to accept the theory that Sam's motive was to get rid of his wife in order to pursue a sexual involvement with another woman.

His firm opinion was that Richard Eberling, not Sam Sheppard, had murdered Marilyn in her bed.

I knew that Dr. Tanay was wrong, and that Marilyn Sheppard's murder had nothing even remotely to do with sexual sadism. All of the elements necessary to classify this as a sexually sadistic homicide were absent. A sexual sadist keeps his victim alive for hours, even days, and torments them. That's how he gets his satisfaction: Their suffering arouses him. This had been a blitz attack, without physical evidence of rape or torture. But what about Richard Eberling as a suspect? Was he motivated by an unbridled sexual lust for Marilyn and a hatred of Sam? Could he be good for the murder?

First of all, Richard Eberling had been a lifelong homosexual. That was initially documented in his foster care records, and that sexual orientation remained fixed throughout his life. Second, the crime scene does not support hatred for Sam, but it certainly supports a hatred for Marilyn. The offender chose to repeatedly bludgeon Marilyn, not Sam. She was the focus of the offender's attack and the victim of overkill. Sam got a bump on his eye, a chipped tooth, and a disputed cervical fracture, depending on which x-ray you looked at. It's also interesting to note that Richard Eberling testified *for* Sam during the second trial, and Sam never even suggested that Eberling might have been the "bushy-haired stranger" with whom he fought twice on the evening of the murder. (Terry Gilbert, Sam Reese Sheppard's lawyer, managed to find a nurse, Kathy Dyal, who claimed that Eberling had confessed to her that he had killed Marilyn, that she had bitten him badly, and that he'd taken her ring. Gilbert didn't seem to realize that the ring had been traced back to Marilyn's sister-in-law after Marilyn's death, making this story suspect.) Eberling took three separate polygraph exams, and when he denied killing Marilyn or knowing who did, each polygrapher found no deception. But what about the staging?

Noncriminals who stage crime scenes generally reveal their lack of criminal sophistication. They typically don't know what real crime scenes look like, because their knowledge of crimes comes from what they've read in books, or have seen on television or in the movies. "The false motives that are staged by criminally unsophisticated offenders," I wrote in my report, "are discernable because they are inconsistent with much of the forensic and behavioral evidence present in the crime and crime scene."

Crime scenes are high-risk environments, and none more so than a homicide scene. Offenders typically spend no more time than necessary there for fear of being interrupted or caught. Consequently, there is a high degree of correlation between the amount of time an offender spends at a crime scene and the offender's familiarity with and feeling of comfort there. Offenders who remain for a longer time often have a legitimate reason for being at the scene and are therefore not worried about being discovered or interrupted. This offender spent an inordinate amount of time at the crime scene.

It was now my job to use the available evidence to describe the type of crime that I believed it to be. I summed up my interpretation in the following tables, using the *Crime Classification Manual* as a guideline:

Red Flags Indicating Staging

Crime Classification Manual	Sheppard Crime Scene
Inappropriate items taken from the crime scene if burglary appeared to be the motive.	The crime scene was staged to appear as though burglary was a motive (drawers pulled out, contents dumped, etc.) but nothing of value was taken from the scene. Ms. Sheppard's watch was apparently taken from her wrist, but left downstairs, and Dr. Sheppard's watch was allegedly taken from his wrist but recovered in a green bag along with other personal articles outside the house. Dr. Sheppard alleged that a small sum of money was taken from his wallet. After a walk-through of the house, he admitted to law enforcement that nothing of value was taken from the crime scene.
Did the point of entry make sense?	No point of entry was determined. Dr. Sheppard indicated that the doors remained unlocked when he was home and if an intruder entered it is most

Crime Classification Manual	Sheppard Crime Scene
	logical that the point of entry was through an unlocked door. There is some speculation that the point of entry may have been a basement door, as fresh tool marks were found on that door two weeks after the homicide. This is not a logical point of entry, as it would make no sense to break in a basement door when the ground-floor doors were unlocked. (It was later established at trial that the door with the marks on it was actually an interior door that was inside the house and provided access to a crawl space under the living room and was not, in fact, an entry door at all.)
Did the perpetration of this crime pose a high risk to the offender?	If an intruder perpetrated this crime, he did so at high risk for detection. If one believes that the intent was to sexually assault the victim, the intruder would have been attempting to do so with both the victim's husband and son in close proximity. This high-risk approach is very uncommon for rapists, who are usually cowardly by nature. If an alleged intruder was in the house to burglarize or rape, he was doing so at great risk for detection.
Excessive trauma beyond that necessary to cause death (overkill).	Thirty-five injuries were noted on the autopsy report. The cause of death was listed as

Crime Classification Manual	Sheppard Crime Scene
	multiple impacts to the head and face with comminuted fractures of skull and separation of frontal suture, bilateral subdural hemorrhages, diffuse bilateral subarachnoid hemorrhages, and contusions of the brain. The number and severity of these injuries can reasonably be considered to be "overkill."
The offender will often manipulate the victim's discovery by a neighbor or family member.	Dr. Sheppard called his neighbors, Mr. and Mrs. Houk, and asked them to come to the house stating, "I think they've killed Marilyn." Once Mr. and Mrs. Houk arrived, Dr. Sheppard remained downstairs and they went upstairs where they discovered her body. Although Dr. Sheppard testified that he had "discovered" his wife's body on two separate occasions he never called the police. Instead he called his neighbors who, once they discovered the body, called the police.

Crime Scene Indicators Frequently Noted in a Staged Domestic Homicide

Crime Classification Manual	Sheppard Crime Scene
The murder weapon, fingerprints, and other evidentiary items often removed.	The murder weapon was removed from the scene and no latent fingerprints of value were developed.
The victim's body is not concealed.	The victim's body was not concealed, rather it was displayed to suggest she had been sexually assaulted.
The crime scene often involves the victim's or offender's residence, as the offender typically has control of the scene and therefore can spend time staging the scene without worry of being interrupted.	The victim's residence was the the crime scene.
Death may appear to have occurred in the context of another criminal activity such as a robbery or a rape.	Marilyn Sheppard's death appeared as though it occurred in the context of failed sexual assault or a burglary.
An offender who has a close relationship with his victim will often only partially remove the victim's clothing (e.g., pants pulled down, shirt or dress pulled up, etc.). He rarely leaves the victim nude.	The victim's pajamas were only partially removed as her pajama bottoms were pulled off one leg and her top was unbuttoned and pushed up over her breasts.
The offender frequently positions the victim to infer that a sexual assault has occurred.	The offender exposed the victim's breasts, pulled off one pants leg, and slightly spread her legs, implying that the victim was the target of a sexual assault.

Crime Classification Manual	Sheppard Crime Scene
Despite the body's positioning and partial removal of clothes, the autopsy demonstrates a lack of sexual assault. With a staged sexual assault, there is usually no evidence of any sexual activity and an absence of seminal fluids in body orifices.	The autopsy of Marilyn Reese Sheppard revealed no evidence of vaginal or anal trauma, no seminal fluid or any indication of sexual assault even though the offender had positioned her body to imply that a sexual assault had occurred.
Another red flag apparent with many staged domestic murders is the fatal assault of the wife and/or children by an intruder while the husband escapes without injury or with a non-fatal injury. If the offender does not first target the person posing the greatest threat or if that person suffers the least amount of injury, the police investigator should especially examine all other crime scene indicators.	The allegation in this case is that an intruder fatally assaulted Mrs. Sheppard while her husband escaped with nonfatal injuries in spite of having two separate physical confrontations with the alleged murderer. I will defer to Dr. White's analysis and conclusions regarding the nature of the injuries sustained by Dr. Sheppard at the time of the homicide, but clearly, they were nonfatal.

The known indicators for criminal staging, as well as the known crime scene indicators consistent with a staged domestic homicide, are abundantly present. I concluded that the totality of the physical forensic and behavioral evidence allows for only one logical conclusion and that is that the homicide of Marilyn Reese Sheppard on July 4, 1954, was a staged domestic homicide. But what about the trial? As it turned out, the path to and through the trial would be circuitous, and justice would be severe, gratifying some, eviscerating others.

[6]

The lawsuit went to the Cuyahoga County Court of Common Pleas, Judge Ronald Suster presiding. While some evidence had not been preserved, and some, amazingly, was returned to Sam Sheppard himself at the formal request of his attorney, F. Lee Bailey, following his not-guilty verdict, there were over 100 pieces still available, including fingernail scrapings, a vaginal swab, and a bloodstained splinter of wood from the basement steps where a trail of blood had been found. There was much argument about whether or not Terry Gilbert, Sam R's lawyer, had actually produced a chip of wood from the house, as the item they offered as evidence had a chain-of-custody record from 1966 to the present that had decades of holes for which Gilbert had no witness or record that could account for its handling, storage or whereabouts. It was just a black chunk of something in a plastic bag that he told the court was wood. It had never been tested to determine if it was wood or not, and there was no way to determine if it came from the Sheppard house or was part of the Sheppard evidence found in a box slated for discard when Paul Kirk's office was cleaned out following his death some years earlier. We did have the pants with the suspect blood spot, which Sam had been wearing, and some other trace evidence, but it quickly became clear that handling evidence by 1950s' standards had corrupted most of it for modern analysis. The coroner sent some of this to Dr. Mohammed Tahir, who directed a serology and DNA lab in Indianapolis. He also received a blood sample from Richard Eberling.

Then the DNA results came in. Dr. Tahir said that he'd found a sperm in the vaginal swab, and then another, but they had come from two different men. He also indicated that the samples had been corrupted by handling, and that there was a possibility of multiple unknown contributors. He could not say that any of this DNA came from Richard Eberling, only that markers present in the multiple contributor sample were also present in Eberling's profile. But, those markers could each have come from a separate contributor and not Eberling at all. Richard Eberling could not be excluded as the possible source, he indicated, but that rather vague conclusion did not exactly pin it on him either.

Tahir admitted that he had been unable to really define Sheppard's DNA profile, so an exhumation was in order. Sam R initially resisted this, but eventually agreed with his team and with Terry Gilbert. On September 17, 1997, he went with Gilbert and a few others to the Forest Lawn Memorial Gardens in Columbus, Ohio. Sam's body had been buried in a tightly sealed coffin, so it was well preserved. After leaving prison, Sam had become a professional wrestler, so his son had buried him in his wrestling outfit, complete with sunglasses and a bottle of bourbon, all still intact. The coroner in Cleveland received the remains, and she collected hair, skin, bone, and tooth-enamel samples.

Then they received the preserved sample from the bloodstain, found on the bedroom closet, that Dr. Kirk had said had not come from either Marilyn or Sam. It was sent for DNA testing. Tahir claimed that it proved to be a mix of two people: Marilyn Sheppard and a profile that occurred in one out of every forty-two people. That was not very discriminating, Terry Gilbert knew, but Richard Eberling could be in that group. To get public support, Gilbert released this information in a press conference. Backed by Dr. Tahir, Gilbert claimed that he now had conclusive evidence that Sam Sheppard did not kill his wife. Gilbert was cunning, but justice can be cruel to those who play fast and loose with the facts.

Bill Mason, with Steve Dever as chief counsel, led the defense for the state of Ohio. Mason had read through the documents from the first trial and had decided that Sam was the killer.

Steve Dever wanted to exhume Marilyn Sheppard to reexamine her teeth and the extent of her injuries. He was also interested in conducting a DNA test on the unborn child to determine if Sam was the father. Sensitive to Sam R's wishes, they gave him notice. Sam was again reluctant, but consented and asked to have his spiritual advisor, Kobutsu, a Buddhist monk, brought in to preside over the procedure. That October in 1999, the defense team agreed to fly him in at the county's expense.

Almost everyone anticipated the arrival of a contemplative, serene oriental monk, perhaps gracefully wearing orange saffron robes. To our surprise, he turned out to be an overweight, chain-smoking Irishman named Vince Malone from New Jersey, and he brought along some friends who wanted to watch. He was dressed in ceremonial garments, mostly black, and carried a purselike wallet. He walked with a pronounced limp, which required an occasional realignment of his layered garments.

The cemetery officials agreed to let him perform a small ceremony before they removed Marilyn's casket from its vault. Apparently reasoning that a stick or two of incense was insufficient, Kobutsu ignited a small brushfire of incense inside the mausoleum. The place filled with smoke and people were coughing, dodging, and ducking. Steve Dever, a regular churchgoer himself and already nervous about the spiritual aspect of disturbing the dead, was pacing with Dean Boland in the back of the mausoleum. He reacted to this simultaneously comic and uncomfortable scene with, "This is a bad situation. A couple of Hail Marys isn't gonna do it."

Kobutsu followed the incense by mumbling either some prayers or meditations, ending with the repeated phrase, "One scream alone in the valley."

Dean Boland thought that was ironically appropriatc. He also thought that Kobutsu's smoke was a symbolic representation of Terry Gilbert's attempt to keep the truth about Marilyn's murder shrouded in a fog of innuendo and misrepresentations. Before long, the smoke cleared and the cemetery workers went about their duties.

Marilyn's remains were not in good shape. As they pulled her coffin out of the ground in Cleveland's Knollwood Cemetery, the bottom fell out. What was left of her was mostly bones, but they ran some tests anyway. The results were somewhat inconclusive because they couldn't run a control, but there was a good probability, based on paternal DNA, that Sam had been the father of Marilyn's unborn child.

Then we got down to the trial. It began in January 2000, in one of the courtrooms on the twentieth floor of Cleveland's Justice Center. Court TV was set, presumably, to cover the entire trial. To begin, Terry Gilbert relied on F. Lee Bailey's opening arguments from the second trial in 1966, but he provided Eberling as a suspect rather than the Houks. He went over past mistakes made by investigators and asked the jury to avoid making Sam Reese Sheppard a victim of those failed proceedings. He named Emmanuel Tanay as his expert on sexual homicide and raised the issue of the blood spot on the closet door.

For the defense, Mason brought out motives for Sam to have been an enraged husband and therefore more likely to be the one who struck Marilyn over and over that night rather than some would-be burglar.

Gilbert's first witness was F. Lee Bailey himself. Relying on Bailey's theory about the Houks, on cross-examination, Dever got him to admit that until now, Eberling had never been a real suspect. Bailey testified that he was certain that Spencer Houk had been acting in complicity with his wife in the homicide. "I bought it initially," he insisted, "and it got stronger through the years, even until today." He had evaluated Richard Eberling as a possibility and had rejected him. "I did not then, or at any time since, form a belief that Richard Eberling killed Marilyn Sheppard." So, ironically, as he protected his own theory, Bailey ended up in this third trial siding with the state—the party against whom he had originally defended Sam.

After Sam R and a few others went to the stand, Gilbert called Dr. Tanay to discuss his theory of sexual sadism. Eberling died before Dr. Tanay could interview him, so he based his opinion on records about the man. The best he could say was that Eberling was "sending signals" that he did it. He called the murder a clear-cut torture, although he had no evidence that Marilyn had been forced to experience pain over any significant amount of time. He did say it would take a monster to do such a thing, but pulled back at the idea that a monster would finish off other people in the house. His ideas were confusing at best.

A prominent medical examiner, Cyril Wecht, was Gilbert's next witness. Dr. Wecht is known for his controversial positions on various high-profile cases. For example, he holds that John F. Kennedy was killed as part of a conspiracy, and he served as a consultant to film director Oliver Stone, who made a movie to that effect. Dr. Wecht also contends that, in spite of being convicted for the crime, Sirhan Sirhan did not murder Robert Kennedy. Dr. Wecht was now involved in this civil case to back up Tanay's opinions that this crime had been a sexual assault and to say that the original coroner, Gerber, had botched the job.

On cross-examination of this witness, Dever had an ace to play. He mentioned that Paul Kirk had made the claim that the assailant of Mrs. Sheppard was left-handed.

"Yes," said Wecht.

"Do you share that opinion?" Dever asked.

"Yes, with reasonable medical probability, based upon the majority of the defensive wounds being on her right arm and hand, I believe that it's more likely than not that the assailant was left-handed. I can't state that with certainty. It's more likely than not."

"Have you said on previous occasions," Dever continued, "that you cannot tell whether an assailant is left-handed or right-handed?"

"In this case?"

"Yes."

"Gee, I don't know," Wecht said. "In my written opinion, I think I said I thought he was left-handed. I don't know if I ever said otherwise."

"To refresh your recollection, do you recall that on the date of October 5 of last year, at the conclusion of the exhumation of Marilyn Sheppard, you appeared on CNN as far as giving an opinion as to the left-handedness of the assailant?"

"I remember being on CNN, but I don't remember the day."

The video of what he said was played for him to see. In it he not only stated quite clearly that he couldn't comment on the handedness of the assailant, but that he also thought it was doubtful that there would be any evidence to support a conclusion about it. "In the best of conditions," he had claimed, "this handedness is more that of fiction than it is of reality." He had spoken hypothetically of the different positions the assailant could have taken while attacking Marilyn, indicating that the issue was too complicated to be definitive, and had repeated, "This business of handedness is more in the realm of the novelist."

"Doctor," said Dever, "are you writing a novel up here on the witness stand?" It was an embarrassing moment for Gilbert's team.

Dever also got Wecht to admit that he could not say the homicide had not been staged and that he could not know if the sperm found inside Marilyn might have been there for a day or more. Thus, one of their star witnesses did them very little good.

There were moments when the trial seemed to me like something produced for television. The judge actually let a dentist testify about a fingernail abrasion on the skin, which is completely unscientific. A dentist would have no expertise in this area, and yet Dr. Michael Sobel went ahead and said that a half-moon scar that had been photographed on Eberling's arm was consistent with a scratch produced by a fingernail. What made this even more incredible was that they had no measurements or scale of comparison to say whether it was a bite mark or a fingernail mark, so this dentist had no real place as an expert witness. He had not measured Marilyn's fingernail in order to compare it with this scar. He hadn't even seen a photograph of Marilyn's hand with the broken fingernail. Even had he taken the time to review the only photograph of her fingernail, that photograph has no scale, was not photographed straight on, and is, therefore, unsuitable for such a comparison. He just thought his explanation made everything fit.

Then came the buildup for the most climactic moment. The piece of evidence on which Gilbert's team members were hanging their hats was the blood they had drawn from Richard Eberling before he died. The plaintiff claimed they had DNA from blood at the crime scene that excluded Sam Sheppard as the donor but that could be Richard Eberling's. They put a blood expert, Bart Epstein, who had been Paul Kirk's protégé, on the stand.

Dever let Gilbert go ahead and have this expert present his evidence. They lined up the DNA probes and looked at the markers, but in the end all they could really conclude was that it didn't exclude Eberling; hence, he could have been the source of the blood on the door. Yet in their quest to conduct the DNA examinations, Dean Boland had uncovered a huge error on the part of Epstein and the Gilbert team and Dever was ready to jump on it. On cross-examination, he raised the point with Epstein that Dr. Kirk had typed the two different blood types from the dried blood on the closet and had determined them both to be type O, albeit a little different from each other. Epstein acknowledged that.

"Group O was, in fact, Marilyn Sheppard's blood type, was it not?" Dever pressed.

"Yes, she was group O."

"And Dr. Sheppard's blood group was group A, wasn't it?"

"Yes, Dr. Kirk determined that."

"And Richard Eberling's group was A also, was it not?"

Epstein shot a look at his team. He'd been trapped. "I don't know his ABO blood group," he admitted.

"You mean to tell me," said Dever, "that when you were there with the consultants and the two hundred hours that you spent getting ready for this case, you never determined what Richard Eberling's blood type was?"

"That's what I'm telling you." He was clearly uncomfortable with the insinuation.

But Dever wasn't letting him off the hook. "What significance does blood group A have for these two blood group O stains?" he asked.

"Well, if you say that's solely group O, that it's not coming from a group A person."

"So that would exclude Eberling as the source of the two blood spots on that door, would it not?"

"I presume that if you have him as group A . . ."

"Can an A be an O?"

"No, I just said that."

"Can an O be an A?"

"No, it cannot."

"So, if Dr. Kirk's testing is correct, and he did all this work as far as typing the blood, and he determined the blood on the door to be type O, then anyone who is type-A blood is excluded as the source on that door. Is that correct?"

"Yes, assuming Paul Kirk's work is correct, which we can." And that was that. Dever succeeded in turning Bart Epstein completely around. Epstein had to reverse himself and conclude the obvious: that the blood at the crime scene so meticulously tested for DNA and boasted about during Gilbert and Tahir's dramatic pre-trial news conference could *not possibly* have been Richard Eberling's.

The other part of the plaintiff's theory was that Marilyn's teeth had been pulled out from biting. They believed that she bit the offender on the hand or arm during the assault and when he pulled his arm out of her mouth, he pulled her teeth out of her head. Then he had dripped blood down the steps. That was a stretch for me. I reasoned that having teeth knocked out of her head was far more consistent with the horrendous facial trauma she had sustained and my suspicions were confirmed later when Mason put the noted forensic dentist Lowell Levine on the stand. He agreed that Marilyn's teeth had not been pulled out of her head in the manner they had suggested. Dr. Sobel also testified in agreement with this conclusion, saying that her teeth injuries were, in his opinion, the result of blunt trauma to her mouth and had not been pulled out.

The plaintiff then brought Dr. Tahir to testify on five pieces of evidence. One was the small chunk of wood from a basement step, with an apparent bloodstain on it; two others were vaginal smear swabs on slides from the coroner's office; and the last two were two stains from the wardrobe door in the murder room.

From these five stains, Tahir had concluded that Eberling could not be excluded as a contributor to the

DNA found in the samples. But the plaintiff's own population geneticist, Dr. Ranajit Chakraborty, whose testimony followed Tahir's, admitted under cross-examination that while Eberling could not be excluded as a contributor to these samples, neither could 90 percent of Caucasian males—except for the stain on the wardrobe, in which case 70 percent of all Caucasian males could have been the donor. In short, they pointed to almost everyone, which means they pointed to no one in particular. Regarding the vaginal smears, no one else ever saw sperm on those slides, not even Lester Adelson, who stained and examined them within hours of the murder and who would not have known what role the existence of sperm might have played. Thus, he would not have intentionally concealed them. Dr. Gerber, the coroner at the time, and Dr. Balraj, the current coroner, also had not observed any sperm on those slides. Only Dr. Tahir had.

Per a court order, he had taken those slides to his lab in Indiana to examine them for possible DNA material. He claimed he put them under a microscope and identified a sperm head (no tails). However, he didn't photograph this earth-shattering discovery, but went ahead and conducted destructive testing on the sample, consuming it all. Then he looked at the second slide and again found a sperm head that no one else had ever seen, didn't photograph this either, and did not preserve the slide. Once again, he conducted destructive DNA testing, consuming the entire sample.

Interestingly, Tahir testified that while he excluded Sam from one of the vaginal smear slides, he could not exclude Sam as being the source of the sperm on the second smear slide, and both smears were taken within seconds of each other. So what was really going on?

The magnification necessary to see sperm existed in 1954. Dr. Adelson was a prominent, competent, and well-respected pathologist. It is unlikely that he would have overlooked the presence of sperm on two separate slides. It is also unlikely that Dr. Balraj, the highly professional pathologist currently working for Cuyahoga County who also examined those slides, would have either missed or intentionally concealed such a significant finding.

At any rate, Gilbert rested his case. Interestingly, right afterward I noticed that virtually everyone from Court TV left town. Only a technician remained to tape the rest of the trial for their archives. But gone were the producers and local on-air talent to provide commentary and witty banter with the hosts back in their New York studio. Only the plaintiff's case was broadcast live. The nation never got to see the state of Ohio's case.

They put on their witnesses, and finally it was my turn to take the stand. Terry Gilbert wanted to keep me off it in the worst way. For the better part of a day, he challenged my expertise, and in a hearing outside the presence of the jury tried to exclude my testimony. One of his ploys was to find another legitimate criminal investigative analyst or profiler to rebut my position. Apparently, he was unable to do so, as he stooped to using a self-proclaimed profiler named Brent Turvey. Not only has Turvey never completed any recognized profiling training programs, such as those run by the FBI or the International Criminal Investigative Analysts Fellowship (ICIAF), he doesn't even have the basic qualifications necessary to apply for those programs. As a matter of fact, he has never completed even a basic police academy training program anywhere. He had, however, authored a flawed textbook on "profiling," which, Gilbert argued, made Turvey an "expert."

In his affidavit, Turvey alleged that my analysis was "not legitimate forensic practice." However, he never qualified as an expert in this case nor even set foot inside the courtroom. Consequently, Judge Suster appropriately disregarded his affidavit. The judge also found Terry Gilbert's other arguments to exclude my testimony insufficient and unconvincing. At the end of the hearing, Judge Suster concluded that I was fully qualified as an expert and that my methodology was sound, so he ruled that I would be allowed to testify before the jury as follows: "Any conclusions must be based on evidence already admitted or based on [McCrary's] understanding of evidence that will be admitted." For example, any of my testimony that related to blood transfer stains "must be taken from evidence already admitted in this case or from evidence that will be offered."

The judge also ruled that I could testify to "the characteristics of domestic homicide and compare them to the physical evidence at the scene; the characteristics of homicide that are drug related and compare them to the physical evidence at the scene; the characteristics of homicide that are robbery or burglary related and compare them to the physical evidence at the scene." In addition, I was allowed to testify to "the aspects, the characteristics of staging in particular as [McCrary's] referring to those areas. . . ." However, neither I nor any other expert would be allowed to offer our conclusion as to whether the Sheppard case was staged. That was the jury's job, and any such expert testimony would improperly invade their province. It was part of what's known as "the ultimate issue."

These were basically the same limitations Judge Suster had put on Dr. Tanay's testimony, and they were the only limitations put on my testimony. I thought they were fair enough. Because I couldn't base my opinions on anything that had not been entered into evidence in this trial, such as Marilyn Sheppard's original autopsy report, I spent the weekend studying the other evidence to ensure that my testimony would comply with Judge Suster's ruling.

(Turvey has claimed in a second edition of his flawed textbook, and elsewhere, that his affidavit was used to "help successfully limit the testimony of former FBI profiler Gregg McCrary in this case," that "McCrary was not allowed to testify about his opinions regarding the physical evidence in this case" and that the judge ruled that McCrary's opinions ". . . were not sufficiently reliable and amounted essentially to profiling evidence." None of these statements is true.)

In my initial testimony, I rebutted Dr. Tanay's assertion that Marilyn Sheppard's murder was a sexually sadistic homicide. She had not been tortured or held for days, the offender did not use restraints or other instruments or devices, and there was no evidence of sexual experimentation. As a matter of fact, there was no evidence that Marilyn Sheppard had been sexually assaulted in any manner. This was not a sexually sadistic homicide.

While I couldn't testify about staging in the context of a domestic homicide, I could and did testify to the physical evidence and how that was or was not consistent with staging. Obviously, the evidence was overwhelmingly consistent with staging and the jury appeared to be getting it. That fact was not lost on Mr. Gilbert. Falling prey to what seemed to me to be an increasing sense of desperation and paranoia, he popped up from behind the plaintiff's table like a wounded weasel, accusing the jurors and me of exchanging some sort of secret communication. I was incredulous, as nothing of the sort had been occurring.

He demanded that the judge stop me from communicating with the jury, which took everyone by surprise, as my job as an expert witness is to do exactly that—communicate with the jury. I asked Judge Suster if I could continue to look at the jurors while I testified and he assured me that I could.

Another issue was the relationship of wife battering to homicide. The plaintiff held that battering preceded almost every spousal homicide, and because there was no record of Sam battering Marilyn, Sam was not likely to have been her killer. The best data available shows that only half of all women who are murdered by their partners were physically abused prior to the homicide (National Crime Victims Survey, 1995).

By the end of the day, I had concluded my testimony; as I was leaving the courtroom, Bill Mason put his hand on my shoulder. Nodding toward Terry Gilbert, Bill quietly said, "He never laid a glove on you."

For the first time, the actual murder weapon might have been identified. While this was not allowed into court, I learned about it from Dean Boland. Back in 1954, Gerber had speculated that it was some sort of surgical instrument, although in all of his searches around the world, he had found no instrument that would make such a mark. That got him crucified in the second trial. To avoid that, this team had looked more deeply into the matter. They wanted to see how the imprint that was found on the pillowcase had been created, so they took forty-eight down pillows with cotton covers and used various techniques. Only one worked: A second bloody object had been touched against a primary bloodstain that had dried. They used ten milliliters of blood to create the primary stain, much less than was actually on the crime scene pillow. It took over two hours to dry. So what was the object that created the image on the stain, and where was it?

When Dean Boland turned the imprint around to look at it from different angles, he perceived the image of a lamp. Dean pursued this idea and found that a man named Paul Gerhard had told the police long before that he had fixed and returned a lamp to the Sheppard bedroom, to the nightstand, thirty-six hours before the murder. Gerhard described the lamp as heavy brass or metal, about seven inches tall with a circular base. It was consistent with the concentric injuries to Marilyn's head. A one-sentence note at the end of a police report identified a small lampshade found by itself on a bookcase in a room on the second floor. No lamp was found in the murder room, yet Sam's notebook lay on the nightstand, ready for late-night calls, so how could he have taken notes without any light?

The conclusion should be obvious.

[7]

After two and a half months of testimony, on April 4, 2000, the case went to the jury. They took three hours to reach a unanimous verdict for the defense, the state of Ohio. In effect, they were saying that Sam Sheppard had not been falsely imprisoned.

When the foreman said the words, Gilbert, sitting

next to Sam R, put his face in his hands and broke down. Sam R received the news stoically.

To my mind, Gilbert's team had made the fatal error of conducting a theory-driven rather than a fact-driven investigation. In other words, they started with a conclusion and then looked for facts that might support that conclusion. That doomed them from the beginning, as Gilbert and his experts had to ignore, filter, shape, bend, torture, and cherry-pick various facts to create the illusion that their theory was valid. Ironically, Gilbert spun his case to careless media in order to shape public opinion and influence potential jurors, which is exactly what the U.S. Supreme Court had condemned as unconstitutional in the first trial. The prosecutors' approach was the antithesis of Gilbert's approach. They were going to become "masters of the facts," as Steve Dever put it, and follow the facts regardless of where they led in order to reach an unbiased and objective conclusion. That's exactly what they did.

After the trial, I heard Sam R and Terry Gilbert interviewed on television. Sam R has said that he is convinced that Richard Eberling murdered his mother, but he has also said that there is at least one other suspect. This is the ABS defense. Anybody but Sam. The reality is that once the jury heard the facts, they had no trouble making the right call. Those jurors who would discuss the case after it was over confirmed that their verdict rested upon the belief of each one of them that Sam Sheppard had murdered his wife. There was no mystery killer, no "bushy-haired stranger," nor any "one-armed man" who got away with murder. The truth is more certain but less exciting.

Sam didn't love Marilyn, he possessed her. Just weeks before the murder, he'd revealed his contempt for her by publicly flaunting his intimate relationship with Susan Hayes. Sam's motive for murder was the most common one among wife-killers: control. As long as he believed he was in control and Marilyn complied, everything was fine. But Marilyn wasn't complying. She was threatening to divorce him, to ruin him financially and to "drag his name through the mud." I believe that her defiance was devastating to him and to dissipate his rage and restore control, he opted for violence. As Dr. Ronald Markman observed in his book *Alone with the Devil,* "Psychically, the [wife-killer] kills out of self-defense. The only way he can preserve his psychic integrity and discharge the explosive anxiety within is to restore control through the most extreme violence." By murdering Marilyn, Sam vented his anger and restored his control over her, but at a hell of a price.

Immediately after the homicide, Sam's thoughts then turned to self-preservation. He couldn't undo the murder, but he could save himself—or so he thought. Although smart, Sam was criminally unsophisticated, and that was his downfall. He staged the scene the way he *thought* a crime scene should look and fabricated different stories to try to support his staging. However, the physical and behavioral evidence actually revealed both the staging and the impossibilities in Sam's story. Like an attack that is redirected back at the attacker, Sam's attempts at staging and fabrication were self-defeating. In spite of the notoriety and controversy that has swirled around this case for decades there is only one logical conclusion that the evidence supports: Sam murdered Marilyn. It's the only way that all of the pieces of this puzzle fit together. The police and prosecutors had been right all along.

Yet that truth won't stop other pro-Sam groupies. In fact, James Neff, an author who sat through this trial and claims to have done years of research on the case, has written a book titled *The Wrong Man* in which he continues to float the fable that Richard Eberling murdered Marilyn. I suppose that this supports Mark Twain's observation that the reason we hold truth in such respect is because we have so little opportunity to get familiar with it.

As I continue to offer my expertise on violent crime, I follow the developments at Quantico in Criminal Investigative Analysis with special interest for after-the-fact improvements from cases I've worked. To finish, let's look at the changes that have taken place since the cases I've just described.

10: The Future

> It is not our part to master all the tides of the world, but to do what is in us for the succor of those years wherein we are set, uprooting the evil in the fields that we know, so that those who live after may have clean earth to till. What weather they shall have is not ours to rule.
>
> —J.R.R. Tolkien

With Criminal Investigative Analysis, the BSU has managed to uproot some evil in the world, but in the larger scheme of things, we may still ask, just "where the fugawae?"

When the FBI began analyzing crimes behaviorally in the 1970s, we believed we were on to something, but we didn't know exactly what or exactly where this approach would lead. Over the years, it has grown in many unexpected and productive ways and has developed into a substantial and respected tool for law enforcement, with many beneficial applications. Enhanced interrogation techniques, more creative investigative strategies, and increasingly accurate detection of staging, signature, and false allegations of crimes are among the advances made as new applications emerge from the ongoing research. All of this has proved beneficial for law-enforcement officers, for prosecuting and defense attorneys, and in civil litigation that arises from violent crimes. Expert testimony has evolved to facilitate the legal process and educate jurors, better enabling everyone involved to make informed decisions.

At first in our underground bunker, we wandered around a bit, wondering where we were and where we were going, but now we know. When I first arrived at Quantico, there were seven FBI agents in the behavioral science operational unit; now there are nearly forty. The reason for that is the exponentially increased demand, which proves that this type of service works. The reason it works is that the analysis and advice come from fully trained, seasoned investigators. The unit has an impressive list of success stories.

Even so, I believe that in developing this discipline, we're still in the embryonic stages, and regardless of how much we know, there is a vast amount yet to be learned. Criminals are always devising new ways to commit their crimes, and because of that, we can best fulfill our potential for tracking and stopping them by integrating the disciplines of psychiatry, psychology, and the forensic sciences with the practical experience of frontline investigators. In fact, this is what I do in the seminars I teach. My vision has been to integrate the best of these worlds through face-to-face dialogue for the betterment of all.

Law enforcement and mental health professionals are known to harbor a degree of mistrust and certain stereotypical misperceptions about each other. Police officers tend to view mental health professionals as soft-headed apologists who excuse a serial murderer's crimes by pointing out that when this killer grew up, he simply didn't have the benefit of a hot-lunch program. Conversely, some mental health professionals tend to perceive those of us in law enforcement as knuckle-dragging Neanderthals, uneducated and as clueless as we are coarse.

When I bring these two groups together, such myths get dispelled. Once the fog of misperception is lifted, these seemingly divergent groups find that they are far more alike than different and that they share many of the same professional goals, concerns, and frustrations. That should come as no surprise, as I explain in my seminars, because we are dealing with the same clientele. The only difference is that law enforcement deals with them in the wild, while the mental health professionals deal with them in captivity. We are united by the common goal of stopping the current violence and preventing future violence, so we should maximize our collective strengths. Like a jug being filled drop by drop, progress is often made on a case-by-case basis. In the wake of the cases that I have presented in this book, for example, many positive changes have been implemented in both fields.

The year after the Unterweger trial, I returned to Vienna to chair the FBI's first international symposium on Criminal Investigative Analysis. Investigators from throughout Europe attended and their enthusiasm for the program led to a multitude of requests from many European countries for additional training and support for specific investigations. Austria and several other European countries have adopted a computerized Violent Crime Linkage Analysis System (VICLAS) to track violent crimes. This is unquestionably better than relying on the memories of retired detectives—who might or might not be reading the newspaper on the right days.

In North America, too, improvements have been made based on what we've learned from particular investigations. After the Harris case, the New York State Police revamped and professionalized their evidence teams and they now rank among the best in the country. The Maricopa County Sheriff's Office learned from their mistakes in interviewing and interrogation in the Buddhist temple case. It is safe to say that they are now among those departments *least* likely to extract a false confession. In the aftermath of the Bernardo case, a comprehensive judicial review resulted in many positive changes for Canadian authorities in handling such a complex investigation, and improved training for their profilers. And let's not forget Waco. After internal, external, and congressional reviews, the FBI adopted a number of changes that significantly reduce the chance of another dangerous standoff like that from ever occurring. Overall, I'd say, we are further ahead than before, but we should keep in mind that we still "have miles to go before we sleep."

Each of us sees the world through a distinctly personal lens, shaped through our unique life experiences. It's no surprise, then, that my approach to criminal investigations and violent offenders has been influenced not only by my FBI training and experience but through my formal education in psychology and the arts, along with my years of study of Shorinji Kempo. Like other true martial arts, this practice is more than simply a style of fighting.

The discipline of Shorinji Kempo cultivates a strong sense of justice, courage, and compassion among its practitioners and emphasizes using those qualities for society's benefit. One must live "half for self, half for others." To defend what is right and stop violence, students learn to develop their own essential strengths and resources. Defense comes first, followed if necessary by counterattack. As Sun Tzu in *The Art of War* noted, "The first move, if not a surprise attack, can be easily withstood or evaded. A good tactician will begin to fight after getting fully prepared for battle, but a poor tactician who knows neither himself nor the enemy will hasten to fight with the enemy. The more timid and unprepared he is, the more apt he is to strike the first blow." Shorinji Kempo strives to be a discipline that contributes to the welfare of all, to be used only to restrain those seeking to harm others.

So how might these principles be applied in the quest to defend our society from violent criminal behavior? After knowing ourselves, we must know our enemy, and that means, among other things, understanding what Dr. Marvin Wolfgang, the late criminologist, revealed to the world years ago. He devised a longitudinal study aimed at observing the extended life courses of the 9,945 males who were born in Philadelphia in 1945 and who attended school there. Focusing on their criminal behavior between the ages of ten and eighteen, he found that a mere 627—fewer than 7 percent—were chronic offenders who by age eighteen had five or more arrests. These "dirty 7 percenters" committed more than half of all the recorded offenses and two-thirds of the violent crimes, including all of the murders committed by the entire group. He found that 70 percent of those arrested three times had gone on to commit a fourth offense, and of these, 80 percent not only committed a fifth offense but kept at it through twenty or more. Wolfgang calculated that if the city's judges had sent each dirty 7 percenter to prison for just one year after his third offense, Philadelphians would have suffered 7,200 fewer serious crimes while they were off the streets.

Wolfgang's study has been repeated not just in Philadelphia, but in other cities throughout the United States and abroad, with essentially the same results. The best way to defend ourselves from criminal violence is to identify those dirty 7 percenters and separate them from the rest of us. Every objective mental health professional who deals with criminal offenders will admit that we don't know how to fix these types of offenders. That means we should at least try to address the threat potential. Know ourselves, know our enemies, and be prepared to restrain others on behalf of the whole.

Another tenet of Shorinji Kempo is that neither thought nor action is sufficient on its own. Thought without action is useless, and action without thought is dangerous. A thoughtful and integrated approach to the complexity of human violence is the best approach, and I am happy to say that it has begun.

The International Criminal Investigative Analysts Fellowship (ICIAF) is a professional group of highly trained law-enforcement officers who practice the full range of activities included under the concept of Criminal Investigative Analysis. The original police fellows the FBI trained in a ten-month total-immersion course taught at the FBI Academy were the ones who founded this organization. But the ICIAF is more than a group of law-enforcement professionals. It also includes among its members psychiatrists, psychologists, geographic profilers, and other relevant professionals. For example, Dr. Peter Collins, a Canadian psychiatrist from the famed Clark Institute, works virtually full-time with the Ontario Provincial Police and other law-enforcement agencies in Canada, the United States, and Europe. The ICIAF has also honored guests, lecturers, and consultants such as Dr. Park Dietz, an expert witness in many high-profile trials, and Dr. Robert Hare, who knows more than any other professional about the behavior of psychopaths. The blending of these disciplines results in a distillation of ideas that produce thoughtful, potent action.

In the continuing struggle to understand the complicated pathology of violence, every avenue must be explored. Law enforcement, psychologists, psychiatrists, neurologists, geneticists, criminologists, sociologists, forensic scientists, and members of society at large are all stakeholders in the results. By working interdependently, the light from each of these unique perspectives becomes a splendid torch illuminating the unknown darkness and offering the best hope for deliberative action and meaningful interventions. We need to make it burn as brightly as possible before passing this light on to future generations.

Acknowledgments

This book could not have been written without the help of many, and I wish especially to thank the following:

Lynde Johnston and all of the first-rate investigators of the Rochester Police Department and the New York State Police, with whom it was a privilege to work and who deserve full credit for detecting, apprehending, and convicting Arthur Shawcross.

The Metropolitan Toronto Police for their professionalism and continued friendship.

Vince Bevan and the Green Ribbon Task Force for the depth of their commitment and success in solving the murders of Leslie Mahaffy, Kristen French, and Tammy Homolka.

The State of Utah Department of Corrections for all of your help.

Ernst Geiger of the Austrian Federal Police and Thomas Muller, criminal psychologist with the Austrian Ministry of the Interior, for their enduring friendship and continued success in professionalizing law-enforcement investigations throughout Europe.

Dean Boland, Steve Dever, Bill Mason, and the entire Sheppard Task Force from the Cuyahoga County Prosecutor's Office, whose exemplary professionalism ensured that the truth prevailed in the Sam Sheppard case.

John Douglas, for all of the ground-breaking good work he has done and for having the "wisdom" to bring me into the Unit at Quantico, and to all of my friends and colleagues from the National Center for the Analysis of Violent Crime (NCAVC) and the FBI.

Sensei Kimura, my Shorinji Kempo instructor, who helped to develop the right perspective for this work.

Charlie Brennan, ace Colorado reporter, true-crime author, and friend, whose literary suggestions helped shape "The Poet's Shadow."

Martha Sasser, Merritt Woznick, Dean Boland (again), Ruth Osborne, Michael Rowe, Tiffany Souders, and Don and Nancy McCrary, who offered assistance in the form of suggestions and proofreading, and Al Sproule, for his interest and support.

John Silbersack, who made many insightful suggestions for this book's direction, and whose enthusiasm for this book helped to launch it and maintain our focus.

Our editor, Henry Ferris. His ideas for the book and his excitement at seeing it come to fruition helped us to stay on track.

Drs. Park Dietz, Robert Hare, John Monahan, and Joel Devoskin for your professional contributions, inspiration, unerring perspectives, razor-sharp wit, and continued friendship.

Ed Grant, David Caldwell, Mike Prodan, Ron MacKay, Carlo Schippers, Kate Lines, and all the members of the International Criminal Investigative Analysts Fellowship (ICIAF) for sharing your dedication, insight, leadership, and the odd glass of late-night whiskey.

To Scott and Sara, who taught me the truth of Gabriel García Márquez's observation that "[We discover] with great delight that one does not love one's children just because they are one's children but because of the friendship formed while raising them."

Index

True Crime Sagas
Ripped From Today's Headlines

MURDER IN GREENWICH
THE MARTHA MOXLEY CASE . . . SOLVED
by Marc Fuhrman
0-06-109692-X/ $7.99 US/ $10.99 Can

KIDS WHO KILL
BAD SEEDS AND BABY BUTCHERS—
SHOCKING TRUE STORIES OF JUVENILE MURDERERS
by Charles Patrick Ewing
0-380-71525-2/ $6.99 US/ $9.99 Can

SON OF A GRIFTER
THE TWISTED TALE OF SANTE AND KENNY KIMES,
THE MOST NOTORIOUS CON ARTISTS IN AMERICA
by Kent Walker and Mark Schone
0-06-103169-0/ $7.99 US/ $10.99 Can

A WARRANT TO KILL
A TRUE STORY OF OBSESSION, LIES AND A KILLER COP
by Kathryn Casey
0-380-78041-0/ $7.99 US/ $10.99 Can

MAFIA WIFE
MY STORY OF LOVE, MURDER, AND MADNESS
by Lynda Milito with Reg Potterton
0-06-103216-6/ $7.99 US/ $10.99 Can